MW00772652

ILLUSIONS AND DISILLUSIONS OF PSYCHOANALYTIC WORK

PSYCHOANALYTIC IDEAS AND APPLICATIONS SERIES

Series Editor: Leticia Glocer Fiorini

IPA Publications Committee

Leticia Glocer Fiorini (Buenos Aires), Chair and General Editor;
Samuel Arbiser (Buenos Aires); Paulo Cesar Sandler (São Paulo);
Christian Seulin (Lyon); Gennaro Saragnano (Rome);
Mary Kay O'Neil (Montreal); Gail S. Reed (New York)

Other titles in the Series

*The Art of Interpretation: Deconstruction and New Beginning
in the Psychoanalytic Process*
  Wolfgang Loch
  edited and commentary by Peter Wegner

The Unconscious: Further Reflections
  edited by José Carlos Calich & Helmut Hinz

Escape from Selfhood: Breaking Boundaries and Craving for Oneness
  Ilany Kogan

The Conscious in Psychoanalysis
  Antonio Alberti Semi

From Impression to Inquiry: A Tribute to the Work of Robert Wallerstein
  edited by Wilma Bucci & Norbert Freedman; associate editor Ethan A. Graham

Talking About Supervision: 10 Questions, 10 Analysts = 100 Answers
  edited by Laura Elliot Rubinstein

Envy and Gratitude Revisited
  edited by Priscilla Roth and Alessandra Lemma

The Work of Confluence: Listening and Interpreting in the Psychoanalytic Field
  Madeleine & Willy Baranger
  edited and commentary by Leticia Glocer Fiorini
  Foreword by Cláudio Laks Eizink

Good Feelings: Psychoanalytic Reflections on Positive Emotions and Attitudes
  edited by Salman Akhtar

The Analyzing Situation
  Jean-Luc Donnet

Psychosomatics Today: A Psychoanalytical Perspective
  edited by Marilia Aisenstein and Elsa Rappoport de Aisemberg
  Foreword by Cláudio Laks Eizink

Primitive Agony and Symbolization
  René Roussillon

In the Traces of our Name: The Influence of Given Names in Life
  Juan Eduardo Tesone

ILLUSIONS AND DISILLUSIONS OF PSYCHOANALYTIC WORK

André Green

Translated by Andrew Weller

Psychoanalytic Ideas and Applications Series

Routledge
Taylor & Francis Group

LONDON AND NEW YORK

Published 2011 by Karnac Books Ltd.

Published 2018 by Routledge
2 Park Square, Milton Park, Abington, Oxon OX14 4RN
711 Third Avenue, New York, NY 10017, USA

Routledge is an imprint of the Taylor & Francis Group, an informa business

Copyright © 2011 to André Green.
Translated by Andrew Weller.
English translation copyright © 2011 International Psychoanalytical
Association

The right of André Green to be identified as the author of this work has
been asserted in accordance with §§ 77 and 78 of the Copyright Design and
Patents Act 1988.

All rights reserved. No part of this book may be reprinted or
reproduced or utilised in any form or by any electronic, mechanical,
or other means, now known or hereafter invented, including
photocopying and recording, or in any information storage or retrieval
system, without permission in writing from the publishers.

Notice:
Product or corporate names may be trademarks or registered
trademarks, and are used only for identification and explanation
without intent to infringe.

British Library Cataloguing in Publication Data

A C.I.P. for this book is available from the British Library

ISBN 9781855753297 pbk

Edited, designed and produced by The Studio Publishing Services Ltd
www.publishingservicesuk.co.uk
e-mail: studio@publishingservicesuk.co.uk

Printed in the United Kingdom
by Henry Ling Limited

CONTENTS

PART III:
ILLUSIONS AND DISILLUSIONS OF
PSYCHOANALYTIC WORK

IPA Publications Committee

The Publications Committee of the International Psychoanalytical Association continues, with this volume, the series "Psychoanalytic Ideas and Applications".

The aim is to focus on the scientific production of significant authors whose works are outstanding contributions to the development of the psychoanalytic field and to set out relevant ideas and themes, generated during the history of psychoanalysis, that deserve to be discussed by present psychoanalysts.

The relationship between psychoanalytic ideas and their applications has to be put forward from the perspective of theory, clinical practice, technique, and research in order to maintain their validity for contemporary psychoanalysis.

The Publication Committee's objective is to share these ideas with the psychoanalytic community, and with professionals in other related disciplines, in order to expand their knowledge and generate a productive interchange between the text and the reader.

André Green's *oeuvre* is a fundamental contribution to contemporary psychoanalysis. With *Illusions and Disillusions of Psychoanalytic Work*, Green goes beyond a comfortable position concerning clinical practice and introduces a deep approach to failures related to the psychoanalytic treatment. He proposes a complex relation between theory and clinical practice, focusing on learning and theorizing from experience.

The Publications Committee is very much pleased to publish this title in the Psychoanalytic Ideas and Applications series.

Special thanks are due to the author, André Green, for his contribution, as well as to Christian Delourmel for the Prologue, and Fernando Urribarri for the Postscript to this volume.

Leticia Glocer Fiorini
Series Editor
Chair, IPA Publications Committee

ACKNOWLEDGEMENTS

My gratitude to Litza Guttières-Green; my thanks to Josiane Chambrier-Slama, for her friendly help, and to Hélène Boulais, for her precious assistance.

My thanks also go to those authors, who, all things considered, have been the most important for me after Sigmund Freud: Jacques Lacan in the early years, and since then, Donald W. Winnicott and Wilfred R. Bion up until today.

For Christian Delourmel

ABOUT THE AUTHOR

André Green is a psychiatrist and full member of the Paris Psychoanalytic Society. He has been Vice-President of the IPA (1975–1977), President of the Paris Psychoanalytic Society (1986–1989), and held the Freud Memorial Chair at the University of London from 1979 to 1980.

He is also a prolific writer, whose books include: *On Private Madness* (reprinted by Karnac Books in 1997); *The Fabric of Affect in the Psychoanalytic Discourse* (Routledge, 1999); *The Work of the Negative* (Free Association Books, 1999); *Psychoanalysis: A Paradigm for Clinical Thinking* (Free Association Books, 2002); *Key Ideas for a Contemporary Psychoanalysis* (Routledge, 2005); *Pourquoi les pulsions de destruction ou de mort?* [Why are there destructive or death drives?] (Panama, 2007).

An international tribute was paid to him in 2000 through the publication of a book in his honour with papers from several contributors: *Penser les limites. Ecrits en l'honneur d'André Green* [Thinking about limits: Essays in honour of André Green (edited by César Botella; Delachaux et Niestlé, 2000).

André Green lives and works in Paris.

Christian Delourmel

"Rather than be told what we should or should not do, it would be more profitable to be clear about what we are in fact doing"

(Green, 1975, p. 35)

Illusions and Disillusions of Psychoanalytic Work is the title the author has opted for rather than that of failure, a term that does not seem suitable to him, in the specific field of psychoanalysis, for recounting and exploring the disappointing and sometimes tragic evolutions of the treatments of certain patients who are resistant to the effects of analytic work. In this book, he reports cases taken from his own experience and that of his collaborators. He points out, moreover, that such cases have never been absent from the series of analysands that he has treated, from the early days of his practice up until today, without minimizing his countertransference reactions or their possible impact on these disappointing evolutions.

"If," as Freud said, "experience has taught us that psycho-analytic therapy—the freeing of someone from his neurotic symptoms, inhibitions, and abnormalities of character—is a time-consuming business" (1937c, p. 216), it also teaches us that it is uncertain and hazardous work, whose success cannot be guaranteed in advance and which sometimes even fails. This is especially so with certain patients where the analytic work meets repeatedly with what Freud saw as a "resistance from the id . . . [where] all the mental processes, relationships and distributions of force are unchangeable, fixed and rigid" (*ibid.*, p. 242). It is this tenacious resistance to the effects of analysis that characterizes the patients whose analytic histories are reported in this book, and which the author reflects on in the theoretical part of the book by reconsidering questions initially raised by Freud in the light of his own contributions on the negative, narcissism, language, the setting, and thirdness. His remarks are centred on Freud's question concerning the change of orientation in the treatment towards interminable analysis, when "the process backtracks, goes into reverse, and follows the model of negativizing regression . . . the analyst is betrayed by the orientation of the psyche which seems more concerned with preserving a state of illbeing than fighting against it" (pp. 46–47, this text.)

While he does not minimize the impact of the countertransference reactions in these disappointing evolutions, they do not seem to him sufficient to account for them fully. Furthermore, the suffering of these patients is situated well beyond the conflict engendered by envy of the penis in the woman and the repudiation of femininity in the man, and also well beyond masochism. It is true that the renewed interest Freud took in the obstacles and difficulties facing analysis, in "Constructions in analysis" (1937d), and the fresh perspectives that resulted from it, have given us a better understanding of the impact on mental functioning, and on the analytic situation, of an *amnesic memory* (Green, 2000b) whose traumatic quality resides in the fact that the traces inscribed in the mind at a time when "the infant could hardly speak" could not be constituted into memory traces and, therefore, have remained unrepresentable and inaccessible to memory. He writes:

> When traumas occur before language is acquired, remembering is impossible . . . The transference is a process of actualization more than one of remembering; for the analysand does not recognize the return of the past in it . . . I propose to call this phenomenon *amnesic remembering outside the field of conscious and unconscious memories.* [*ibid.*, p. 89, original emphasis]

With regard to this notion Green affirms that the aim of psychoanalysis, which transforms the past investment into knowledge (through recognition), is to allow the present to be. Thus it is crucial not to minimize the importance of the risk of reviving early painful traces in patients who are compelled to repeat an encysting and sterilizing relationship in an identical mode, and for whom the transition from a closed relationship to an open relationship is fraught with "the danger of renewing, *in vivo*, the trauma that was at the origin of the more or less deadly repetitive formation" (*ibid.*, p. 132). But, even though the childhood of these patients was marked by major traumas, the situation was often no worse than for other patients whose treatments have taken a more positive course. So this risk of painful reliving does not seem to him sufficient either to account for the tenacity of the resistances of the patients whose histories are reported in this book, nor for "a particularly clear expression of the work of the negative in which the action of the destructive drives predominates" (p. 172, this text.). In fact, "No description, however complete," he says, "enables us to understand the reasons for the suffering of these patients so that we can come to their help" (*ibid.*). Why does the prospect of being cured represent such a danger for them, leading them to defend themselves against it so actively and with such determination, even at the price of their psychical life, and in some cases even at the price of their somatic life? What can justify such sacrifices? As with Nanon, who remains "an enigma" for her psychoanalyst, both in terms of the diagnosis and in terms of the rigidity of her defences, these cases constitute a "challenge thrown down for psychoanalysis [which] must be met, and [which] must stimulate research so that these discouraging effects can be tackled more effectively" (*ibid.*)

This is the challenge, then, that André Green takes up in the theoretical part of his book, while being careful "not to confuse all the forms of failure of analysis with the negative therapeutic reaction . . . which sets in after a satisfying phase of analytic work" (pp. 45–46, this text). In this book, which constitutes a follow-up to *Key Ideas for a Contemporary Psychoanalysis* (Green, 2002a) where he revisits his principal concepts in order to identify the lines of force for future research, André Green pursues his enquiry by focusing on the causes of these psychoanalytic nonsuits, elaborating, as Fernando Urribarri puts it in his Postscript, a "dynamic core . . .

around which bundles of reflections unfold, grouped together in chapters whose titles themselves function as vanishing points towards a realm beyond the text" (p. 191 in this text). This "beyond" enters into multiple resonance with the essential threads of André Green's work as a whole, knowledge of which is necessary in order to penetrate deeply into the intelligibility of what he is saying. The conceptual "dynamic core" in relation to which he examines a certain number of notions, seems to me to be organized around the contrastive use of two notions: *the metaphorization of analytic speech under the effect of the setting* and *the internalization of the negative*. The common resonance of these notions with the concept of the framing structure of the mother, put forward in his structural approach to primary narcissism (Green, 1967), confers on them the quality of a notional pair.

The metaphor of the weaver that Freud employs in the interpretation of *the dream of the botanical monograph*, citing lines from Goethe's Faust,

> ". . . a thousand threads one treadle throws,
> Where fly the shuttles hither and thither,
> Unseen the threads are knit together,
> And an infinite combination grows." (1900a, p. 283),

provides a good illustration of Green's approach to analytic speech and its metaphorization under the effect of the setting. This process of "decentralizing metaphorization", which is operative in the heterogeneity of the signifier owing to the effects of the work of the negative in its structuring function, is characterized by

> progressive and retrogressive movements that facilitate the emergence of the transference. Alternating erotic and aggressive impulses punctuate the development of communication, the web of which has to be constantly untangled to reveal the movements of the unconscious. . . . In fact, these movements of analytic communication must be understood as the expression of the oscillations of the transference: more precisely, of the tensions between the transference and the resistances . . . [a] mode of expression [which] favour[s] the underlying demands of fantasy activity. [pp. 40–41 in this text]

The notion of the metaphorizing power of the setting which "transforms the dual relation analyst/analysand into a relation of thirdness" (*ibid.*) follows on from his psychoanalytic conception of language (Green, 1983a), the main lines of which he recalls in his book. It also resonates with the model of free association presented in "The central phobic position" (Green, 2000a), a text in which André Green speaks of "arborescent structure and associative irradiation in which retroactive reverberation and anticipatory annunciation act in concert or in alternation" (p. 143). In this model, we find an echo of his conception of "exploded time", since "free association gives us access to a complex temporal structure . . . which means that psychic organization is constantly being reshaped over the course of its history" (*ibid.*). In the same text, this model of free association finds its negative counterpoint in the notion of "associative avoidance", a manifestation of the destructuring influence of the negative in the analytic session. Associative avoidance refers to the use of negativity in analytic speech as an active defence, using "destructivity which is directed, *first and foremost, at the subject's own psychic functioning*" (*ibid.*, p. 146). This defence is mobilized, he says, to protect the subject against a traumatic threat whose essence resides not only in the risk of reawakening the most significant trauma, but in the combination of different traumatic constellations, where the awakening of any single one of these traumas enters into amplificatory resonance with the others. More specifically, it protects against a danger engendered by the resonance and correspondence between certain themes whose full efflorescence and complete revival in consciousness pose a threat to the organization of the ego. These relations of mutual reinforcement are experienced by the subject as a terrifying invasion by uncontrollable forces, creating a potential disintegration and unleashing incredible violence against the patient's ego (*ibid.*, pp. 136–137).

In the cases reported, the resistances are not limited to this associative avoidance characteristic of borderline functioning, but are revealed in the shape of a global and radical attack by the patient on his or her own mind, and by an equally radical opposition to analytic work which manifests itself by what one patient of mine called a "state of non-life". This state was a mark of the intensity of the *psychic desertification* (Green, 2005), which invaded, diffusely, her psychic functioning and manifested itself in massive acts of forgetting. These forgettings were not a result of repression, but of negative hallucinations of thought and speech in the session, combined with negative hallucinations of her image in the mirror as well as with bodily negative hallucinations (Delourmel, 2009). During many years, she told me in her sessions about instantaneous and massive forgetting of what she had just said and of what I had just said to her—acts of forgetting which left her in a state of painful emptiness comparable to the void she experienced when she saw her image in a window or mirror, a perception which give her "a strange sensation". This void, she told me later, "is a sense of nothingness, of inexistence; I have the impression that a part of me is dead. I am like a jellyfish; there's nothing to get hold of, nothing." Such *psychic desertification* results from the activation of a process of *internalization of the negative*. To help the reader understand this new concept which is introduced in this book, it will be useful if I make some clarifying remarks on three Greenian concepts, the *work of the negative*, the *instinctualization of the ego's defences*, and the *framing structure of psychic space*, remarks that are complementary to the study made by Fernando Urribarri in his Postscript, where he recalls the main Greenian concepts via a chronological reading of André Green's work. In counterpoint to his Postscript, I would refer the reader to a paper (Delormel, 2004, 2005) I wrote a few years ago, in which I tried to take a dialectical approach by giving prominence to the mutual theoretical resonances between these theoretical concepts, on the one hand, and their resonances with the concepts elaborated by André Green from the point of view of analytic practice on the other.

First, *the work of the negative*: for Green, the *negative* is not limited to "all the psychical operations of which repression is the prototype, and which later give rise to distinct variations such as negation, disavowal, and foreclosure" (Green, 1993, p. 269), that is to say, to the mechanisms of defence whose grouping together under the term of primary defences resides in the fact that, unlike the others, their common aim is "the treatment by 'Yes' or 'No' of psychic activity falling within their jurisdiction" (*ibid.*, p. 12). He extends the work of the negative beyond the sphere of the ego to all the psychical agencies, which leads him to envisage a "No" of the ego, a "No" of the superego, and a "No" of the id. In short, the work of the negative

> brings together the aspects inherent to the most general psychic
> activity, which is common to all human beings and which cannot
> avoid the negativization of an excess (drive activity); among the

principal vicissitudes met with are repression, identification and sublimation. [*ibid.*]

It is within the context of this extensive approach to the work of the negative that he makes the hypothesis of both its structuring and destructuring influence in psychic life. In the service of psychic organization, the work of the negative operates through a process of "decentralizing metaphorization", which he conceives of as a play "of oscillations which allow for the function of lack"; and, as he has already pointed out, "everything resides in the structuring or destructuring value of the lack" (*ibid.*, p. 283). The theoretical echo of this process is present in his elaborations concerning the metaphorization of analytic speech under the influence of the setting. In the service of disorganization, the work of the negative is operative when

> narcissism takes over from masochism to ensure the closure which makes it impermeable to change; when disavowal, whose effects seem at first to be limited, subjects splitting to a withdrawal of investment causing the subject to experience extreme states of disengagement. [*ibid.*, p. 13]

(A process of disengagement theorized in his concept of the "subjectal unbinding of the ego" (1993, pp. 148–149).)

Second, the instinctualization of the ego's defences

> . . . is connected with the destructive drives. By virtue of their act of refusal, the defences, which are supposed to ward off the effects of these drives, themselves acquire a potential for annihilation akin to that against which they are erected. [1993, p. 132]

For André Green—and this is very important on the practical level—the disobjectalizing function of the destructive drive, whose mode of expression is negative narcissism—that is, "the dark double of the unitary Eros of positive narcissism . . . which tends towards non-existence, anaesthesia, emptiness, the blank, whether this blank cathects affect, representation, or thought" (1976, p. 10)— does not always exist in the active state, but is activated in certain configurations where the limits between inside and outside are thrown into serious crisis. This may be seen as an extreme solution of struggle against "invasion by the Other", illustrated by "states of fusion" where the danger is one of "implosion or explosion", states in which the tendency towards the zero object, neither the One nor the Other, but the Neutral, becomes the object of investment (*ibid.*, p. 28). This is the case in those primordial moments of psychical life that underlie psychosis, where the infant, subjected to his mother's intense instinctual activity, "not only has to fight against internal instinctual excitement . . . but also has to fight on a second front against the external source of the object's instinctual madness" (1980, p. 244). In such circumstances the destructive drives are mobilized because the ego cannot constitute itself and seem to play the role of a last ditch attempt to neutralize the object in order to "put an end to the fusional relationship with the primordial object . . . psychosis is a *conjuration of the object*" (*ibid.*, p. 243). This is also the case in non-neurotic modes of functioning, but in a less absolute way, for these modes of functioning always present oscillations between unbinding and rebinding. The resultant *psychic desertification*, maintained by this compulsive and blind recourse to disobjectalizing disinvestment, is at the same time a means of survival:

> . . . the death of the object has to be both sought after and warded off. The only way of satisfying these contradictory requirements is to freeze the experience of time and to deny the phantasies connected with them. [2002a, p. 185]

Third, *the notion of framing structure*: here I just want to point out that it is through this complex process, involving drive activity and the negative, the metapsychology of which André Green explores in his structural approach to primary narcissism, that the work of mourning the primordial object occurs; and, further, that this concept offers a model of primary identification concerning simultaneously the mother and the father (Green, 1966). By conferring on the psyche the quality of holding mental functioning, this framing structure of psychic space attests to the structuring function of the work of the negative and assures its functionality in the work of *représentance*[1] operating in the heterogeneity of the signifier.

This is how he introduces the notion of the *internalization of the negative* in his book:

> These cases were marked by more or less incapacitating psychic events. When the evolution shows that these after-effects marking

the organization of the mind are long term, I think that we are in the presence of what I propose to call the *internalization of the negative*. I mean that the mind has introjected these defensive primary reactions as a mode of unconscious defence, altering the psychical organization and preventing it from developing along the usual lines of the pleasure-principle. In other words, the mind escapes the models of behaviour dictated by positive experiences. The outcome has made it lose its flexibility of adaptation and called for reactions dictated by acquired defensive distortions, attesting to the internalization of the negative, a form of negative primary identification.

Of course, this case is not always constituted as a model induced by pathogenic mechanisms. It is often the sign of a certain vulnerability that leaves no other option than repetition. This repetition has nothing automatic about it, but indicates a rigidity governing psychic reactions, without a capacity for adapting to circumstances better. What has happened, then, with the internalization of the negative, is that the manifestations of negativity have become identificatory introjections that are not so much chosen as obligatory; they have become what might be called second nature, artificially grafted on to a mind that has been precociously modified by pathology and its defensive reactions. The latter become so deeply rooted in the subject who has been subjected to them that they can appear for a long time to be constitutional, forming part of an innate nature. [p. 174, this text]

What becomes anchored in the psyche of these patients is to be understood, then, as the internalization of an early defensive mode of functioning which resides in resorting defensively to the disobjectalizing function of the death drive, an internalization which concerns the past beyond time and beyond remembering, evoked by Freud in "Constructions in analysis" (1937d). This internalization of the negative is a form of those returns of the past which consist, as Freud said, in "the repetition of reactions dating from infancy", and which are actualized through the revival of reactions to which the emerging ego had once resorted in emergency to cope with a traumatic situation—reactions that are repeated in an identical manner. Resulting from "the introjection of primary defensive reactions", and consisting in a "negative primary identification", this internalization of the negative should be conceived of as a counterpoint to the processes involved in primary identification. It is a sign of the

failure of the subject to come to terms with the loss of the primordial object, and also a sign of the failure of the work of the negative
in its structuring function. It is a primordial failure with which all
the "childhood experiences and the scars they have left in the mind,
often for a very long time after the events that caused them" (p. 173,
this text) will echo in an amplified way. Moreover, each of these
experiences will reactivate and amplify this negative identification.
In these clinical configurations, the *internalization of the negative*,
maintained and reinforced by the permanent echoing of these multiple scars with this primordial failure to mourn the primordial
object, is at the origin of an organization of psychic functioning
under the sway of a radical negative, in a sphere beyond masochism. Over the course of time, this radical *negative* has become for
these subjects the sole reality. This is because the patient's life experiences have convinced him or her that only these states of non-life
have the power to restrain the endless pull towards the psychic
abyss. This process is constantly actualized in and through the
instinctual investment of a significant object, which contains the
danger for these patients of reactivating in the deep layers of their
psyches their failure to mourn the primordial object. "These forms
of resistance to recovery," the author writes, "feeding on destructivity, prove to be a way for the patient of hanging on and, no
doubt, of surviving as best he or she can" (p. 172, this text). It is this
compromise–survival which the patient feels he/she has to defend
against the effects of analysis, but at the high price of psychic desertification. It is a very unstable compromise, which is at the source
of a vicious circle self-perpetuated by this paradoxical defensive
recourse to destructivity. This defensive mode, which consists in an
"instinctualization" of the ego's defences, in fact amplifies the danger that it aims to avoid, confining the ego within a vicious circle
that is short-sighted. The danger is one of losing the representation
of the object induced by "the primary murder whose aim is to carry
out an *excorporation of the abandoning* [and/or too exciting] *object*"
(2002b, p. 162). All this helps us to understand better the impasse
that the analytic situation constitutes for these patients: their incapacity to use the metaphorizing power of the setting makes the analytic situation permanently traumatic for them, with the result that
they feel they have to defend themselves against it by resorting to
forms of resistance which immobilize their psychic life. And they

will continue to employ these resistances as long as they are convinced that this state of non-life has the power to prevent the danger of breakdown (Winnicott, 1974).

We are indebted to André Green for enriching our understanding of the drama of these patients, and of the meaning of the defensive vicious circle that they are locked into. This understanding not only allows the analyst to have greater tolerance in himself for these analytic journeys, where there is a great risk of getting bogged down in the jungle of psychic rifts and the defensive systems employed to deal with them, but also to understand why it is necessary to respect these defensive nooses for as long as possible. The patient will then feel that his or her distress and sense of confinement are understood deeply, and it is unnecessary to stress the narcissistic importance for the patient of the analyst's understanding of his or her drama, which goes beyond words. Sometimes the underground work that is accomplished in these analyses—when the analyst has survived (in the sense of Winnicott's *use of the object*, 1969)—allows the patient to acquire an internal confidence which enables him or her to take the risk of loosening his or her defensive grip a little bit. It is within this transfero–countertransference situation, where the subject can take the risk of letting go to some extent of these measures to which his or her emerging ego had once resorted in emergency to cope with a traumatic situation—measures that will be repeated in exactly the same way as in the past as long as the ego does not dispose of functional means capable of transforming the traumatic revival into reminiscence—that "these disillusions . . . sometimes lead to an entirely unhoped for surprise, even if it turns out to be limited" (p. 51, this text). This deeper understanding that André Green has brought to these extreme clinical configurations also allows psychoanalysts to reflect better on the limits of analysability, which "can only be those of the analyst, the patient's alter ego" (1975, p. 36).

This notion of internalization of the negative leads him at the end of his book to question the relations between "the negative of individual clinical practice and the socio-cultural expressions of the negative" and to defend "the idea of a unified negative assuming diverse forms". "The first", he says, "has succeeded in passing itself off as unconscious"; the second results from "an aggression from outside, from an 'externalization', which attacks the inner truth". It is the product of a dissimulated falsification [of truth] combined with violence:

> Nobody really believes in it; no one listens to those whose task it is to spread it around, no one backs their statements up with faith, but it is the so-called official truth, the only one that is admitted. . . . It only gathers accomplices and specialists of terror. [p. 185, this text]

However, for André Green, both these forms of negativity are connected, an articulation he elaborates by contrasting "masochism and perversion, two forms of attack on the life of the mind: one turns against itself, and the other is subject to a cynical domination that has force of law" (pp. 185–186, this text). This notion of *delusional perversion*, operative in collective life, echoes with the notion of the *"perversion of the Ego"* (Green, 1993, pp. 122–130), which he uses to characterize the alienation of the ego invaded in its defences by the destructive impulses.

André Green's lucidity (like Freud, he is animated by the love of truth), combined with his rigorous approach, underlies the elaboration of this book as well as that of his work in general, but it does not lead him to radical pessimism. On the contrary, it opens out on to a note of hope, for, after giving a lucid account of these disappointing and sometimes tragic evolutions, the author seeks to account for their causes. This also attests to the depth of his psychoanalytic and human commitment to these difficult patients, a commitment that he does not regret in spite of these evolutions of which he has "recollections of disappointing experiences, but not bad memories" (p. 133, this text).

Note

1. Translator's note: a general category including different types of representation (psychic representative, ideational representative, representative of the drive, etc.), which implies the movement, the activity, of representation.

Introduction

This book is the result of more than fifty years of practising psychoanalysis. It brings together the ideas gathered from my experience. Not all my experience, which is more diverse, and has often been a source of great satisfaction when I have succeeded in helping, and sometimes curing, some of my patients. I am grateful to them for having helped me to understand the nature of their difficulties and to resolve the problems that they presented.

"I treated him, but God healed him."[1] A good many qualities are certainly needed to successfully remove the obstacles that have impeded a patient's personal development, but, alas, I have experienced disappointing evolutions more often than I would have liked, either because I was unable to avert the outcome, or because I was unable to reverse its course towards a better direction.

I have gathered together the ideas derived from my least fortunate experiences and set them out in the theoretical part of this book. I have also wanted to include in this volume some clinical observations: some of these have been kindly communicated to me by collaborators and others come from my own practice. What I have retained is the result of a choice that is far from exhaustive. None the less, it allows the reader to form quite a varied picture of the clinical experience involved in these cases. This collection is not contradictory, and reflects a reasonably homogeneous set of views. It is a pleasure for me to present the reader with what I believe, or at least hope, is a coherent vision of what my experience has taught me. I hope that the reading I am proposing, assisted by others, will ultimately throw light on a clinical picture which has seemed to me, rightly or wrongly, to have been somewhat neglected by my contemporaries.

Last, I would like to refer the reader to the chapter on *The Beast in the Jungle*, by Henry James, in my book *L'Aventure négative. Lecture psychanalytique d'Henry James* (Green, 2009).

Note

1. Translator's note: the oft-repeated motto of the sixteenth century French surgeon, Ambroise Paré.

Marilyn Monroe: death of an icon

"Some time after the death of their common patient (M.M.),
Milton Wexler and Ralph Greenson envisaged a research
project for the Foundation for Research in Psychoanalysis in
Beverly Hills, and a book which would have treated of the
Failures of psychoanalysis. This book was never written"

(Schneider, 2006, p. 223)

When America woke up, and the whole world with her, on 5
August 1962 to learn of Marilyn Monroe's death, it came as a very
bad surprise. Suddenly, tongues were loosened. Dead? How? From
an overdose? From suicide? Or had she been assassinated by those
who wanted to silence her? Or alternatively, had she passed away
as a result of the poor medical care that she had received from her
doctors, and particularly from her psychoanalyst, the renowned
Ralph Greenson? And yet, those who had met her a few hours
before her demise had found her full of life and showing no signs
of wanting to die.

She had not had a date with anyone the evening before, which
in itself was rather unusual. Little was known about her future

plans. She seemed ready to separate from her famous lovers; she had said goodbye—at least, she had intended to do so, even though she was unable to do it—to the "Prez", as she called him, but it seems she had stayed in contact until the end with his brother Bob Kennedy, with whom she was having a steady love affair. As Attorney General, was he afraid that rumours about him might be divulged? Was Greenson mixed up in intrigues that were supposed to remain secret?

Marilyn Monroe had made it clear that she wished to leave her psychoanalyst, although nothing had as yet been decided. I do not pretend to see clearly into these mysterious circumstances. The fact remains that her death came as surprising news for the anonymous crowds that had elected, celebrated, and adulated her, even though they knew nothing of her. For who could really say they knew who Marilyn Monroe was?

She had been in psychoanalysis, then, for thirty months with Greenson, and a lot of rumours had been circulating about this treatment. It was common knowledge that Greenson did not confine himself to practising "classical" psychoanalysis. He also saw to it that she respected her professional engagements and that she arrived on stage on time. He kept a close eye on her chemotherapy and had employed Eunice Murray, a cross between a warder, a head nurse, and an appointed spy, to administer her drugs and generally watch over her.

Marilyn was born Norma Jean Baker. She was abandoned very early on by her mother, who was mentally ill. Of an unknown father, she never bore his name: Mortenson. When her mother was declared unfit to take care of her, she entrusted her to one of her friends, Grace McKee, who looked after her in a slapdash manner before sending her back at the age of eight. Marilyn was placed in several orphanages and was accustomed to saying that her mother was dead. No doubt she also preferred this version of her history. She was forced to give up her schooling before her secondary studies in order to get married, out of economic necessity. And yet she had a great deal of intellectual curiosity, and had read the major works of literature.

In adolescence, she posed as a model. When she became anxious, she would behave like an abandoned child, like an orphan. It is probable that she had a precocious sexual life, not out of interest or personal curiosity, but because she understood very early on that this was what men expected of her. Her second husband was the baseball champion Joe DiMaggio, who undoubtedly loved her sincerely until the end. She divorced him and married Arthur Miller, whom she found too cold, but she tried to make him happy as best she could. By all accounts, she never enjoyed a satisfying sexual life. She confessed to Greenson that she had never had an orgasm, in spite of her many lovers. One of these, who seems to have counted for her, was André de Dienes, her photographer and friend. It should be added, moreover, that Marilyn was afraid of the cinema because it involved speaking; she much preferred photos, including pornographic photos (as early as the age of twenty-two) which her photographers took very successfully and sold very dearly. De Dienes used to say to her, "Look bad; not just sexy, but dirty." She played the game, but repeated that she wanted to be an artist, not a sex machine. This hope was constantly disappointed.

On her death, Gladys Baker, her mother, showed no reaction. So she had been quite justified in claiming, ahead of time, that her mother was dead.

So, what were her personal ambitions? We have seen that she wanted to play the greatest theatrical roles on the stage, including Lady Macbeth. Her dream was to act with Laurence Olivier, who was accustomed to neurotic actresses, having been married for a long time to Vivien Leigh, the unforgettable Blanche Dubois in *A Streetcar Named Desire* and also one of Greenson's patients. Marilyn would also have liked to play the role of Blanche DuBois, but was unsuccessful. Laurence Olivier, who loathed her, gave her just one piece of advice, "Look sexy." She was labelled as a titillating woman. She was not given the opportunity of playing the role either of Cecily Koertner in John Huston's film on Freud, or of Zelda, the crazy wife of F. Scott Fitzgerald.

Among her famous lovers must be included Frank Sinatra (another of Ralph Greenson's patients), a friend of the Kennedy's, and a provider of women for John Kennedy. It was not until 1962 that she broke off her relationship with Sinatra. She would sometimes spend hours in front of the mirror, and when she was asked what she was doing, she would say, "I'm looking at her." She always said that her fear of the cinema was linked to her fear of words, to her panic at having to speak in front of the camera. She used to say, "The cinema is like the sexual act, the other person uses your body to live out fantasies in which you play no part . . . I have never belonged to anything or anyone—only to fear!" She was referring to Rilke, who had written that beauty was nothing but the beginning of terror.

It was through one of her professional contacts that she had the idea of resorting to psychoanalysis. She had taken courses at the Actors Studio and Lee Strasberg, who believed in psychoanalysis and used it in his teaching, recommended her to Margaret Hohenberg, who had her in treatment for five years. After that, she was in analysis with Marianne Kris, the daughter of Freud's paediatrician, and also one of Freud's former patients, who was now a well-known analyst and a close friend of Anna Freud. When Marilyn left the East coast, Marianne Kris referred her to Ralph Greenson. He was a psychoanalytic celebrity, undoubtedly the most renowned psychoanalyst on the West coast. He had had many Hollywood stars as patients, enjoyed a considerable reputation, and flirted with the cinema. He frequented the corridors of 20th Century Fox, who paid him to get Marilyn to respect her engagements. He supported her in her court actions against her producers, supervised the scenarios of her films, and was on friendly terms with the directors, many of whom could not tolerate Marilyn's unpredictable and capricious character. Some of those who directed her in films detested her, Cukor and John Huston, in particular. But when she died, they missed her.

Greenson was known as "the lady-killer". He was very respectful of sexual taboos and was never reproached for having taken advantage of Marilyn's physical attributes. He supplemented the psychoanalytic treatment by prescribing medication, whether in the form of sedatives or sleeping pills. Marianne Kris had asked for her to be hospitalized at the Payne Whitney Clinic in New York, an experience that Marilyn found very difficult to tolerate. She became violent and was finally let out when Joe DiMaggio intervened on her behalf. She later wrote to Greenson to complain about very distressing feelings of solitude. For his part, Greenson said he was struck by the emptiness of her object relationships and the intensity of her defences against homosexuality. None the less, Marilyn had two homosexual affairs, one of which was with Joan Crawford, whom she disliked intensely.

It seems to me that she was trying to explore and test out her sexuality, without ever finding anything that could satisfy her. She yielded without much resistance to the sexual demands of men, sometimes strangers, and described herself as a "whore". She suffered from an incurable feeling of being the child of an infanticidal mother. She was also treated by Dr Engelberg, who assisted Greenson and took responsibility for administering chemically-based treatments, very often Nembutal. During the inquest following her death, one of the investigators concluded that murder was evident. Duly noted.

What can be said of Greenson, who met her when he was about fifty? Romeo Greenschpoon was the twin of a sister, Juliette Greenschpoon, a musician whom he accompanied on the violin. His first analyst had been Stekel, who was a dissident of Freud and excluded by him, and then Fenichel, the major authority on psychoanalytic theory in the USA, and finally Frances Deri (a student of Simmel).

Greenson had a very renowned clientele: Peter Lorre, Vivien Leigh, Inge Stevens, Tony Curtis, and Frank Sinatra, among others. He first proposed that Marilyn have sessions in *her* home, then in *his.* Marilyn became a regular visitor to the Greenson's home, on the suggestion of Greenson himself, who wanted to offer her what she lacked. She was a friend of Hilde Greenson, the psychoanalyst's wife; she also became a friend of his children, and gradually became increasingly dependent on the family.

In fact, Greenson was a cinema enthusiast. He once admitted that his secret desire was to become a film director. He minimized the fact that he had partially written the scenario for the films in which Marilyn was the star, and that she had also created—unconsciously—his own role. He collaborated closely with 20th Century Fox, and they referred to him as soon as Marilyn's behaviour created a serious problem (showing up late for filming). His countertransference eventually caused problems. His associate, Milton Wexler, had realized this and tried to warn him. Milton Wexler had understood that the method chosen by Greenson was doomed to failure and that there was no limit to his reparative tendencies. Moreover, he had sensed that what Greenson offered Marilyn—a home where she seemed to be adopted—could only aggravate in his patient the suffering of having been deprived of a home in the past. But Greenson, persuaded that he had made the right choice, would not listen. It is not altogether impossible that he had received the backing and support of Anna Freud, with whom he was on close terms.

He eventually asked Max Scheler, Freud's doctor, and a psychoanalyst, to give him a new analysis, which he accepted. But that was not enough. In fact, Greenson became more and more dependent on Marilyn. So he decided to go on a long trip to Europe with his wife, which Marilyn found very difficult to tolerate. Greenson had to maintain their relationship by giving her a chess piece, a knight, which was supposed to serve as a transitional object. Her lovers could do nothing to help, and she begged him to return.

If we turn towards Marilyn's lovers, her husbands obviously have to be included: Joe DiMaggio and Arthur Miller, as well as other more regular lovers such as André de Dienes, Frank Sinatra, and Yves Montand, who finally dropped her as if she was nothing but an incurably immature child. There is also the remarkable case of someone who was never her lover, Clark Gable, about whom she said that, although she did not want to sleep with him, she loved him *like a father*. She had met him during the shooting of *The Misfits*, and admitted to having felt authentic physical sensations during the filming scenes.

Marlon Brando was her friend, and Dean Martin, too. She had an abortion during one shoot, when she was married to Arthur Miller. Sexuality had no effect on her. She could not overcome her frigidity. She is reported to have given herself to strangers (taxi drivers), and to have asked to be sodomized, without experiencing any particular excitement. She wanted to be told that she had a soul, which would have allowed her to "offer a part of her body".

Also on this impressive list were the Kennedy brothers. She sang "Happy Birthday" at the President's birthday party, while Jackie refrained from attending (May 1962). Marilyn's dress, which had been sewn on her (for 6000 dollars), allowed her to make a dazzling appearance. Peter Lawford had announced her arrival by saying, "The late Marilyn Monroe", the double meaning of which is evident. The circumstances surrounding her death were mysterious. Even Greenson was implicated, suspected of being Bob Kennedy's accomplice. He observed a silence that was justified by professional secrecy, which must have weighed heavily upon him.

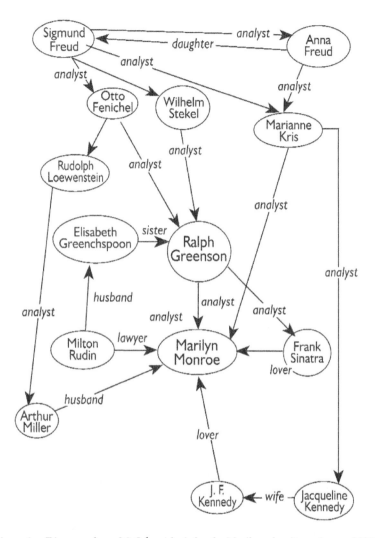

Figure 1.   Diagram from M. Schneider's book, *Marilyn, dernières séances*, 2006.

Her funeral was organized by Joe Dimaggio, who loved her without any question and who selected the guests, leaving out those who were connected with the cinema. Shortly before her death, Milton Wexler had no doubt understood that Greenson's countertransference reactions were *a structure*—that is, a network of entangled relationships—that could not be undone. The relations between the highly interconnected members of this society constituted a rather endogamic world in which analytic neutrality had given way to the generalized mediatization of its members. On Marilyn's death, Greenson, who was very affected by it, had the impression that she had slipped away from him, just when she was getting better and planning to leave him. She had found the solution, she said.

She had understood what analysis was—that is, she had understood the fundamental role of associations. But she had recognized her inability to supply them during sessions. So, she had decided to record tapes, alone, and to send them to Greenson afterwards. She was no longer afraid of words, but could not link them up with her transference object. Thinking and speaking did not go together. Overcoming the slanderous things that were said about him, Greenson was to call Marilyn, "my child, my pain, my sister, my insanity".

What should one think of this failure? It has to be recognized, first of all, that Marilyn was perhaps, certainly even, beyond the resources of psychoanalysis. She had experienced traumas too early on in life, traumas that were too deep and too incurable for her to be able tolerate the inherent frustrations of analytic treatment. Furthermore, she had too many easy solutions available to neutralize the effect of the frustrations. It goes without saying that she had not experienced love; and, above all, she had not allowed herself to become a mother, feeling too ambivalent towards her own. She was afraid of repeating what she had suffered. Behind her fabulous success, she had experienced nothing but failure in relation to her ego-ideals. She could not believe in anyone's love, and she was inhabited and haunted by fear. Rather than being a guarantee of love, her beauty had turned her into a prey. She had not known either her father or her mother, who, struggling with her psychosis, had not even realized that she had a daughter. She had been abandoned by her various foster mothers one after the other. In short, she was very much an orphan in search of her unknown or mad parents.

Greenson believed that her unhappiness stemmed from having waited for her father in vain. Perhaps. In fact, it seems to me that he was unaware of the studies devoted to primary deficiencies in relation to maternal pathology. I do not know what would have happened if he had been aware of them, and if he had been able to integrate the ideas of Donald Woods Winnicott. It might not have changed anything, but it is certain that his professional attitude would have benefited a great deal from it. Anna Freud, who, as Freud's daughter, was considered the legitimate heir of his thought, saw Marilyn for a few sessions, and advised Greenson. It is not certain that she was the best choice that English psychoanalysis had to offer American psychoanalysis. At any rate, it has to be said that American psychoanalysts took a very long time to understand Winnicott's ideas. For them, he passed for a Kleinian, which is the worst misinterpretation one can make. When Marilyn wanted to consult a prominent person in the discipline, she turned quite naturally towards Anna Freud, without much benefit. The latter's notes concerning her are extremely trite. One might have expected better.

Marilyn is an exemplary case of a failed psychoanalytic treatment due to the catastrophic effects of fate, the constantly faltering love of her husbands, her lovers, and her friends. She elicited everyone's love, but no one was prepared to pay the price. She stands as a paradigm, a martyr, and sacrificial figure. She will remain in our memory, wreathed in our pity and our compassion.[1]

Note

1. I am indebted to Michel Schneider and his book *Marilyn, dernières séances* (2006) for the documentation for this chapter. I would ask the interested reader to refer to the References section of this book.

PART I
THEORETICAL STUDY

CHAPTER ONE

From the treatment of neuroses to the crisis of psychoanalysis

During the last years of his life and up until his death, Freud was constantly asking himself questions about the obstacles standing in the way of psychoanalytic therapy. This was the reason he wrote "Analysis terminable and interminable" (1937c). He returned to the question shortly after, in 1938, in *An Outline of Psychoanalysis* (1940a [1938]). There he notes the causes for the lack of success of psychoanalysis without giving any definitive answers, but emphasizes the effect of the destructive drives. He affirms his interest in forms of regression akin to psychosis, but not as serious as the latter. In other words, he was already wondering about what would subsequently be called borderline cases, and he seems to have foreseen the evolution that would make them a major theme of interest in the future.

In 1999, the *Newsletter* of the International Psychoanalytic Association published the results of a vast survey on psychoanalysis and related therapies. This survey masked a certain degree of concern about what appeared to be a loss of ground by psychoanalysis, accompanied by a corresponding progression of the psychotherapies. Admittedly, the various psychoanalytic movements do not always give concordant results. In North America, psychoanalysis

and the psychotherapies are no longer separated by a sharp dividing line. The only difference is in the number of weekly sessions.
The survey revealed many disillusions concerning the method and
the rules that had governed the practices of earlier generations.

In Northern Europe, "psychoanalytically trained" psychotherapists are exerting pressure to have their activity better recognized.
Elsewhere, in certain countries where there is a policy of reimburs-
ing sessions fully, irrespective of the number of weekly sessions,
few patients are ready to undertake an analysis of four or five
sessions a week. By way of a curious exception, the British Psychoanalytical Society did not respond to the survey. But it subsequently
published interesting results concerning practice in the UK. Sixty
per cent of cases were reckoned to be in analysis. Concerning the
remaining 40%, the information is not very precise regarding the
setting of the therapies proposed to the patients. Yet it may be esti-
mated that 30% at least of the patients treated by psychoanalysts in
the UK are proposed psychotherapies. This significant figure gives
no precise idea of the modalities or principles of the psychotherapies practised. There is every reason to be astonished by the scarcity
of information published under this rubric concerning what
amounts to a considerable proportion of cases, and by the scarcity
of observations concerning psychotherapeutic practice.

However, elsewhere in Europe, and especially in France, the
difference between the classical treatment and the face-to-face treatment is still maintained, even if, in certain cases, psychodrama is
recommended alongside the psychotherapies (particularly in
France).

This leaves South America. The survey notes a high proportion
of psychotherapists who seem to suffer from problems of identity
compared with psychoanalysts. This situation is the result of the
choice made by many psychoanalytic societies, which, following
the example of the American Psychoanalytical Society, have long
considered psychoanalytic practice as the exclusive reserve of
doctors. This has not prevented the prominent analysts of these
societies from participating in the training of psychotherapists in
those institutions that sought their expertise. Over the course of
time, psychotherapists have pointed to the quality of the training
received from prominent practitioners of psychoanalysis in order to
demand recognition for their field of competence. The change of

policy in psychoanalytic societies, many of which have made psychoanalytic training available to candidates without medical training (following the English and French societies), has already modified the situation.

Finally, current generations are affected by a mutation related to the historical and socio-economic changes affecting psychoanalytic activity:

- the increase in the number of analysands presenting narcissistic and identity-related pathologies, borderline states, etc.;
- the variation of indications, which shows that more and more neuroses are treated face-to-face, with fewer weekly sessions.

These observations raise questions about psychoanalytic activity today; or, more particularly, about the relations between psychoanalysis and psychotherapy. Generally speaking, it is accepted that psychotherapy conducted by a psychoanalyst has better chances of success. Moreover, contributions on the face-to-face setting by authors who are experienced psychoanalysts are often of great value (see Brusset, 2005a,b; Cahn, 2002). Yet, the idea of a crisis in psychoanalysis has to be considered.

In 1999, I already had the project of writing on a subject that goes beyond the well-known problem of the difficult cases, which had already been the object of many publications. My intention was to consider the question of the failures of psychoanalysis. I had to change my mind, for reasons that I shall explain later. I noticed, not without surprise, that the bibliographical references were particularly scarce, as if psychoanalysts sought to avoid this theme. Was this because they did not want to admit to themselves or acknowledge that their activity could meet with failures? At any rate, I felt truly alone in embarking on this undertaking. Was I going to be the psychoanalyst who had revealed a well-guarded secret, and who had risked being anathematized for daring to speak a truth that one would have preferred to keep quiet about?

Fortunately, I was mistaken. For several years, I had been running a seminar on case studies posing problems for young analysts. The seminar was well attended and I had the opportunity of admiring the talent of several of the participants who had accepted submitting for discussion the difficulties that they had encountered. The cases were presented in detail, often over several sessions. For my part, I commented on the material presented each time I had the opportunity of doing so, interweaving my thoughts with those proposed by the participants. These exchanges, associating the participants' comments with mine, were very rich. The basic rule was to take one's time and not to feel constrained by any particular time limit. Without losing sight of the general theme of our meetings, I understood that if I wanted to publish something in connection with what had been discussed in the seminars, rather than going it alone, it would be much more interesting to join forces with my colleagues and to present their cases in order to show that we seemed to share a common concern. So, I decided to pool our respective experience. Far from seeming to be an isolated effort, this collective undertaking offered us a broader horizon for our reflections. So it was that I decided to present my colleagues' contributions, naturally with their agreement.

What are the reasons for the impression we have that the difficulties of analysis have increased in recent years? It is difficult to say, precisely, and even more so to demonstrate that this is indeed the case. Are we not dealing, once again, with an idealization of the past? Or perhaps it will be said that the same obstacles to cure or recovery existed just as much in the past as today, but that they were less well identified. Or, alternatively, it may be thought that in the past we were content with more modest or more superficial results, without being aware of what remained unanalysed and continued to stand in the way of a more complete analysis. It is worth making a comparison here. Many analysts today accept continuing an analysis conducted by other colleagues a long time before, but which had resulted in only partially satisfying results. They venture to conduct a second or even a third analysis, which allows them to follow up the analytic work already done, and quite often to arrive at more satisfactory conclusions for the patients concerned. I, too, have experienced arrests of the analytic process, and blockages that led some patients to give up analysis. Sometimes this was because they themselves had tried working as an analyst without success, and, in other cases, it was because analysis had shown the limits of the benefits that they were able to derive from it.

While there are no statistical studies that allow us to make a valid quantitative evaluation, we can at least draw attention to certain facts and venture certain hypotheses. The first case, familiar to us for a very long time now, is that of interminable analysis. Freud discussed it in his article "Analysis terminable and interminable" (1937c). If I search my memory, I can recall a time when, for an analyst as experienced as Nacht, interminable analysis was a scourge to be avoided at any cost; to such an extent that, at the end of his career, one was surprised to see him encouraging the resistances of the patient against continuing the analysis, and pushing the analyst to precipitate the end of the treatment, to the great astonishment of those whose task it was to train others.

Alongside this technique, motivated by a phobia of interminability, Lacan opted for a different solution. We heard about his interminable analyses exceeding fifteen or twenty years, except that the sessions of these analysands, chained to their transference, rarely exceeded five minutes! Clearly, neither of these techniques coincided with our analytic ideals.

However, the generation that followed these pioneers of French psychoanalysis proved to be more ambitious. Mention should be made here, in particular, of Bouvet, whose influence was remarkable. When we refer to the golden age—if ever there was one—of psychoanalysis in France, it is noticeable that more attention was paid then than it is today to carefully establishing the indications of analysis, often after careful thought. In the case of patients who were considered regressed or too fragile, a negative decision was frequently taken with regard to analysis. Nevertheless, new ideas emerged. The first that should be mentioned was the categorization by Bouvet (1967) of genital structures in contrast with pregenital structures. This division corresponded approximately to the Oedipal neuroses in contrast with those in which fixations prior to the Oedipus complex predominate. The "good cases", the real indications of analysis, were those in which Oedipal organizations and genital structures dominated. The transference was not too ambivalent, parental imagos were sufficiently differentiated, conflicts were centred around castration anxiety, problems related to bisexuality were limited, and, above all, the influence of aggressivity and destructivity was neither too invasive nor too much under the sway of repetition compulsion, so that an appropriate interpretation was sufficient in the majority of cases. Still more frequently, a formidable stumbling block was the discovery of a form of masochism that did not yield to the transference-analysis, while resistances persisted that were firmly anchored in the patient's psychical organization. These often unforeseen, not to say unforeseeable surprises had discouraging effects on the analyst which he/she had to learn to anticipate and to tolerate. So, the prospect of the psychoanalytic process getting bogged down seemed less formidable, and psychoanalysis was practised increasingly for the satisfactions that could be derived from it.

But, however influential the contributions of Bouvet were (see Bouvet, 1967)—he was the author of an original conception of the object-relation founded on the notion of distance from the object—other themes aroused interest: the study of character neuroses (Diatkine and Favreau, Sauguet); the renewed description of narcissism (Grunberger); the first innovations in psychosomatics (Marty and Fain), etc. Moreover, now that Freud's work had ceased to enjoy a veneration that brooked no criticism, Viderman (1970) did not hesitate to raise a number of questions that shook more than one of his colleagues, at least for a while. He had the weakness, however, of ignoring foreign authors belonging to the Kleinian or American movements. As for "Ego psychology", theorized by Hartmann, Loewenstein and Kris, it did not have much success in our country. Compared with the UK, and sometimes the USA, countries to which many of Freud's disciples had emigrated and transmitted what remained of his teaching, French psychoanalysts suffered at the time from certain limitations in their clinical experience. France had benefited from the direct teaching of analysts who had only known Freud indirectly. Marie Bonaparte had been close to him, but only had a limited influence. Certainly Hartmann, for a very short time, and Loewenstein, for a longer period, played this role of transmitters. The latter was the analyst of the pioneers of French psychoanalysis: Nacht, Lacan, and Mâle. However, after 1945, France could only count on the first generation of French analysts, who analysed the majority of the future most prominent analysts in Paris.

In addition, the civil war in French psychoanalysis between the adversaries and followers of Lacan had a sterile influence on exchanges between analysts. Without going into the details of a story that is now well known, the splits that took place in 1953 and 1963 encouraged different and sometimes opposing attitudes.

Lacan succeeded in having his dissident technique accepted: short sessions, the analyst's systematic silence, abstention from analysing the negative transference, and the application of a theory in which everything connected with the maternal transference was more or less ignored, emphasis being placed almost exclusively on the paternal transference. This new way of understanding analysis attracted a lot of people owing to Lacan's charisma. On the other hand, those who tried a Lacanian analysis—a considerable number initially—often ended up changing analyst in order to follow more established and tested practices. Many analysands preferred to break off their Lacanian analysis and to continue their experience in more classical analytical movements. Those who had left the Lacanian School found themselves, as a result of a second split, in the ranks of the SFP (Société française de psychanalyse), which grouped together the former Lacanians and those gathered around Daniel Lagache, whose thinking was often akin to that of American analysts. Although they had separated from Lacan, relations none the less remained very distant with their former colleagues from the Paris Psychoanalytical Society (SPP: Société psychanalytique de Paris). The new style that they adopted, often influenced by by their former allegiance to Lacanian circles, did not always facilitate their exchanges with those whose training remained marked by the spirit of the Paris Psychoanalytical Society. Much time was needed before genuine exchanges took place between the societies. As for the members of the mother society, the SPP, they developed a clinical tradition that was often appreciated, but frequently criticized, of which Nacht was the leader. Later, the creation of the "Fourth Group" allowed for greater diversity and richness of contacts, especially through Aulagnier.

The *Nouvelle Revue de Psychanalyse*, directed by Pontalis, practised a policy of openness encouraging exchanges with colleagues of the British Psychoanalytical Society as well as with American psychoanalysts. Thanks to translations, French analysts were able to familiarize themselves better with foreign publications worthy of interest. Links were soon established between certain French analysts and their colleagues from across the Channel. Winnicott's work created a great stir in France. Henceforth, Lacan was not the only one to represent novelty. Thanks to Winnicott's influence, there was a revival of the technique of borderline cases. So, French analysts made the transition from Bouvet's pregenital structures to borderline cases, which they came to understand better through their reading of Winnicott. Moreover, the work of Bion, who was analysed by Melanie Klein, was becoming increasingly widely read. An original author, Bion could not allow himself to be confined by Kleinian theory, to which he gave a decisive new impetus by developing his own way of thinking. Bion's thought finally distinguished itself from the model that had inspired it, liberating itself progressively from its major lines of thinking in order to venture out far from its horizons. The exchange between British and French psychoanalysts is still being pursued, with limited but reciprocal interest (see Birksted-Breen, Flanders, & Gibeault, 2010). No one knows what will emerge from it, but the exchanges have deepened, and mutual understanding has been improved.

It cannot be denied, however, that in recent years there has been a growing sense that psychoanalysis is going through a crisis. It has been more frequently and more vigorously attacked by adversaries who have tried to impose new techniques inspired by cognitivism. Psychoanalysis has resisted well these vigorous assaults, which were intended to eliminate it, albeit without success. It is pursuing the advances of its caravan without being troubled by the rantings of its detractors. Today, it is still doing well.

CHAPTER TWO

Lacanian thinking on language

I have expressed myself on various occasions on Lacan's ideas concerning the relations between language and the unconscious. I have made a number of contributions to the subject, of which one, in 1983, treats of the problem in detail. I have come back to this topic several times, in particular in 2005, in the preface to Castarède and Konopczynski's book *Au commencement était la voix* (Green, 2005) and more recently still, in 2007, in an article "Langue, parole psychanalytique et absence", published in the *Revue française de psychanalyse* (Green, 2007a).

Language in psychoanalysis (Green, 1983a)

Around 1950, French psychoanalytic thinking turned towards the study of the relations between language and the unconscious under the influence of the structuralist movement. In 1953, Lacan presented his Rome Report, "The function and field of speech and language in psychoanalysis" (Lacan, 1966), an event that coincided with the split which divided the SPP and the future SFP. The allusions in this text linking psychoanalysis to structuralism are rare. It is only in the second half of the Rome Report that one comes across any mention of the thinking of Lévi-Strauss, and the proposition: "This law reveals itself clearly enough as identical to a language order" (Lacan, 1966, p. 229). The allegiance to the work of Lévi-Strauss would not be returned. The latter waited until Lacan's death to explain himself. He subsequently admitted that he had never understood anything of what Lacan was writing about, while stating his disagreement with the theoretical foundations of psychoanalysis (see Lévi-Strauss & Eribon, 1988, pp. 107–108; also Green, 2008). But this was only one stage for Lacan. He strived to pursue the linguistic inspiration by extending it towards mathematics. Psychoanalysis was supposed to open up a "first language" for us. He cited the example of poetic texts, justifying an investigation into poetics (Lacan, 1966, p. 244). And he reminded us opportunely that the function of language is not to inform but to evoke (*ibid.*, p. 247).

The relations between Lacan's thought and structuralism are not clear. It has been debated in turn how he differentiated himself from it and how he belonged to it *de facto* (Miller). Those who analysed his thought—of whom I was one—nevertheless finally understood the role that Lacan attributed to linguistics, before detaching himself from it because the linguists had not followed him. So, he then called it *"linguisterie"* out of derision. But before arriving at this irrevocable condemnation, it was necessary to have a clear conscience about it. This is why, in the year that we celebrated the thirtieth anniversary of the Rome Report, I decided to put the question of the relations between language and the unconscious to a thorough examination. (In my contribution to the *Cahiers de l'Herne* on Saussure (Green, 2003a), I tried to clarify the relations between the unconscious according to Saussure and the Freudian unconscious. In this same article, I discussed the ideas of Charles Bally, Saussure's successor to the chair of Geneva, who, in his work *Le Langage et la Vie* (Bally, 1965), opposed the ideas of his teacher by emphasizing the role of affect. See also Green (1979).) The result was the long work which I entitled "Le langage dans la psychanalyse" (Green, 1983a, 1997). Unfortunately this text, which was probably too long and arduous, discouraged the reader and was largely ignored when it came out. Subsequently, however, a few readers have examined it carefully. It was a long time before it was cited in the literature. Among its commentators, I will mention Gilbert Diatkine who has studied it in detail, Julia Kristeva, and, finally, Christian Delourmel, who has not hesitated to refer to it. If I am referring to it today, it is to recall certain ideas which still seem valid to me and which deserve to find their place in this book.

I shall just recapitulate briefly on three stages of my study of 1983. (For the section that follows, I am grateful to Christian Delourmel for the help he has given me in refinding passages relevant to my present work.)

First stage: initial Freudian contributions

At the beginning of my study (pp. 20–33), I set out the basis for my investigation, which affirms the need for a psychoanalytic conception of language. I referred to the *Minutes of the Psychoanalytic Society of Vienna*, to the scientific session of 3 March 1909 (Nunberg & Federn, 1967, p. 167), when a lecture on word and thought was discussed. Freud begins by emphasizing the link between conscious thinking and its verbal expression: "Our consciousness", he says, "behaves like a sense organ; it is at first turned in only one definite direction—that is, toward the *perception of the external world*, and only secondarily toward psychological processes". Already, at that time, Freud maintained that words have the function of making the relations between internal processes and ideas perceptible.

From the outset, the differences between conscious and unconscious psychical processes are related to a structural heterogeneity, which obliges us to think about the modalities of their coexistence and their reciprocal transformations. Now, these questions were only dealt with in 1909, whereas one would have expected them to have been discussed from the outset. They did not receive any more attention during the subsequent evolution of the theory, and, generally speaking, apart from Lacan, the major authors of psychoanalysis have refrained from devoting a particular conceptualization to language.

The question arises as to how ordinary language leads us to the unconscious without a symptom of the discourse (a slip of the tongue) revealing its connection with desire by making this stumbling of speech audible.

One further remark: it was necessary to wait for the work of those psychoanalysts who succeeded Freud for attention to be drawn to the importance of the setting; one would have considerable difficulty finding allusions to the setting in his work. But after Bleger, and especially Winnicott, the usefulness, and even the necessity, of this concept was widely recognized. There is thus *an implicit disavowal of the setting* in Freud's work, owing to a blindness concerning its psychical function. Freud was only interested in the negative conditions that mark analytic communication (motor restriction, the fixedness of perceptual conditions, relaxation of censorship, etc.), and did not accord sufficient importance to the reasons for its power.

Analytic technique arose from a series of refinements, the final result of which was the limitation of contact to verbal exchange. Before discovering the conditions of psychoanalytic practice, Freud had first been a scientist who was very aware of the relations between the procedure of dividing up an object and what is revealed from the discovery of its properties. This revelation only acquired meaning later, through studying the relations between the method which made it possible to individualize the properties of the unconscious, an object discovered by means of the scientific method, and the dream work. Consequently, it was easy to deduce that the unconscious object could not be thought of independently of the method—the free association of language and its relations with dream functioning—that permitted its exploration. But Freud overlooked this relationship. Turning his back on biology to devote himself to psychoanalysis, he did not think about defining more clearly the relations between the method and the object of his discovery in the psychoanalytic field.

This observation is fraught with consequences; it reveals a rift in our identity as analysts. For if the analytic exchange is reduced to verbalization, this requires us in turn to clarify the relations of correspondence uniting and separating the two orders of language and the unconscious. If we do not clarify the relations between these two orders of the mind, it boils down to saying that we do not know what we are doing when we analyse. These are the prolegomena that come to mind when one reflects on the questions that are raised, not by psychoanalytic theory, but by the foundations of its practice.

Second stage: the particularities of the poetic function

When we examine the different branches of linguistics in order to contrast them with the analysis of unconscious processes, we soon realize that it is probably the field of poetics that suggests the most evocative comparisons (see Cohen, 1966). The poetic function "is co-present in the speech of every human being from early infancy" (Jakobson, 1973, p. 485). Among the six functions described by Jakobson, the one that is mentioned first, coming from the addresser (sender), is the emotional function. This coincides with Cohen's remark concerning the affective logic which impregnates the poem (Cohen, 1966). These observations must have escaped Lacan, who was determined to claim that affect had scarcely any place in psychoanalytic theory. This allows me to recall the role of traces of the mother's voice in the psyche (Green, 2005). I will come back to this later.

When dealing with unconscious material, the problem arises of the relations between the exercise of speech elicited by the setting, and the extra-linguistic dimension, which is so important in psychoanalysis; in other words, of envisaging this extralinguistic dimension in its relation to the drive.

The transition from phonetics to the linguistic analysis of poetry requires a shift to other levels of organization of language, in particular, that of syntax. In this case, one notices the desire to flout meaning, where the fiction of a language devoid of all ambiguity persists. On the other hand, the paradigmatic axis transcends mere formalization. The poetic function reaches another level in poetry proper, described by the poet Gerard Manley Hopkins as ". . . speech framed . . . to be heard for its own sake and interest, over and above its interest of meaning" (quoted by Jakobson, 1973, p. 489). There is a parallel here with Benveniste, for whom the meaning of ordinary speech is more than the sum of the significations of the contents of the sentence, even though this extra meaning cannot be recovered by grammatical analysis. Baudelaire wrote: "In the word, in the verb, there is something which prevents us from seeing it as a matter of chance. Handling a language skilfully involves practising a kind of evocative sorcery" (cited by Jakobson, *ibid.*, p. 488)

This takes us back to Lacan's proposition that language *evokes*. In other words, it *suggests*. Poetry goes *vers l'arrière* (backwards) (*vers*, which in French means "towards", and "verse"), whereas prose goes forwards. This bidirectionality of language was understood by Freud. Baudelaire, once again, underscores the "regularity and symmetry which are among the primordial needs of the human spirit" and the "slightly misshapen curves which stand out against this regularity: the unexpected, the surprise, and astonishment constitute in turn an essential part of the artistic effect, in other words, the indispensable condiment of all beauty" (*ibid.*, p. 491). The poetic function consists in treating unities of higher rank differently. Between formalization and poetic effect a gap appears which can be accounted for by other criteria: affective logic, imagination, fantasy, etc. Poetic potentiality exists at the basis of all speech. The transition from ordinary speech to poetic speech must be sought in the context of the enunciation, or even as the effect of the analytic setting, which allows the enunciation to be heard differently. It is clear that the problem cannot be reduced to a combinatory system.

For Benveniste (1956, p. 82), a reader of Lacan, unconscious symbolism is *infra*- and *supra*linguistic. "*La langue* (language as a general system) is an instrument for ordering the world and society; it applies to a world considered as 'real' . . ." and not as a world of "non-existing things" (*inexistants*). Benveniste designates the veritable comparative term of dream language at the heart of *la langue*. Style, rhetoric, metaphor, fiction, and myth have their place here. Lacan finally abandoned the reference to *la langue* in favour of *lalangue*, symbolizing an earlier, more primary language than its later aspect.

Thom (1980, p. 127) once wrote: "What circumscribes the true is not the false but the insignificant", and also, "Everything that is rigorous is insignificant" (1968, p. 10). The extension of the field of representation allows us to speak of *représentance* (see note 1 in the Preface). *Signifiance*—the act of signifying—and *représentance* have to be articulated within the context of the reference. Saussure had placed hope in a formalistic orientation. His successor, Charles Bally, was to oppose this theoretical vision (see Bally, 1965; Green, 1979). According to him:

1. Thinking is not under the domination of the intellect, but subordinates it to its ends.
2. Thinking is essentially subjective.
3. Thinking is affective to different degrees.

At this point we need to turn to Peirce and his conception of *representamen*:

> A sign, or *representamen*, is something which stands to somebody for something in some respect or capacity. It addresses somebody, that is, creates in the mind of that person an equivalent sign or perhaps a more developed sign. That sign which it creates I call the *interpretant* of the first sign. This sign stands for something, its object. It stands for that object, not in all respects, but in reference to a sort of idea which I have sometimes called the ground of the *representamen*. [Peirce, 1931, Vol. 2, p. 228]

This leads me to propose a model:

- of a double *signifiance* of sign and meaning;
- of a double *représentance* of words (linguistic) and objects (extralinguistic);
- and of a double *reference* to external reality and internal (psychic) reality.

For Martinet (1961), who argued in favour of the linguistic concept of double articulation (of phonemes and monemes), sounds are subordinate to meaning. What is situated at the limits of physiology (sounds) is thus articulated with meaning which touches on social communication.

What is the truth status of the objects of psychical reality? By way of a response, Linsky (1974) suggests that it may be necessary to resort here to the logic of what Lacan called *lalangue* rather than that of *la langue*. But it still has to be constructed. The double object comes into play here: object of speech to the addressee of speech and object of speech which designates what it refers to. This is where the place of the imaginary is situated. According to Meinong (cited by Linsky, *ibid.*, p. 35), "There are objects of which it is true to say that there are no such objects". This is an application, in my view, of the Freudian distinction between the judgement of attribution and the judgement of existence (negation).

If the signifier is the material side of the linguistic sign, the object *is not* the material support of representation, since there are imaginary objects which are based on their representation alone, and which do not depend on any form of reality. Bühler's schema and von Foerster's model can help us here. The Freudian concept of the drive prompts us to study their relations. Remember that Freud postulates that the drive is anchored in the somatic (a position he held from the second topography—1923—onwards), but that it is the expression of what is already psychical "in forms unknown to us". ("Its source is a state of excitation in the body; its aim is the removal of that excitation. On its path from its source to its aim, the instinct becomes operative psychically" (Freud, 1933a, p. 96).) The conclusion cannot be avoided, then, that the idea of a signifier separate from the signified seems, by definition, to be an error.

Let us come now to the essential issue. In Freud's work, it can be found in the wooden reel game: the *Fort! Da!* What must be emphasized here are the alternations between what is far away and what is near, the actions of throwing away and retrieving, the absent and the present, etc. The reference is unquestionably on the side of *movement*. The drive is movement, contrary to all the other interpretations. And this movement is that of a game. The subject can only be defined as a *sujet joueur* (a subject who enjoys playing)—Winnicott comes to mind here—which refers to all the aspects of the notion of double that I have identified. This duplicity presupposes a gap between the terms. From the point of view of language, the double *signifiance* of words (exclusively linguistic) and things (extralinguistic) must be taken into account. The third is an emerging quality of the relations between the two polarities. The relations between word and thing suppose their intersection. A third order can emerge from this, such as Winnicott's category of transitional objects. So, the problem cannot be resolved by perception and representation alone. It is not difficult to understand the role that Winnicott attributes to playing. This leads us to contrast the homogeneity of the linguistic system with the heterogeneity of the system of representations (extralinguistic).

Third stage: some hypotheses on the conception of language in psychoanalysis: the setting must be taken into consideration

> The necessity of resorting to the setting is based on a simple implicit presupposition and yet, to the best of my knowledge, it is one that

has never been made explicit. If language is *mediation* towards the unconscious, then speech and the conditions of its production must be subjected to a modification in such a way that the mediating function becomes audible. [Green, 1983a, p. 118]

In other words, the transformation of the psychical apparatus into a language apparatus, and vice versa, is a permanent work.

> The setting thus favours the emergence of a third reality created by objects of the third order (transitional), with the "language" objects replacing all the types of objects of psychical and material reality and bringing into existence a *"sujet joueur"* . . . [*ibid.*, p. 119]

"The function of the setting is to accomplish a *polysemic metaphorization*" (*ibid.*, p. 120). You can see that the idea was already there, even if its theoretical exposition came only much later! This metaphorization is closely bound up with thirdness. The setting thus has the possibility of bringing the *other* of the object into existence. The enunciation of the analytic discourse thus acquires the status of a metaphor. Such a metaphorization also relates to the work of the negative. The double transference unites the transference of the psychical on to speech and the transference of speech on to the object.

> Analytic speech takes the mourning out of language. It gives back to the other the representation of objects of desire which have been relegated to the shadows through renunciation. Such is the effect of the analytic setting on *la langue*. [*ibid.*, p. 136]

Thirdness finds its illustration in tertiary processes. We can notice, too, that the focus is more on the message than on the code.

For me, the symbolic order does not rest on language alone, but on the ensemble of bindings–unbindings occurring in the three agencies of the psychical apparatus. Tertiary processes form the bridge between the psychical apparatus and the language apparatus. The relations between Lacanian theory and its practice can be deduced from this.

These remarks can be applied to the different forms of interpretation in contemporary practice.

The voice, affect, and the other (Green, 2005)

The voice is a component of speech. In linguistics, sound and mean-ing (Jakobson, 1973) are treated both by phonology and poetics. Sublimation and pathology join forces in an effort to go beyond an approach that is too restricted. And it is true that "before being the one who speaks" (Rolland, 2006), the infant comes into the world in a bath of language, even if he cannot perceive words during the period of pregnancy while he is in his mother's womb from where he can already hear noises. In any case, the baby has a faculty of discrimination that enables him to recognize his mother's voice (recorded backwards by the tape recorder, experiments conducted by J. Mehler) from the first day. In other words, the voice is much more than a physiological mechanism. There is a destination before there is an addressee (Sebeok, 1974). A pure, "scientific" linguistics, without subjectivity, without affect, without a speaking subject, seeks implicitly to eliminate the human dimension of language.

The exchange of words requires a study of the *vocal relations between two voices*. The voice has been the object of special investi-gation. Listening needs to be conceived here from two points of view: the expression of the mother's voice and its reception by the infant. This is another form of binarism, which can be linked to the negative selection defining phonematic pairs where one can desig-nate the place of the one who is absent.

These observations can be summed up by the famous Lacanian formula: "The signifier is what represents a subject for another signifier", which means that a subject only exists for another subject. However, no branch of linguistics processes language in a way that has any resemblance whatsoever with the psychoanalytic approach to language.

There is a search for a complementary voice that will provide a sense of harmony. Here, the demand for pleasure is encountered. *The expectation of seduction* is inferred as being essential after the event. Sharing. Encounter between the different constitutive modes of heterogeneity (the voice in speech, poetry, song, dance, etc.), between the different modes of *représentance*. The question of the primal. The mother's voice is a voice that sings. Further-more, speech produced lying down (Green) cannot fail to excite affect.

Let me conclude now with a word on the pathology of autism. The autist manifests speech disorders that are consequences, rather than causes. It seems to me that the subject is not so much speaking as reading a text. One of Diatkine's patients (reported by Danon-Boileau (2007, pp. 1341–1409)), said, "It has to interest my mind completely, which unfortunately is very rarely the case". This is the voice of an absence of self. It is not a failure of speech that is in question, but the shield that it constitutes against an unsignifiable world. The study of autism calls for theoretical hypotheses concerning subjective psychical functioning. The reference to sound gives us nothing to see. Signifying is not sufficient; evidence of the sense of existing is lacking (Bion). All language refers to the drive. The poetic problem is one of knowing what remains of the voice when it is no longer sound (Meschonnic): the subject who includes the other in us. Tribute should be paid here to Rousseau, who, in his "Essay on the origin of languages", put the passions in the forefront. Likewise, Freud put forward the hypothesis that the first cry was at the origin of *mutual comprehension:* the cry, thus, comes first. This touches on an aspect of life that I shall define as a subjective form "for another".

Language, psychoanalytic speech, and absence (Green, 2007a)

The following comments were written on the occasion of the Congress of French-speaking psychoanalysts in 2007. The reports discussed were presented by Dominique Clerc and Laurent Danon-Boileau. The latter presented a paper entitled "La force du langage" (Danon-Boileau, 2007). This text constitutes the most recent contribution to the question of language in psychoanalysis. Its author is a linguist and a psychoanalyst, which gives a certain weight to his contribution. For my part, the text that I am commenting on here represents, without any question, a break with my earlier contributions. This change of direction was taken after reading the work of Rastier (2007), who has influenced me in a decisive manner.

The unconscious structured like a language? This aphorism, while famous, appears over the course of the years to be more than questionable, and the temptation to build a bridge with psychoanalysis has proved illusory. In fact, thanks to the writings of

Bouquet and Rastier, it appeared to me that Lacan's theorization was attached to the logico–grammatical pole, whereas one might have expected the efforts of psychoanalysts to be focused on the rhetorico–hermeneutical pole. We need to remember that psychoanalytic speech is the product of free association (and, more generally, of the setting).

It would be a mistake to think that interpretation only refers to the elements of language. Interpreting is also a form of elaborating. In the material of a session, three fundamental components can be noted: language, affect and, by extension, sensations (somatizations involving the body), and last, the component linked to force, in relation with quantity. Between language and affect is the hallucinatory realm (see the case of nightmares).

For Culioli (1999) "the activity of language is significant in so far as an enunciator produces forms that can be recognized by a co-enunciator as having been produced in order to be recognized as interpretable". (I would like to emphasize here the interest that I have taken in Culioli's ideas. He has helped me a great deal in understanding contemporary ideas on language, and I am grateful to him.) Language is an activity that comes from the inside (Culioli). I concur with the positions defended by Rastier. He shows that the theories of the origin of language take no account of the history of languages. This approach tends to make a parallel between genetic code and language. By contrast, Rastier argues,

> It could very well be that human language arose from the contingent encounter between a phonatory apparatus (quite ordinary in primates), an exceptionally developed prefrontal cortex *capable of imagining objects in their absence,* and finally complex social interactions. [2006, pp. 297–326]

Language is, thus, a *social* phenomenon. It is not so much in the field of the brain that we need to pursue our investigations as in the domain of society and history.

We only know human languages. As a result, we must investigate human *surroundings*, which, according to Rastier, can be structured in three zones: the distal zone (strangeness), to which we must add the proximal zone (adjacent), and, finally, the zone of identity. The particularity of human languages probably resides in the fact of referring to what is not present (the distal zone).

It is my contention that *psychoanalytic discourse as a whole depends more or less on absence. Everything that is said there is interpreted in connection with the transference as if concerning someone else, in a relationship which refers to another space and another time.*

*   *   *

The 1950s saw the emergence of the first theoretical investigations into the concept of the setting. In Europe, Winnicott (1954) laid the foundations in an article that marked a milestone. At the same time, and, it seems, without any concern to harmonize these undertakings, Lacan inaugurated his studies on language. What has to be understood *a posteriori* is that Lacan's effort, in fact, constituted an alternative to the contributions of Anglo-Saxon origin, in particular concerning language, without even referring to them. In other words, what Lacanian technique had proposed as an innovation, centred around the study of language, already constituted another path that was quite distinct from the route taken by the Anglo-Saxons, concerning what could be deduced from this focus on language. Under these conditions, the Lacanian technique proposed another way of understanding what would subsequently be called the setting. From this point of view, short sessions, the practice of scansion, the exclusion of a theory of affect, all lead in the same direction. The insufficiencies of the Lacanian conception of psychoanalytic practice are masked behind the brief allusions that are made to it in the *Écrits* concerning the variation of the duration of sessions (always in the sense of shortening them), scansion, and even practices verging on physical violence. I have had testimonies. The evolution of the rules of Lacanian practice thus finds its true meaning, even though it has never been made explicit in a convincing manner.

If the other orientation, followed by the majority of analysts, saw a conception of the setting develop which took several years to acquire its coherence, it cannot be questioned that the efforts of Winnicott, for example, allowed genuine innovation in the way we understand the justifications of the technique. Subsequently, those French analysts who followed the direction taken by English psychoanalysis were, thereby, able to join up again with the general current, and to distance themselves from what has to be called the

Lacanian deviation, which was abandoned over the course of time by many of Lacan's followers.

Thus French psychoanalysis, under Lacan's impetus, was articulated around an exploration of language as a central, guiding axis. In this respect, studies on linguistics supplanted the interest which elsewhere was taken in the setting. It is to Winnicott that we owe this other orientation. But it was already present in Freud's time, even if it had not been theorized in a sufficiently explicit manner. It was an approach that would prove fruitful for psychoanalysis.

CHAPTER THREE

The setting and its interpretation

The relative rarity of contributions pertaining to the evaluation of psychoanalytic work cannot be explained solely by the wish to avoid a thorny issue; there is also a real difficulty in speaking about it. A few years ago, analysts who were concerned about the fact that they did not possess sufficiently reliable criteria for such evaluations made up their minds to examine this problem "scientifically". It cannot be said that the results, which were supposed to be based on objective criteria, met the expectations that they had raised. It rapidly became clear that the methodology (analysis observed from behind a screen) was highly questionable, and it was soon concluded that the attempt to elucidate our understanding by means of an "objective" approach had failed.

The primary difficulty stems from the fact that we lack a model for reflecting on these evaluations. The temptation is to apply criteria that govern the medical model to an activity that is recognized as therapeutic. We would like to reason in terms of cure, improvement, stagnation, aggravation, and, ultimately, failure. But it seems that this model is false on two counts. First of all, applying modes of evaluation derived from medicine to psychoanalysis is a questionable procedure, as the medical model proves itself to be quite inappropriate. Second, even the advances of medical therapeutics no longer conform to these old and unsuitable criteria. However, a person who wants to undergo an analysis will say that they want to get better. Whatever the causes of their anxiety or ill-being are, the wish to change in order to experience relief from this suffering is expressed, even if these aspirations turn out to be more complex than it seems.

The wish to be cured turns out to be more ambiguous than one might at first think. The symptoms that push someone to undertake an analysis are extremely various. We observe an increase in signs of ill-being, and in the wish to be free of neurotic or "existential" impasses. It is clear that the comparison with medicine is not valid. The wish to enter analysis remains a singular experience that is not self-evident. The conventions of the setting are often poorly understood. Sometimes, the future analysand resists the frequency of sessions proposed. It will take a long time before the analysand accepts that this rhythm is necessary, or before he is able to recognize that he misses the analysis during periods of interruption.

The entire analysis rests on the analysand's capacity to apply the fundamental rule. Many analysands have difficulty in respecting it and in recognizing what it involves. The analysand will often begin his analysis only after having recounted his life story in great detail, without realizing that this review is only of limited interest. It is only after this that the transference can open out and that the analytic process can unfold. Much has been written about the analytic setting. It is well known now that the model underlying analysis is derived from the Freudian theory of dreams. More precisely, the fundamental rule aims to bring mental functioning during the treatment into close approximation with dream functioning. In other words, the lowering of the censorship facilitates associative linking, making it possible to gain access to modes of expression close to those of dreams (the Botellas have drawn attention to topical regression in Freud's work). But if there is a dream work, it implies there is a processual work that requires the integrity of psychical mechanisms.

Beyond these comparisons, it is especially important that the analysand recognizes that the fundamental rule facilitates an original mode of expression that he acquires by surprising himself. This is a discovery that gives analytic functioning the meaning of a new way of speaking and signifying to this other to whom the discourse is addressed, and of transforming this interlocutor into a symbolic figure.

The fundamental rule involves asking the patient to say what he/she knows, but also what he/she does not know (see Freud's *Outline*, 1940a (1938), p. 174). Freud understood the full importance—and, I would say, the necessity, as well as the impossibility—that underlies this rule of rules which governs the entire practice of analysis. Since the initial observations, the fundamental rule has been the object of in-depth studies, notably by Jean-Luc Donnet, who has given it all the attention it deserves (2001, 2009). It has also been freed from the restricted field in which it had been reduced to a technical obligation, and has become the object of epistemological reflection.

When one reflects on the origins of the mind, any work of thought (*Denkenarbeit*), any work of judgement (*Urteilarbeit*), any act of thought (*Denkakt*), involves a collaboration of body and thought. Thought arises out of representation. Negation specifies the double connotation of the judgement of attribution or existence, which are functions of the oral drives. Here we have a new dualism between inside and outside which implies the existence of the other. It is here that the role of the digestive (bodily) models of thought (as in Bion's work), and their application through the idea of transformation, comes into play. In this way, the body is represented, symbolized.

As we have seen, the rules governing the specificity of communication in psychoanalysis are reduced to the essential. What is the significance of this fundamental rule that has caused so much ink to flow? While updating myself on recent positions, I came across the view among the contributions of English authors that the fundamental rule does not exist. This is a somewhat hasty statement. The problem cannot be disposed of so quickly. Certainly, it is true that the rule faces the analysand with an impossible task: it is very difficult to wholly respect what amount to both simple and radical requirements. But, paradoxically, their heuristic value is due precisely to the difficulty of fulfilling these aims. It is more interesting to try and uncover the fantasy which pushes us to state it.

The fundamental rule is designed to facilitate the functioning of supposedly free speech. The theoretical assumption of Freud, who was perhaps thinking here of the psychical functioning of dreams, is based on the idea that the speech of ordinary conversation is subject to constraint in more than one respect. On the one hand, in ordinary exchanges, neither participant can escape the conditions of social censorship, and so cannot say what they think without first having silenced those thoughts, fantasies, desires, and intentions that it would be inappropriate to reveal. This first censorship of a social and moral origin is backed up by others. All supposedly correct communication requires a certain respect for grammatical rules. But one cannot accept a form of expression that is lacking a minimum of grammatical correctness, for, while the patient is asked to free him/herself as much as possible from the constraints of language, it must be remembered that in all cases the language expressed according to the fundamental rule is a language addressed to someone, and it is therefore required to be intelligible so that he/she can comment on it. Ordinarily, we do not think about all these necessary conditions for respecting the fundamental rule. Such free verbal expression, without any form of criticism, is a very difficult task for the patient to fulfil. It could be concluded, ultimately, that the analyst's fundamental rule is an impossible task to accomplish. Nevertheless, when the patient succeeds in respecting it sufficiently, it allows thoughts to be expressed that are ordinarily suppressed. Not only can they be expressed, but they find a new, more relaxed mode of expression which brings the patient nearer to primary thinking, bypassing the secondary processes inherent to language.

To these conditions of the production of analytic speech must be added the complementary role of the analyst's mode of listening, which Freud called "evenly suspended attention". This aims to replace the differentiated attention of the listening of ordinary conversation, which, on the contrary, demands attention to be directed to the point required by the expressive style. This, then, is what respecting the fundamental rule aims at, and it permits the construction of psychoanalytic interpretation. Here we have one of the conditions of the transformation of verbal communication, which, in psychoanalysis, makes it more metaphorical.

This metaphorization is the result of a mysterious transformation. From a prosaic analysis of the contents of the discourse, it can only be concluded that what constitutes the psychoanalytic exchange is apparently quite ordinary. As Bion says, the nature of what is said resembles "ordinary conversation". How, then, can this ordinary conversation be transformed into metaphorized discourse? Many psychoanalysts who endeavour to grasp the mysterious quality of what unfolds during an analytic session refer to the "slow magic" of words (Rolland, 2006); at the same time, they are astonished by the power of associative language. Freud (1890a) had already noted this. And it is a fact that in certain, if not in many, sessions, what is exchanged undergoes a transformation that sometimes confers it with a mysterious quality. But it is precisely this transformation that allows us to suppose that analytic communication cannot be reduced to the prosaic exchange with which it might be compared. Furthermore, when language is no longer infused with this aura, there is reason to think that one has lost the thread of the analysis. In such cases, the analyst suffers from a certain platitude in what he is hearing, the content of which can lose its transferential quality. The analyst then sometimes becomes bored with listening to what is being said to him. "Empty speech", said Lacan, in the place of full speech that is not forthcoming. One might say that what is being said is approaching a centre that it avoids, and from which it could radiate out, and, at the same time, it is fleeing this centre and distancing itself from it. This movement to-and-fro gives analytic speech its respiration. The contents are rarely approached head on, but more often obliquely or sometimes allusively. As one listens to what is being said, one gets the feeling that there is an important issue that is difficult to identify and grasp, and sometimes obscure, which is in danger of disappearing, as if the ambiguity sustaining the discourse made it a fragile message. These are impressions that can only be obtained by attempting to follow cautiously the thread of the discourse. One can understand how the attempt to follow the progression of the meaning of what is being said often occurs in a discontinuous manner: one has to wait until the themes encountered acquire the beginnings of some sort of unity, or a set of unities, which fortunately sometimes lead to an emerging understanding. But no linear thread is constituted. Meaning is gradually woven and unwoven before it emerges. What had seemed to be constituting itself by letting itself be approached may suddenly come undone. Resistance then gains ground once again, and one sometimes has to wait a long time until the patient recognizes that he or she has gained fresh insight or awareness into their situation.

CHAPTER FOUR

Die Entstellung

I n a recent contribution, Ludin (2009) points out that Freud
attaches value to the notion of *Entstellung*, of distortion. Starting
out from hysterical speech, which has the tendency to distort
the event it is speaking about, Freud finally concludes in *Moses and
Monotheism* (1939a) that this tendency has quite a wide-ranging
significance, and that it plays a role in the way we construct history.
So, it is necessary to abandon the idea of objectivity. Every narrative is tendentious:

> What is specific about psychoanalysis with regard to the construc-
> tion of history is the fact that, according to Freud, it is necessarily
> distorted; not because we lack the necessary information to
> construct it objectively—which is certainly true—but because there
> is a more or less unconscious need in us to distort it; our desire to
> construct history always involves a distortion, and this movement
> is scarcely avoidable. [Ludin, 2009, p. 56]

From this we can conclude that the analysand *necessarily* distorts
when speaking to the analyst. To understand this better, it is necessary to refer to the transference. Thus, as Ludin says, "we are
always 'liers', more or less" (p. 56). Fortunately, there remains

metanoïa, that is, the return of narration. *Proton pseudos.* The reference to an involuntary memory brings us closer to transference and distances us from objectivity.

I was the third analyst of a female patient who had already had a long analytic past. During this psychotherapy, this patient unearthed a very old memory, which, to the best of my knowledge, had not been analysed in detail by the two preceding analysts. Being the youngest child of a long line of siblings, and belonging to a very pious Jewish family, every month, when her mother had her periods, she had to give up her own bed to her mother, and share her parents' bed with her father for four or five days. She had never been given any explanation for this. Her father was very concerned to observe religious practices, which did not allow his wife to sleep by his side during her menstrual period, and was very modest by nature. The patient had no recollection of ever having been kissed by her father, of any manifestation of physical tenderness between them. We spent a long time thinking together about what this experience, which I qualified as a trauma, might have meant for her at that time when she was still a child. This ritual stopped when she was about twelve, without any further precision; it may have coincided with her mother's menopause and her own puberty. Her father was respected for his religious knowledge, while her mother was almost illiterate. In other respects, she was a model mother— ignorant, but full of common sense. As for the patient, she was a brilliant pupil; her father was proud of her academic successes, even though they had been achieved in a different culture from his own.

I was surprised by the poverty of the patient's sexual life at that time, since she had immigrated to France for her studies and, having left her parents, now enjoyed complete freedom. She herself was astonished by this. She eventually acknowledged her identifications with her mother. When she left her family of origin, these identifications had suddenly rendered her incapable of pursuing her success at school and university. Everything had come to a stop without any apparent reason, and her love life had not flowered at all. She had got married and had had two children, whose education she had watched over closely, enabling them to achieve the prestigious success that she had not allowed herself. Moreover, her marriage had brought her nothing but disappointments and financial problems owing to her husband's conduct. She had thought about separating from him, but had been unable to decide to leave him.

I sometimes had the feeling that certain details were not clear in what she communicated to me about her life. I pointed this out to her in passing, drawing sharp protests from her. She insisted on her absolute sincerity, which had been praised by her father in the past and more recently by her previous analysts. I was very surprised by the contrast between the hostile feelings that she expressed towards her husband, whom she constantly criticized, returning continually to the absence of any affective ties between them, and the fact that she continued to stay with him, even though she repeatedly mentioned her wish to separate. As I expressed my surprise at this indecision, and assumed that there was no physical relationship between them, my patient corrected me, as if in passing, saying, "But I still have sexual relations with him." Upon this admission, which nothing had allowed me to imagine, I pointed out to her that although she had been coming for three years, she had never told me this. On the contrary, I had been struck by the poverty of their relations and the sterility of our sessions. She claimed that she had had more important things to tell me, which had led her to pass over this detail in silence. I felt bound to reply that this consisted in an important transgression of the fundamental rule, and that for me it was as if it was a lie by omission. She reacted to this very violently, abandoning her usual depressive tone, which had blocked the evolution of the treatment, and began to defend herself by accusing me of inflicting a treatment on her that amounted to a "chainsaw massacre". She complained about my unbearable violence, and ended the session by telling me she wanted to put an end to our work. She seemed so determined, and so little disposed to try to understand what I had qualified as a "lie by omission", that I did not even try to hold her back. I was no doubt rather disappointed to see my efforts lead to such a failure, but I did not go back on what I had said. She demanded explanations or justifications. I refrained from giving them, pointing out that I was there to analyse and not to excuse myself. I really thought I would not see her again. A few days after, I received a phone call in which she told me she had got over her anger, and that she wanted to continue her sessions. I agreed, and we were finally able to overcome this impasse.

I returned to the "trauma", saying that we had only considered what in my view constituted half of the trauma, represented by this obligation to share her father's bed. I asked her, "How long does a woman's period last?" She replied, without surprise, five or six days, perhaps a week. I added, "And the cycle?" "Every month," she replied. So, I said to her, "So there were three whole weeks during which your mother went back to her place and you to yours in *your* bed." I added that if the week spent in her parents' bed had given her the impression that nothing happened there, she must have wondered, all the same, if anything ever happened between her mother and her father during the three weeks when they slept together. She reacted sharply to this remark. So now I offered an interpretation: "You stressed the mysterious reasons for these visits, when you had the impression that you were preferred to your mother, without talking to me about the questions you had asked yourself about the three weeks during which your father and mother were together, preferring to imagine that nothing happened then, either, so as not to have to face the other half of the trauma." *In our relationship, she had managed to make me relive her past by putting me in her position, a victim of her parents by omission, not allowing herself to wonder about the physical relations between her father and mother. Let me add that the patient slept permanently in a little bed that was in her parents' bedroom, and only joined her father in his bed when her mother was excluded from her place there owing to her periods. So she went from her small bed to her father's bed, without explanations. In fact, this blank and projected transference was aimed at avoiding the revival of the content of the trauma, which was not mentioned.*

I had interpreted the resistance, but my remarks went largely unheeded. "Resistance to what?" she replied. "Resistance to discovering resistances," I said. My interventions were poorly tolerated: "It's for you to do the explaining!" she said, which seemed pointless, given the context I was dealing with. The patient did not seem to understand that it was for her to discover what stood in the way of the emergence of her truth. She expected me to tell her what I could infer about it, as if this cause had determined her from the outside. In other words, she did not want to know anything about it. And she insisted on her good will, reminding me of the laudatory comments of her father and of her previous analysts concerning her good faith, saying I had no right to call into doubt what she was claiming. It had required this transferential reactivation and her projections concerning my sadism and my violence—which, I believe, were related to her father's sexuality—for us to be able to overcome this situation.

However, that was not the end of the matter. After a short relapse into her resistances, she talked to me about an incident that had occurred shortly after; she was thinking once again about a difficult period of her life when she had employed all her resources of ingenuity to escape the creditors who were persecuting her. She told me about the sharp sense of anxiety and surprise that she had had recently when her doorbell rang unexpectedly, making her think about this period in the past when she had to escape from her pursuers who were hot on her heels. I interrupted her and said, "You are mistaken, it was not your creditors, but the police." This association had come to me as I recalled the existence of a brother, an inveterate compulsive gambler, who had caused serious trouble for the family. The mother could not face seeing him sent to prison, and the father bled himself dry to reimburse his debts and save him from a very disagreeable situation. My patient had told me that this brother, whom she never spoke about, had loved her a lot, even though she was only a child. One day, the doorbell had rung—this time it really was the police—and she was terrorized by the idea that they had come to take her brother away, which was in fact the case. Although only five years old, she had answered curtly, "He's not here." The police were about to leave, but her father, who could not tolerate lying, answered, "Yes, he is here." The patient recognized immediately the link between the two doorbell rings, and had a decisive moment of insight. She understood that in her desire to reduce her parents' worries, she had intervened to prevent the intolerable consequences of her brother's arrest. She recognized that, later in her life, she had always been inclined to defend those who were accused of something, sometimes with good reason, coming to their defence. She went further and maintained, making certain connections with what she had had to put up with from her husband, that he had received threats from the police which had led on one occasion to his being taken into police custody. And she concluded without prompting from me, "I realize now that I have married my brother."

From this point on, the atmosphere became less tense between us and the analytic work ceased to be sterile and aggressive. She was able to relive in the transference the ambivalent nature of her feelings towards her husband and, before him, towards her brother. Owing to the constant worries that the latter's gambling debts caused his father, who strove to repay them to prevent his son from going to prison, something his mother would not have been able to bear, he brought upon himself the disapproval of all the other members of his family. So, her husband had inherited the hostility aroused by her brother. But, in a more secret manner, my patient, who at the time was very young, had difficulty in resisting his attempts to seduce her, for her brother was very affectionate towards her. "Come and have a siesta with me," he would say to her, putting his arms around her neck. Secretly, I guessed that she had loved him and, being attracted by him, had yielded to his invitations. So, as an adult, she felt the need to hide from me the fact that, in spite of his reproaches and his complaints, she continued to have sexual relations with her husband, probably not without pleasure. Hence, the whole gamut of contradictory childhood feelings were experienced again in adulthood. The treatment continued in a relaxed atmosphere in which the usefulness of our exchanges was recognized. Finally, we were into the transference analysis.

The process of remembering, and the links that she was able to forge, allowed considerable progress to be made in the lifting of her repression; proof, if it is needed, that resistances do not give way all at once and have to be elaborated in several stages.

It is true that the example I have chosen is taken from psychotherapy and not from psychoanalysis. So, I find myself here in contradiction with the positions that I usually defend, tending to distinguish the work of psychoanalysis from that of psychotherapy. It is clear that it would be inexact to contrast the "always good" work of analysis with the "approximate and incomplete" work of psychotherapy. Some nuances are needed. Rather than sticking rigidly to clear-cut and no doubt schematic oppositions, it is better to give a more precise account of the differences. I would contrast the fecundity of the work that opens up interesting perspectives for psychoanalytic dialogue with the sterility of work that does not leave the paths of repetition–compulsion. How are we to characterize the situation? The creative work of the analytic exchange, set in motion by the patient's analytic discourse, sometimes without his realizing it, is capable of arousing in the analyst a response whose effects make it possible to go beyond the stereotyped bloc of resistances which freeze or rigidify the exchange. It is clear that what is expected of the dialogue is not limited to action–reaction, to what the patient says and to what the analyst says in return, but to a veritable fabric in which the patient's words are woven together with the analyst's words. The latter depends, of course, on the way he has experienced and heard what has been communicated to him. It is this type of mutual resonance that is sought after. In short, in the good cases, whether in the couch–armchair or armchair–armchair position, psychoanalysis and psychotherapy differ, but it should not be concluded that the effects hoped for are always obtained by psychoanalysis and never by psychotherapy. What I would say is that the psychoanalytic setting is generally more appropriate for obtaining the result desired, even if it sometimes prevents the psychoanalytic process from developing. So, we must distinguish between the therapeutic work of psychotherapy and the transformational effects obtained by the psychoanalytic setting.

Hence, I will not distinguish psychoanalysis and psychotherapy in terms of the differences of the couch–armchair situation within the setting and armchair–armchair outside the setting. My hypothesis is that psychoanalytic work differs from that of psychotherapy, not in terms of its depth, nor in relation to the superficiality of the work of psychotherapy, but owing to the multiple ramifications that are deployed in the psychoanalytic setting. Provided, of course, we are dealing with good indications of analysis.

CHAPTER FIVE

The metaphorization of analytic speech

The major themes of the theory of the neuroses or of border-line cases are identifiable through listening. The sense of finally grasping something belonging to the poetics of meaning can sometimes lead to a sense of jubilation. Much patience is often required before one is lucky enough to capture a fragment of truth. It will be understood that the process I am describing here is one that develops in a way that is globally satisfying, but this is not always the case. This schematic description is underpinned by the process of the transference, and the idea of processuality gradually forces itself upon us to characterize the links that ensure the progression of the communication under the impulse of unconscious affects and more or less lively transferential movements.

It is not my intention here to describe in detail the characteristics of the analytic exchange. I will just emphasize certain points to help the reader grasp the originality of this situation. Submission to the fundamental rule is closely bound up with the acceptance of regression, which marks the originality of this mode of knowledge. The relaxation of defensive control goes hand in hand with its antagonist—that is, a certain restraint placed on regression in order to avoid slipping towards a mode of functioning perceived as psychotic, or towards acting out, which thwarts the work of elaboration.

Defensive flexibility authorizes, and even espouses, progressive and retrogressive movements that facilitate the emergence of the transference. Alternating erotic and aggressive impulses punctuate the development of communication, the web of which has to be constantly untangled to reveal the movements of the unconscious.

This manner of addressing oneself to someone who may be experienced either as being there, elsewhere, or eventually lost, is the mark of what is known as a polysemic condition. Furthermore, this uncertainty can also concern the identity of the addressee. Who is listening, then, to what is being said? Is it X, or has he been replaced by Y, or by someone from childhood who today is no longer there, but who is represented during a moment of illusion. In short, who is speaking to whom, and about what? All of this induces the metaphorical quality of the discourse. This new condition is responsible for an original dimension that promotes transferential communication. Once again, we must notice the nature of what is experienced in the transference. To speak authentically about the transference, it is necessary to take account of what characterizes this form of love. We should emphasize here what gives it its originality. One can only refer to the transferential dimension provided one recognizes in it the quality of illusion that gives it its originality. Transference love is always marked by this ambiguity. It is a real, true love, capable of surges of passion, and, at the same time, something makes you feel that it is not real, as is reflected by the ambivalence. It is the product of an illusion, but this does not justify its rejection and makes it serve multiple transformations. It is an illusion that will be believed in the full sense of the term and is destined, under the influence of analysis, which facilitates its emergence, to wear itself out, to recognize its illusory nature, to dissipate, but not without leaving behind it the memory of an unforgettable experience. In short, it is a resurrection of childhood that one has to accept leaving behind. So, the reason for the metaphorization acquires its full meaning before fading away progressively until it is nothing but a memory. Everything that I have just described could be summed up by saying that this metaphorization transforms the dual relation analyst–analysand into a relation of thirdness (Green, 1989). It is as if the original dual relation gave birth to a third term uniting the two others, binding them to the chain that holds them together, revealing the uneliminable third. It binds and unbinds alternately, producing unforeseen effects of meaning.

In fact, these movements of analytic communication must be understood as the expression of the oscillations of the transference: more precisely, of the tensions between the transference and the resistances. This explains the sense that the analyst has of simultaneously approaching and moving away from a core of meaning that reveals itself to his understanding or, on the contrary, eludes it. To speak of the transference without distinguishing between its positive and negative aspects is once again to simplify things. To be honest, the transference is not always easy to identify, and the analyst sometimes loses his way and is unable to get the patient to recognize it. In contemporary analysis, recognizing the transference, without being preoccupied systematically with it, is undoubtedly what is most fundamental. The transference can make the analytic process richer, or, in some cases, it can prevent it from unfolding. It is focused on the more or less stereotyped reproduction of unconscious relations with the principal figures of childhood. The process is the current that allows the progressive and retrogressive movements that guarantee the march, the procession, of what is apprehended through listening to the material. The particular nature of analytic communication resides in the fact that, by virtue of free association, a disguised or defensive fantasy activity is expressed that the analyst is able to recognize. I have emphasized the existence of the transference, but there is no transference without underlying fantasy activity. In short, association is always the expression of the transference. It is clear, then, that free association, fantasy, and transference are interwoven.

What does this "metaphorization", transforming the prosaic communication from the analysand to the analyst, ultimately depend on? I have already stressed the role of free association, which gives a new form of binding to the elements expressed. It seems to me that this mode of expression favours the underlying demands of fantasy activity. Is that enough, though, to account for what can be surmised? Another factor, characteristic of the production of analytic speech, plays an equally important determining role. As I have pointed out on many occasions, this factor is *speech in the lying position to a hidden addressee*. That it is delivered lying down makes its production akin to the speech of dreams, even if it remains in a more or less waking state. What is more important is its quality of being addressed to a hidden addressee. The addressee's invisibility obliges the analysand to comply with the new condition of addressing himself to someone who is both present and absent, and, consequently, to accept the contradictory status of his speech: namely, that it is addressed both to a disguised presence and to a virtual absence, as with the patient I was speaking about before. Elucidating the defence against recollecting her parents' relations outside the menstrual cycle was not enough to lift all the repressions of childhood.

However, for analysis to take place, it is also necessary that the "distortions" imposed on the analysand's communication do not simply modify the truth of the communication that is supposedly undistorted. The distorted communication has, in fact, succeeded, through the distortions, in producing a new enunciation, but also in engendering a form behind which one detects not only the work of distortion, but a new manifestation that is closer to the truth than the lost literalness. In short, the transformation allows a new vision of the truth to transpire under the appearance of what has been distorted. This effect of analysis succeeds in overcoming the resistances opposed to the transferential communication—the only one that is real, the only one that is reliable, more real than the so-called authenticity that is deceptive.

When the patient's structure does not permit this triangulation, which is evocative of the Oedipal structure and gives access to the expression of two parental imagos, the analysis risks falling back on to a relationship that is overly limited to the duality between a subject and an omnipotent instinctual object. Bouvet designated this as a sexually undifferentiated "phallic personage", and contemporary analysis characterizes it as a dual relationship. Two before three? This succession calls for reflection.

It can be seen that it is the thread governing unconscious desire that allows us to construct hypothetically what can be glimpsed through the disguises of the resistances. We will be very attentive to what governs the dynamic organizations that appear under the light of examination. Analysis reveals the pressure of the regressive movements and the antagonistic interaction of the drives and resistances. By virtue of interpretation, the analysis continues without undermining the communication by causing too many regressive or disorganizing jolts, and without hindering the unfolding of the analytic process. As the latter develops, it allows for the progressive integration of moments of insight or awareness. This expression is very relative, for the analyst sometimes observes, in certain exceptional circumstances, that the transference remains too intense, so that its affective quality compromises the distance necessary for its intelligibility. But even in these cases, these flare-ups die down soon enough, and are no longer characterized by the excessive intensity that prevents comprehension. The contrary situation can also sometimes be observed in which the transference appears to be reduced and anaesthetized.

Once termination has been decided on by both parties, after there has been an evolution towards the resolution of the transference, it is not uncommon for regressive movements to result in a new resumption of the conflicts. This generally allows the transferential embers to be progressively extinguished.

I would like to say a word now about the phase of termination. Many analytic relationships do not terminate with a "classical" ending. Things can evolve towards interminability, prolonging unduly an analysis that does not reach its natural term. Alternatively, the analysis can be broken off unilaterally. Often, the analysand is disappointed at not having obtained what he or she had hoped for from the analysis, and has developed more or less resentful feelings about it. The separation then occurs in an atmosphere tainted with rancour.

So far, I have not considered in detail the encounter, alas, all too frequently, of real difficulties affecting analytic work. The picture I have painted, which I have tried to make as clear as possible, turns out to be simplified in comparison with the reality. The reference to free association can make the clinical material difficult to decipher owing to the bi-directionality of the psychical processes. The regression that can be surmised behind their apparent expression disturbs the meaning that is attributed to them. The opposition of the resistances conflictualizes and obscures what is striving to make itself heard, to the point that one is led to envisage an *instinctualization of the defences* (Green, 1993, p. 132). The drive has burst its banks, as it were, and invaded the entire communication, leaving nothing but itself.

All these reasons complicate the work which would allow us to arrive at an understanding that differs from that which is ordinarily based on secondary processes alone. And yet, everything that I have just described is considered by the analyst as part of his daily practice, and does not elicit any protest on his part concerning the difficulty of his work. Throughout his technical articles, Freud referred constantly to the multiple factors with which the analyst is confronted, and he dealt with them as he encountered them. Of all those that posed him problems, it was resistance that progressively took first place, and continued to acquire sharper relief until the end. Others were recognized, then abandoned—for instance, the transference, which was considered first as a resistance, before being regarded as the lever of the treatment. Others, too, appeared, in turn, such as the discovery that repetition takes the place of remembering to the point of becoming a compulsion. New defences were identified, like splitting and masochism, the second of which sometimes neutralizes the pleasure principle. It would seem that the ideal Freud had of analytic communication eluded him, and led him to complain about how he was unable to obtain it from his patients. He was constantly obliged to lower his sights.

Freud rarely admitted to his failures. Certain cases have become exemplary, such as the analysis of the young homosexual woman whom Freud finally got rid of, calling into question her analytic sincerity. But the case that raises the most discussions is that of the Wolf Man. A rereading of this analysis raises many questions. Admittedly, one can point out that Freud's aim was first and foremost to oppose Jung, whom he wanted to persuade of the reality of the primal scene, while somewhat neglecting the adult neurosis.

But one cannot agree with him when he claims that the patient had fully recovered by the end of his analysis. Freud never admitted his failure, considering that the continuation of the analysis with Ruth Mack-Brunswick simply had the aim of resolving or removing the residues of the transference that had been insufficiently analysed. Subsequent events, after Freud's death, show that it was scarcely possible to take this opinion at face value. In fact, Freud did not want to recognize that the analysis of the Wolf Man had reached an impasse. But this affair had taken place well before 1930. Thereafter, analysts experienced the difficulties of analysis more and more frequently. It is time now for us to consider them.

CHAPTER SIX

The negative therapeutic reaction

I t is necessary to distinguish between these diverse and uncertain factors and the serious problems that Freud encountered. It was in 1920 that Freud eventually recognized the undesirable new development known as the "negative therapeutic reaction". It is not simply a perspective that he would have preferred to ignore. In fact, his description is the consequence of a major theoretical discovery. It proceeds from this new finding, which changes the direction of the government of psychical processes. Henceforth, it is no longer the pleasure principle that holds sway over the psyche. Not only are the experiences attached to the pleasure principle repeated, *but also* the disagreeable and painful experiences that elude it. The sovereignty of the pleasure principle gives way to repetition. The negative therapeutic reaction is one example of this. But we must be careful here, Freud does not claim that it is *primarily* the distressing or disagreeable experiences that tend to repeat themselves, but rather that they do so *just as much* as those that are attached to the pleasure principle. From now on, the final outcome is governed by binding or unbinding.

We know that it is important not to confuse all the forms of failure of analysis with the negative therapeutic reaction, which has a particular profile. It sets in after a satisfying phase of analytic work and, from a certain moment onwards, reverses the general progression of the treatment. What, up to that point, had seemed to be a treatment that was evolving favourably, suddenly changes direction and takes a negative turn.

Negativity thus seems to be the product of an inverted orientation. It is as if the aims had been reversed, giving priority to an orientation independent of the pleasure principle, or even contrary to it, following the paths traced by unpleasure. This paradoxical trajectory develops under the sway of prevalent masochism. Subsequently, Freud was to reconsider his options, defending the existence of a primary masochism that is responsible for many disappointments of analysis. This evolution would be explained by theses related to the death drive.

At the same time, Freud's increasingly marked adherence to his final theory of the drives takes account of the predominance of negativity, where the compulsion to repeat obstinately resists favourable change and repeats the adverse orientation of the course of the analysis. We may ask ourselves if what had hitherto been considered as resistances were not, in fact, the expression of the death or destructive drives. However, we cannot examine the causes of failures without seeking to shed more light on their mechanisms. Analysts have studied with meticulous care those factors that, according to Freud, favour the domination of the death drives. If we examine the psychoanalytic literature around 1930, we are struck by the number of contributions that proposed explanatory hypotheses concerning the causes of failure in analytic work, without obtaining general recognition.

It seemed to me that the most specific feature corresponded to the formation of a mixture with deleterious characteristics. This mixture is made up of a combination of traits connected with virulent destructiveness, combined with a component which increases its negative potentialities and is linked to narcissism, particularly, that form of narcissism which I have called negative narcissism, which aims to return to the zero level of investment—in other words, to hinder the synthesizing process of Eros. The negative therapeutic reaction thus inverses the orientation of the resolution of the transference and poses a threat for the success of the treatment. The process backtracks, goes into reverse, and follows the model of negativizing regression, choosing the path of the worst rather than of the best. From this point on, the analyst is betrayed by the orientation of the psyche, which seems more concerned with preserving a state of ill-being than fighting against it. Interminable analysis often sets in. Freud said this in his *Outline* (1940a [1938]). It is as if everything that happened to an individual served only to nourish his need to be unhappy. Such cases are met with in real life, prompting those who witness them to conclude that they are dealing with inveterate pessimists.

CHAPTER SEVEN

The notion of failure

I t is time now to look further into what we understand by failure in analysis. If we agree to abandon the medical model, we
have to give up certain easy solutions. When are we justified in
speaking of failure in analysis? A well-known scenario is one where
the two partners of the analytic couple have a different appreciation
of the situation. It is not uncommon, for instance, to find the analyst
expressing an opinion that is totally contrary to the analysand's.
The analysand proclaims, to anyone who is ready to listen, that he
(or she) is more than satisfied with the experience he is having, and
cannot praise his analyst's qualities enough. But when one has the
opportunity of hearing, confidentially, the analyst's opinion (he is,
of course, careful not to express out loud what he thinks of the work
he is doing with this patient), one is struck by the lack of concor-
dance between their opinions. From the analyst, who is thinking
about how the analysis is unfolding, one hears the sharpest criticisms, to the effect that there is no analytic process, and that what
is being expressed during the sessions is not worthy of being
described as analysis. Further, the analyst has the feeling that, in
spite of the superficial progress that is being made, the analysand
has not really understood the nature of analytic work; his or her

discourse is factual, and there is no real willingness on his or her part to engage in an analysis of the unconscious, etc.

The converse situation can equally be observed. This time, it is the analysand who complains that the analyst does not understand him, or says things to him that are incomprehensible or unrelated to what he is feeling. From his point of view, the analysis is stagnating, while the analyst is repeatedly hammering out his interpretations to the analysand in the hope that the latter will finally understand what he feels is pertinent. On the other hand, when one listens to the analyst speaking about the analysis, one is surprised to hear him/her expressing a certain degree of satisfaction with regard to its progress. The problem becomes even more complicated when both partners of the analytic couple share the same negative impression, although when this analysis is presented to third parties, their opinions sometimes turn out to be less negative than those of the analytic couple. Alternatively, when both partners seem satisfied with the result, third parties sometimes prove more sceptical than the parties concerned. In other words, no opinion is reliable.

The problems related to failure cannot be considered without taking into account what the analyst feels about this judgement. For when one speaks of failure, whether it is the analysand or the analyst who is to blame, one is attributing responsibility for the outcome to the analyst, who is seen as having failed in his task. Irrespective of whether this judgement is objectively true or not, what counts is the reaction of the analyst who has conducted the analysis.

In fact, the analyst cannot escape the sense of guilt he experiences. Was the indication for analysis established correctly? Would it not have been better to refrain from undertaking the analysis in the first place? Did he conduct the analysis properly, and interpret what was addressed to him appropriately? Could he not, perhaps, have done better? All of which are potential reasons for reproaching himself. It is unusual for the analyst to emerge from this examination of his conscience and to totally reject the responsibility for this outcome on to the patient. Such a reaction is understandable, but it makes him feel he is a poor therapist, and, in short, a bad analyst, irrespective of the causes. And the nagging question always returns: would another analyst not have done better? Sometimes, the opposite reproach is made: was it not imprudent to undertake an analysis with such a fragile subject, encouraging him/her to undergo an experience that he/she was not able to tolerate? There are any number of good arguments nourishing the reproaches that an analyst can make of himself.

In these cases, the transference appears to be frozen, repetitive, dominated by stereotyped mechanisms. The situation barely evolves at all, and the process is exposed to interminable repetitions. The analyst's inventiveness is undermined. The patient no longer seems to notice that this analysis has long since been doomed. A decision will have to be made to terminate what has long since been nothing other than a moribund analysis.

Sometimes, when a long analysis has taken a course that is considered to be calamitous, the analyst is ready to throw in the towel. And one is surprised, in many cases, to see how the analysand insists on his analyst continuing the treatment in spite of everything. Certain analyses that seem interminable are sometimes broken off after a unilateral decision by the analyst. The analysand, who seems to have settled into a sort of analytic addiction, insists on the analyst continuing a treatment that has shown its limits. Every means is used to make the analyst renege on his decision, including the proposal to increase his fees. And yet, it cannot be said that breaking off an analysis is always followed by deterioration in the patient's state. I see confirmation here of the narcissistic predominance of the relationship. What should these discrepancies be attributed to? It is questionable to speak of failure when there is no consensus about the outcome of the experience, and even when such a consensus exists. The wish to prolong the analysis is akin to keeping someone alive who has long since been doomed. Failure? It is better to stick to the formula I have adopted and to speak of "the disillusions of psychoanalytic work". These disillusions also sometimes lead to an entirely unhoped for surprise, even if it turns out to be limited. It is clear that referring to the idea of failure is not really a psychoanalytic criterion, as its reliability is too uncertain. It remains true that the course of an analysis is rarely foreseeable in advance. And if it is true that prevention is better than cure, it is still important to think carefully about the pros and cons of the decision to propose an analysis—especially when the person concerned is only moderately inclined to make the venture. It is not enough to make the decision; the consequences will have to be borne. When someone is not enthusiastic about the idea of beginning an analysis that is likely to prove difficult, it is probably better to leave them the time they need to think it over. But let us leave some room for hope: the analyst who has bungled the analysis, or who has not been successful with it, should not erect his judgement into an absolute criterion. Where one analyst has failed, there is still a chance that another, more inspired, analyst may succeed.

CHAPTER EIGHT

Variety of traumas

Various factors can be invoked to explain the deceptions of analytic work that has proved insufficient—among others, the early nature of traumatic experiences. It is true that very early traumas can play a determining role. Yet, some subjects, in spite of undergoing significant and prolonged traumatic experiences, escape pathological destinies which are difficult to overcome. The appreciation of these traumas is often partial; for example, attention is attracted by the departure or loss of one of the parents, especially if he/she has not been replaced, and there is often a failure to take into account the overall family situation. Particularly serious for a young child is the situation when one of the parents has committed suicide, and mention is no longer made of their name and memory. Another equally serious situation is when the father has abandoned his family, giving no further signs of life, and the children are then forbidden by the mother to speak about him or even to refer to him. If the mother remarries, it is as if the original father had never existed. We can see that the trauma is linked to a relatively isolated consequence of this loss, which has led to the erasure of a part of the children's history. I can recall a psychoanalyst telling me about a couple who had gone to celebrate Christmas Eve with their neighbours; on their return, they found several of their children dead from carbon dioxide poisoning. Other children, who had been given the same first names, had since replaced the ones that had died, even though the photos of the latter had been preserved. How are these traumas, which could not be verbalized, to be elaborated? The analyst who had the task of analysing one of the survivors had a tough job on her hands. (This case is the subject of a chapter in the second part of this book. See "From the intergenerational transmission of grief to intrapsychic questions", observation by Catherine Kriegel.)

Early parental separation is often the cause of serious regressions. These can be attenuated by later, more advantageous circumstances, but, none the less, they leave deep and lasting psychical scars which can lead to difficulties later on in life. In spite of positive developments in many areas, relational life continues to bear the traces of the past. The general impression one gets of many of these patients, whose lives are marked by the bitter taste of failures and disillusionment, is somewhat reminiscent of chronic depression. The analyst is often perplexed by this inversion of erotic values and this orientation opposed to the search for pleasure. We are bound to question the opinion that Freud gave in "Analysis terminable and interminable" (1937c), where he states that, of the three factors mentioned, the trauma was the one whose influence was the least noxious. What I have just reported must cast doubt on this. The very early occurrence of traumas, prior to the accession of language, has very disturbing pathological effects that cannot be worked through successfully. Freud (1937d) had already said as much in "Constructions in analysis".

In spite of a long analysis, which has otherwise led to significant changes, certain fixations, originating in the past, remain unmodified. I am referring, in particular, to perverse fixations that acquire the significance of antidepressive forms of behaviour, aimed at combating a permanent sense of frustration. For instance, the disappointment at having failed to create a successful relationship with an object capable of soothing internal tension may justify the search for substitutive satisfactions by resorting to practices devoid of any sense of guilt, such as flirting with homosexuality, or paying regular visits to prostitutes with whom personal relations are established to the point of nourishing fantasies of companionship or even of marriage.

Another cause of indelible psychic wounds may be attributed to parental structures whose pathology and harmful effects have left wounds that never heal. This is often the case for families where the children share the pathological traits of their parents, actively repeating the traumas that they have suffered. Under these conditions, what is inscribed in the psyche of the children involves striking mechanisms of identification that are the consequence of traumatic experiences that have not been elaborated. As the years pass, the regression towards pathology is increasingly accentuated in conformity with the first traces. We should also emphasize the role of masochistic fixations to the mother, who is sometimes physically or mentally ill: the patient is in search of love that she cannot give, but, none the less, never gives up hope of obtaining it. These forms give rise to very ambivalent fusional relationships, producing a transference to an omnipotent internal object which favours fixations that are resistant to time.

The negative manifestations of the transference can sometimes take a turn that verges on delusion. The analysand then suspects the analyst of wanting to harm him or her, even to the point of wishing him or her dead. In these cases, the recommendation to take medication may be experienced as a disguised attempt at murder by poisoning. Sometimes, the patient's acting out takes on the form of a demand—for instance, that the analyst should agree to his or her applying for some sort of training programme, even though the patient is totally incapable of doing it. Fortunately, in most cases, these delusional moments of agitation do not persist, and eventually peter out. At any rate, the countertransference is sorely tested, and it is not uncommon for the analyst to end up doubting his competence, and even his mental health, or his capacity to understand the direction that things are taking.

Other patients seem to bring misfortune on themselves or on their families. These polytraumatized persons carry wounds which have been repeated throughout their lives ("cumulative traumas", see Khan, 1964), making them psychic invalids who can never get over the blows that fate has dealt them: early bereavements, unhappy childhood relationships, more or less invalidating illnesses affecting their parents or themselves, professional failures, disappointments in love, and so on. One is surprised that they have survived so many misfortunes without having broken down completely.

Certain more complex characteropathic organizations are more difficult to interpret. In such cases, depressive tendencies, or attempts to flee possible happiness, are sometimes subject to unexpected periods of respite. The analyst nourishes the hope that the subject will implement changes in his life and make contacts with people that will allow him, temporarily at least, to experience happiness. But soon enough, these hopes give way again to disappointment, for no explicable reason. One understands, in fact, that as soon as a favourable perspective opens up, pessimism gains the upper hand again. In fact, the subject, who, for a moment, had hoped for a happier life, cannot allow himself to envisage it and retreats to the unconscious pleasures of his masochism. It is as though his superego could not allow him to betray his negative ideals. He remains firmly attached to the deadly aims of his existence, as if he felt he had to remain faithful to a mourned internal object which he has to nourish by his own unhappiness—that is, the unhappiness of his object, becoming a hapless double who shares its fate. In fact, the fusion of the drives can lead to a temporary success of happiness, followed by the erotization of suffering which inaugurates a new victory of unhappiness, just when pleasure had momentarily seemed possible.

For reasons that are not clear, we are not all equal in the face of the misfortunes of life. As Freud had already remarked, experience teaches us that some individuals manage to avoid being overwhelmed by physical and mental misfortunes, while others, who have been relatively less affected by them, seem to be constantly scratching their wounds. No doubt the former have been lucky enough to be blessed with an unassailable optimism which has helped them stand firm in the face of what might have destroyed them, as Potamianou (1992) has clearly shown. All of this relativizes the notion of trauma.

A final point: the sometimes massively traumatic character of what some subjects have suffered can induce compulsive reactions that feed countertransference resistances. Yet, the consequences of these traumas deserve to be analysed. For it is not uncommon that if we break down their different combinations or mixtures, reactions are provoked that involve a variety of impulses, leading to composite formations in which inhibiting and depressive effects as well as exciting and aggressive effects are combined, not to mention masochistic reactions. It is important, then, that the analyst's countertransference is not parasitically invaded by desires for reparation, and that he strives to preserve his lucidity. The analyst's priority is to analyse the transference, while resisting the patient's efforts to seduce him, modelled on his masochistic desires.

It is important, though, to avoid oversimplifying. As one analyses more deeply, one witnesses initially an organization cultivating unhappiness, indulging itself in pain, immersed in negativity. The erotization of suffering allows for an indirect return to pleasure via the path of masochism, indicating the fusion of signs of negativity with those of secondary pleasure. While it is essential to perceive the alloy of the structures, it is often very difficult to get the patient to recognize the pleasure underlying his masochism.

In particular, these patients do not allow the analyst to work with free-floating or evenly suspended attention. In other words, the analyst no longer has the freedom to associate. He will soon notice that instead of letting his analytic listening "float", in order to gather up what the analysand lays before him, he finds himself obliged to react to the communication of his analysand with extreme concentration. But this inversion of suspended attention is contrary to the application of the analytic method. The least that can be said is that it prevents the patient's speech from letting unconscious fantasy emerge. Freud attributed great importance to this capacity of evenly suspended attention, which should be understood as an equivalent of free association.

CHAPTER NINE

Some effects of the primitive superego

T he cases I have just described are, for the most part, ones that began as cases of analysis, but continued as face-to-face relationships. The change of setting was supposed to facilitate the lifting of resistances. But there are other cases, which, from the outset, were not indicated for analysis, and so the patient was proposed therapy on a face-to-face basis, at a variable rhythm, usually two sessions a week. If some of them benefited from favourable evolutions in spite of the slowness of the process, others followed the path of interminable analyses. At the end of a very long journey, patients sometimes decide to put an end to their treatment, not because they consider the work as finished and as having achieved satisfying results, but out of a desire to finish with the repetition and sterility of the process.

The outcome we hope for is that these patients will be able to organize their defences better in order to cope more satisfactorily with their difficulties, even if we are unable to get rid of their symptoms. Think of the number of cases in medicine today where it is not possible to cure the patients either, and where all one can do is to try and improve their lot. An attenuation of their suffering is the best that one can hope for. Sometimes the analyst's patience eventually bears fruit. Some suggest switching to other forms of therapy, psychodrama or group psychotherapy, for instance, but the psychoanalytic point of view is still maintained, albeit adapted to the circumstances. Donnet has suggested the term "psychoanalytic assistance".

How has the profile of analysands changed? We may wonder about the wisdom of extending psychoanalysis in the 1950s to mental states outside the limits of neurosis. It was referred to at the time as the "widening scope" of analysis (Stone, 1954). The pertinence of this change, however, has never been called into question, and we have waited in vain to know if we were right or wrong in promoting it. The result was an increase in the proportion of "difficult" patients taken into analysis, but it was not clear whether this was beneficial or not. While some have claimed that results can sometimes be obtained with borderline cases that are just as good as those obtained with neurotic cases, others (Garcia-Badaracco, 1992) have called borderline patients the "specialists of non-change". In other words, the criteria of analysability had to be clarified. In any case, English psychoanalysts—Winnicott in particular— have furthered our understanding of these patients a great deal, without seeking desperately to cure them. Faced with the situation as it was at the time, Winnicott contended that analysts no longer had any choice. By way of example, we can cite the case he presents in *Playing and Reality*, in the two chapters on "Playing" (Winnicott, 1971).

Can we arrive at a better understanding of the nature of the obstacles that stand in the way of therapeutic progress? It seems to me that these patients often suffer from the excessive weight of a very severe, paralysing superego, impeding a positive evolution. In short, we are dealing with the effects of a primitive destructive agency, which obeys the injunctions of a regressive form of masochism. The result is a merciless struggle aimed at opposing change for the better. In these cases, a deeply rooted unconscious sense of guilt prohibits any lasting improvement following analytic treatment. Bion has also described patients who are in the grip of masochistic submission or negative omnipotence, and who have little hope of seeing their psychic state change for the better.

CHAPTER TEN

The ego prior to repression

This pathology of the superego is very often matched by a corresponding pathology linked to the ego. Freud's description of the fundamental mechanisms of neurosis in the early stages of psychoanalysis was only achieved due to the discovery of repression. He later completed them with other mechanisms, such as splitting. Here, it is not so much repression that is involved as disavowal, which succeeds in associating recognition and denial, paradoxical forms which lead to a state of paralysis because they contradict and neutralize each another.

In short, where repression is content to say "No", pushing away what it refuses to accept, splitting simultaneously affirms and denies what it claims both to defend and to challenge. In other words, it recognizes superficially the existence of castration and, thus, the anxiety that accompanies its recognition, while unconsciously continuing to deny it, as if castration anxiety did not exist. This exemplary case extends to a multiplicity of forms that arouse anxiety, accompanied by pronounced denial.

In structures dominated by splitting and disavowal, the clinical material is often incoherent, insensitive to interpretations, and marked by an insurmountable contradiction. This is why there is a real difficulty in recognizing the strategies of defence based on splitting. It is clear that this defensive solution is not the result of masochistically determined mechanisms of the superego, but of a sort of reciprocal invalidation between affirmation and negation. At the extreme pole, we witness what I have called a *subjectal* disinvestment, that is, where the ego disconnects from its own subjectivity (Green, 1993, p. 148).

Analysts have expressed very different evaluations on working psychoanalytically with such patients. It is uncommon, however, for this evaluation to be totally negative. Generally, it is considered that even though the work accomplished has its limitations, it has impeded other developments, which, left to themselves, might have paved the way for even more worrying regressions. That remains to be proved. In many cases where the therapy has been broken off, the patient's condition, reassessed occasionally years later, seems neither to have deteriorated appreciably nor to have improved by one iota. The benefit was to put an end to a repetitive relationship of which little more could be expected. What poses a problem here is the fear that the patient, left to his or her own devices, may collapse into depression.

It is worth observing here that when the therapy has just been broken off and there is a risk of the clinical picture deteriorating, an evolution towards outright psychosis is rarely observed. This outcome, the rarity of which calls for reflection, pleads in favour of the relative stability of these forms, which succeed in maintaining a state of equilibrium in spite of the danger of a deeper disorganization. In these circumstances, one is fearful of seeing an increased threat from destructiveness and hate.

In these clinical forms, attitudes can be observed that ultimately discourage the analyst, leading to interminable or repetitive analyses, even though it has long been evident that the experience is not worth continuing, both because the clinical picture is threatened by a form of paranoia, and because progress is intermittent, of short duration, and more often than not followed by relapses. It does not need adding that the analyst's decision to put an end to the treatment is not taken without a sense of guilt.

There remains the case of suicide, when the patient has the feeling that his (or her) life is futile, that no one cares about him any longer, neither the patient himself nor those with whom he or she has had intense or fusional relationships. After inconsolable losses, life has not returned to normal again; other relationships have not replaced those that have been broken off, and what remains is not worth living. Suicide, none the less, remains very difficult to foresee, unless the clinical picture has a melancholic character.

This admittedly incomplete panorama is intended to give an overall view of the difficulty of expressing an opinion on the evolution of psychoanalytic work. It is clear that these evaluations cannot be treated schematically. As a rule, they call for a nuanced examination in the light of criteria derived from the specific characteristics of the psychoanalytic approach, but there are still other factors to consider.

CHAPTER ELEVEN

Libidinal styles

I n "Analysis terminable and interminable" (1937c), Freud had already attempted to describe a certain number of characteristics which he linked to poorly defined libidinal qualities. Thinking about them *a posteriori*, they could be considered as constitutional factors. Today, we would not be satisfied with invoking an innate libidinal nature; rather, they would be seen as a product of early experiences, fixed by the vicissitudes of development. These influences marked the emerging psyche with characteristics that shaped individual style. Without adopting a position on the genesis of the impressions affecting the libido, I will simply remind you of some of them.

Freud postulated a libidinal viscosity or a certain adhesiveness of psychic investments. This is marked by a resistance to displacing investments, to mobilizing the libido when it seems to aspire to change and a modification of its aims. Adhesiveness has been the object of renewed interest on the part of Kleinian authors (adhesive identification), who have proposed new descriptions.

Another contrasting configuration is the quasi-manic flight of investments, where the subject is constantly attracted by novelty and given to ephemeral and passionate flights of enthusiasm. Such changes are unstable and do not last. This excessively mobile and fleeting libidinal form, frequently found in hysterics, espouses changes of mood that deny frustration and strive to offer distraction from disappointment and even pain, often resembling a manic defence.

Alongside these contrasting forms, which are often dependent on variations of mood translating the vulnerability of a psyche that is struggling as best it can against a more or less disguised threat of depression, one finds other modalities that can be linked to obsessional anality or hysteria; these are so extreme that they exclude any possibility of psychical elaboration bearing witness to a certain solidity or psychical maturity.

Both of the above forms represent a disorder in the economy of the object that is affected by diverse vicissitudes. The form we are going to consider now involves a modification of the relations between the object libido and the narcissistic libido. There is a state of disequilibrium between the two. In this case, we are dealing with a prevalence of narcissism, manifested by character defences. The libido refuses to venture along the often complex paths of objectalization, which not only has to take account of the libido directed towards the object, but also of the libido belonging to the object, that is, the libido of the other which demands to be taken into account.

The narcissistic economy is difficult to analyse. This is because it is mainly turned in on the ego, and because it does not risk venturing out towards horizons far from its base. It is always afraid to move away from its centre and concerned to preserve a potentially endangered ego, weakened by the investments that it has to displace from its own organization in order to serve the aims of the object libido. It is as if the object could not be conceived as a source of enrichment for the subject, but always as a danger that would result in making the psychical organization still more vulnerable. One feels that these subjects are constantly on the alert, surveying the limits of their ego, monitoring its frontiers. Under these conditions, the analysis of the transference is fragile; and cases are even signalled where it seems to be non-existent. The apparent indifference which makes narcissistic subjects seem so distant is simply a mask they wear to protect themselves from the demands they fear from the object, or, worse still, from themselves, when their defences give way, revealing the imperious and tyrannical character of their unconscious desires.

CHAPTER TWELVE

Drive fusion and defusion

The relations between drive fusion and defusion provide a good indication of the way in which the life drives and the death drives have succeeded in blending together internally, giving coherence to their union and according a certain homogeneity to the psychical organization. Sometimes, both of these drives live in a state of mutual coexistence, without interpenetration, and without imposing tensions on the mind that are too disorganizing. In those forms where defusion seems to get the better of fusion, it is not always the unbinding of the destructive drives that prevails, but sometimes the coexistence of the two groups of drives living side by side, without reciprocal exchange. Just as the manifestations of erotic life seem to have no link with the destructive manifestations, so, too, destructiveness seems to have no relation with the forms of erotic life. It looks as if the work of unbinding continues as far as the id, succeeding in dividing the two groups of drives and accentuating the defusion between erotic or libidinal impulses under the stamp of Eros and the destructive impulses marked by hate. Ultimately, when the work of defusion carries the day, it is the destructive impulses that prevail and the forces of defusion that dominate. But when defusion prevails, the cohesion of the psychic structure is weakened, and the field left to destructiveness is increasingly extensive. The result of this is that the forces of the life drives, which are supposed to accomplish a work of binding, are no longer up to the task, and the whole psychical organization, which is less organized and often overwhelmed, becomes concentrated around a narcissistic configuration where it is difficult to see the impact of the life of objects.

If we follow Freud's opinion to the effect that the death drive is a psychical manifestation that seeks to restore an earlier state, it is clear that, since its principal aim is conservation, it could be understood in its most elementary form as a force that is opposed to the differentiations of psychic structure and that hinders the processes of transformation. In pronounced forms of regression, the drive conserves a form of existence that is always dependent on its primitive nature. It is by virtue of the positive effects of Eros—a synthesizing and unifying force—that instinctual transformations can be accomplished in a form that is less crude and more united. In short, the closer the state of fusion is, the more the death drives are bound by the life drives, and the more unbinding is neutralized. It is illusory to hope for a total suppression of the effects of the death drive; the ambivalence one always discovers, which never disappears completely, is proof that they will never be completely suppressed. As the drive forms the primitive basis of the mind, it is clear that this action has repercussions on the other agencies of the psychical apparatus which suffer the consequences of it.

CHAPTER THIRTEEN

The modifications of the ego and the work of the negative

I t remains for me now to consider those manifestations which are the most difficult to describe. When Freud envisages in "Analysis terminable and interminable" (1937c) the factors that are attributable to the modifications of the ego, he admits his perplexity and recognizes that there is much that could be said about it, but remains discreet. We cannot be satisfied today with mentioning the characteropathic distortions of the ego, the description of which is very partial. I have described a *syndrome of psychic desertification* (Green, 2002c) to characterize cases where, when one tries to establish the analytic setting with a patient, one finds that he or she is, in fact, unable to tolerate it. One witnesses functional psychical paralyses caused by the traumatic effect exerted on the mind when it is required to abandon itself to free association. In such cases, patients experience a state of psychic emptiness, a libidinal desert, with the feeling that what is required of them simply faces them with their vacuity, with intense feelings of anxiety linked to profound distress, entailing a serious danger of disorganization. The sense of the ego's unity is jeopardized and the psychic desertification brings with it a risk of psychic annihilation. The analyst is soon obliged to break off an experience which has all the signs of an impending catastrophe, and to return to a more reassuring face-to-face setting, reinforcing relations with reality and avoiding the danger of mental breakdown. It is clear that the face-to-face situation mobilizes defences against a regression that does not just involve the libido, but also concerns the ego, which is seeking to overcome the distress of this state of psychic helplessness.

Other regressive forms are striking, even though the dangers they involve are more limited. These are forms that I have described elsewhere, or that have been encountered by others. (The objectives of René Roussillon's work are often convergent with mine.)

The *feeling of psychic emptiness*, described by Winnicott, is rarely missing. This feeling can even involve an experience of non-existence or, to a lesser degree, of futility. The *vitality of the body is not felt*. The body is experienced more as a burden than as a source of pleasure. A frequent sign of this is *negative hallucination in front of the mirror*. The subject cannot recognize himself, or he says that he cannot see anything: "Yes, I can see something, but I can't recognize myself." Alternatively, the first, blurred, vague, and unidentified image has to be reflected by a second mirror. In other words, a third party is necessary to facilitate recognition, as if the second mirror made it possible to go beyond what the first mirror reflects of a primary maternal gaze that is felt to be negative.

Absence is poorly integrated. This is borne out by statements such as, "I cannot think about anything when you are not there", or "There is something crazy about thinking that someone is there when they are not there." The sense of absence is equivalent here to a sense of loss. The absence is accompanied by the loss of the hope of refinding the object. Narcissistic fragility is omnipresent: *"I'm going away, I am being dragged into the void."* Or, still more radically, *"I am just a negation"*, or *"My life boils down to a long period of waiting in the void."* These are examples of remarks heard by different analysts. It seems to me that these cases illustrate what I have described as the *subjectal unbinding of the ego* (i.e., a defensive operation whereby the ego disconnects itself from its own subjectivity). The injunction to say everything and do nothing prohibits acting out, as if the recourse to acting represented a guarantee of reality that would otherwise be missing.

All these varieties involve the work of the negative. They are related to disorders of the narcissistic economy that concern the ego's sense of existence. The above statements constitute closing remarks, which put an end to associativity; they are threats, and are accompanied by the danger of the *ego's self-disappearance*. This pathology is, no doubt, the richest and the most interesting from the point of view of its consequences on the ego's economy.

I will conclude by mentioning the more well known manifestations, where early, important, and lasting traumas have imposed serious limitations on the ego; Freud had already recognized this in his articles of 1924 on the relations between neurosis and psychosis (Freud, 1924e), where he described the rifts, impingements, and wounds afflicted on the ego's constitution.

CHAPTER FOURTEEN

Diverse critical situations and acute somatizations

Among the difficulties encountered in analytic work, some appear in an acute form and may catch the analyst unawares. Critical states occur unforeseeably, unexpected somatic accidents, for instance. These can range from cardiovascular conditions, a heart attack, for example, or other no less worrying conditions such as ulcers or sudden haemorrhages—prodomal manifestations of an underlying affection that remains to be discovered. Many other symptoms of somatic decompensation can manifest themselves suddenly. In all these cases, the analyst must refer the patient to the doctor. But it is important to add that he should not adopt an artificial or indifferent attitude as a demonstration of his neutrality. I even think that while the patient is receiving medical care, the analyst should stay in contact with the medical team, perhaps even visit the patient and, above all, recommend the resumption of analytic sessions as soon as possible, naturally with the doctors' agreement.

Psychical symptoms can also be a cause of concern for us. For instance, the deterioration of a depression that was initially concealed, but which becomes patent under the influence of circumstances that have since made the situation intolerable. The analyst then feels bound to recommend recourse to medication. In this case, it is better to ask a psychiatric colleague to make the prescription and to follow up the patient's treatment, but this may entail interrupting the analysis, and may even require the patient's hospitalization. It is preferable to work together with a colleague whose qualities one recognizes, and with whom it is possible to collaborate, than to feign indifference under the pretext of neutrality.

Without resulting in situations requiring such clear-cut decisions, the patient's anxiety sometimes becomes a source of perplexity, and even concern for the analyst. I am thinking now of certain cases where the patient is prey to symptoms that escape the analyst's comprehension: for example, a sudden fear of madness, without it being clear what the source of the danger is, and what justifies it. The various hypotheses that the analyst proposes are not convincing for the patient. He or she cannot see how this anxiety, whether of recent or distant origin, can be analysed. It is not characterized by any specific manifestation. The danger that the ego may be overwhelmed by an incoercible instinctual pressure—but which?—is to be feared, as is the risk of breakdown, even though it remains unclear what is involved. In these cases, the analyst needs to maintain a reassuring attitude and not to lose hope that some instinctual insight will emerge to throw light on the patient's uncontrollable fear. Often enough, the patient gets back on top of the situation and his or her anxiety diminishes to the point where he or she is able to analyse it. No doubt there are other worrying manifestations that can be encountered, such as the danger of a transition to irresistible acting out, but here, too, the analyst's unruffled attitude (Bouvet) is often sufficient to calm things down.

Each of the constitutive elements of the psychical apparatus, the superego, the id, and the ego, can be the object of specific regressions; in other cases, it is the psychical apparatus as a whole that suffered in childhood. One cannot emphasize enough the role of early wounds and traumas that leave the patient with vulnerabilities that are more or less curable.

Two types of outcomes can be proposed to summarize the most frequent reactions:

1. *The depressive solution*: this is very frequently encountered and poorly understood, for the depression is treated symptomati-

cally, without sufficient time being taken in some cases to understand the ins and outs of the crisis.

2. *The delusional solution*: what is involved here are poorly structured and badly organized erratic delusions which are not constituted according to a delusional mode of structuring. It is limited to vague, labile, and transitory delusional configurations, without malignancy. Patients sometimes qualify them by saying: "That is my madness."

These two poles include the majority of the observable phenomena. In these cases, they never have serious repercussions and retrocede quite well, without becoming chronic.

CHAPTER FIFTEEN

Causes and remedies

Questions

However obscure the content of this chapter may seem, its importance should not be underestimated. The issues raised here can scarcely be avoided. Which questions are more pressing than the following: Why speak of the disillusions of psychoanalytic work? What are their causes? And, last, how are these states to be overcome? How do psychoanalysts manage to get the better of them? Can they hope to achieve this or are they doomed to accept a chronic state that leaves no other outcome than a palliative treatment for the rest of the patient's life? There has been much criticism in recent years of the inefficacy of psychoanalysis, with the miracle solution of cognitivist treatments being proposed as an alternative. Although psychoanalysts have often not come up with much to counter the criticisms of the cognitivists (apart from their partiality or bad faith in seeking to get rid of psychoanalysis and the treatments inspired by it), the best results of cognitivist therapies have, in practice, proved illusory. In the long run, the cognitivist criticisms of psychoanalysis have only succeeded in turning away a small portion of those who had resorted to the treatment of psychoanalysts, without their being obliged to make a call to arms in order to recover those patients who had temporarily been shaken by the vigour of the attack before pulling themselves together and continuing to put their trust in psychoanalysis as the only reliable method.

But the questions still remain unanswered. After conducting a careful examination in psychoanalysis of the types of cases I am concerned with in this book, only partial responses are available. The disillusions of psychoanalytic work cannot be compared in any way with the noxious effect of an iatrogenic factor. There is nothing that can be compared to a pathogenic cause that attacks the particular individual who is exposed to it from the outside.

We must force ourselves to reason differently. Experience teaches us that in psychoanalysis there are only *personal, individual causes*, due to circumstances that cannot be generalized. These must always be appreciated in the light of the history of the subject, the weight of pathogenic factors, and of the psychopathological structures cementing their organization. The pathogenic factors cannot be appreciated independently of the context in which they were observed. They depend in particular on the early age at which they occurred, the massiveness of the regression, on their effects on the environment, and, conversely, on the reaction of the environment, which tolerates or accentuates the weight of the pathological factors.

For a long time, it was thought that the specificity of neurotic symptoms was linked to their intrapsychic effect. The symptom was not so much the consequence of a pathological process acting from outside as an expression of the suffering caused by internal conflicts: castration anxiety, fantasies arising from unconscious productions, the effects of poorly integrated impulses, rigid narcissism, inflexible defences, and so on. This is how neurotic complications manifested themselves, as if they had been created by the subject's internal psychical organization alone, or principally at least.

Initially, the difficulties of analyses characterized by too much regression were attributed to the earliness and depth of the early fixations. This was verified quite frequently, but the descriptions of these forms in which pregenital traits dominated were too vague and allowed for little understanding of the basic mechanisms.

With Winnicott (1954), a new set of difficulties began to emerge. At variance with both Klein and Freud, Winnicott pointed out that neither of them had paid nearly enough attention to the role of the environment. Winnicott contended that analysts had not taken sufficient account of the external factors influencing the structure of patients. He was criticized for these positions. Above all, he wanted account to be taken of factors linked to the quality of the parental imagos, which were generally not mentioned: for instance, the mother's psychological structure. In other words, he considered that there is a difference between being brought up by a "good enough" mother and a psychotic or borderline mother. The repercussions of the latter situation can be responsible for the creation of a false-self organization, or of distortions that need to be identified or brought to light, even though they do not prove to be so patent as recognized psychotic symptoms.

A completely new symptomatic organization was recognized, to which analysts became accustomed. Since then, the symptoms in which analysts have been interested are not only those that have their origin in the intrapsychic world, but also those originating from outside, owing to the quality of the environment.

These recent findings modify our understanding of the transference, helping us to understand the patient's violent reproaches of the analyst. The transference is often expressed very directly. In the examples described by Winnicott, it sometimes manifests itself in a distorted way: patients force the analyst to recognize that he or she is a bad therapist, that he or she has no understanding of their problems, and that his or her shortcomings are much more important than the benefits of the treatment he or she offers. It would be an error, in his view, to confront the patient with his projections in an attempt to make him admit that he distorts reality according to his desires. In any case, that is what Winnicott recommended: one has to acknowledge the patient's reproaches, otherwise one would be ignoring the particularities of the causality that he or she has experienced, which must be accepted as such without discussion, trusting in the reality of the transference.

Winnicott was very critical of Kleinian technique. He considered that the paranoid–schizoid position was already a late mode of psychic experience. He had an original conception of the primitive psyche, and attempted to describe the early phases of development, where it is extremely difficult to differentiate between what belongs to the mother and what has its source in the infant. He even went so far as to say that this was a way of thinking that could seem crazy. He found this ambiguity in the transference of his patients, when he found he no longer knew what came from him and what came from the patient.

Contrary to common belief, Winnicott was not an unconditional advocate of object-relations theory. He never agreed to recognize the existence of object-relations from the beginning of life, and even less, as Klein did, the presence of manifestations linked to the object and to the ego as early as birth. His conception of the mother, as we shall see, is more complex than Klein's. He defended the idea of a duality in the conception of the object. He proposed the existence of a subjective object present from the very beginning, followed by an objectively perceived object. In other words, he conceived of an evolution in the construction of the internal object oriented towards the external object.

At the outset, the subjective object is an object created almost exclusively by the subject, a manifestation of his omnipotence, without any relation to the real object. This evolution obliges him to recognize the existence of objects which are no longer purely subjective emanations and which are recognized as being situated in a space outside the subject. This represents liberation from the tyranny of the internal world. In this situation, the subject is forced to recognize the limits to his or her omnipotence. Along this path from the extreme inside towards the objectively perceived outside world, we encounter Winnicott's discovery concerning the object and transitional phenomena.

Transitionality is essential for recognizing not only the spatial situation between inside and outside, but also the subjective property of the third. The transitional object both *is* and *is not* the breast. In other words, it is a category that belongs neither to the psychic reality of fantasy nor to external reality. Transitionality has been studied closely by Roussillon (2008), who has taken an interest in borderline cases. Recognition of the transitional realm is of capital importance for structures linked to play, and for the comprehension of the nature of analytic communication.

The transference relationship makes the patient relive experiences that are supposed to reflect the most primitive relations, which find a means of expression in it that would otherwise be unthinkable.

It is clear that the new ideas concerning these deceptions apportion a much greater role to very early factors. These are given an opportunity to express themselves so that, hypothetically, they are treated in a very different way from neurotic symptoms.

Winnicott used to say that because Freud was a whole person, he treated whole persons. In other words, after him, whether they wanted to or not, analysts had to take on patients who had not reached this stage of development. Generally speaking, psychoanalysts understood these very deep regressions as the expressions of a primitive psyche. But actually everything depends on how the latter has been recognized, understood, supported, and sometimes interpreted. What counts is not so much that the patient agrees with what the analyst proposes in his interpretations, but that he is able to recognize the experience that this has allowed him to have.

Bion is undoubtedly the most influential author of the contemporary period. Although he started out as a member of the Kleinian movement, he modified Kleinian theory so deeply that his independence should justly be recognized today. Many authors claim allegiance to his ideas without completely sharing those of Klein. In fact, Bion reformulated psychoanalytic theory, not only the theoretical foundations established by Freud, but also the theory that has emerged since Klein's innovations.

We could sum up the situation by saying that Bion takes as his starting point the interpretation of the psychoses rather than the neuroses, as Freud had done. And yet, in many ways, in particular with respect to the attention he gives to the phenomena of thought processes, Bion seems closer to Freud than Klein. He himself acknowledged that Klein represented an important contribution to psychoanalytic theory, but, he added, no more than a contribution (personal communication).

Now, the Kleinian understanding of the psychoses is based on the hypothesis of archaic phantasies, the recognition of primitive anxieties, and the fragmented state of the primitive mind dominated by fundamental mechanisms such as splitting, denial, projection, and projective identification, characteristic of the paranoid–schizoid phase. If Klein recognized the fundamental role of splitting, which plays a role in the genesis of a large range of phenomena, she none the less proposed to make a distinction between *ordinary splitting* and *minute splitting*—or instantaneous, multiple splitting—to characterize an action that divides the mind intensely and brings into play microscopic scission. This phase evolves towards a more accomplished state of wholeness, tending towards the corresponding unification of the object and the ego during the depressive phase. This evolution, far from always being linear, often seems to oscillate between the paranoid–schizoid phase and the depressive phase, alternating from one to the other, so that the state of wholeness is never achieved, as the post-Kleinians have observed. For Winnicott, too, access to the depressive phase inaugurates the capacity to feel concern for the object.

Bion continued to make use of these basic hypotheses, but reexamined them within a new context. For him, the fundamental dilemma of the mind may be expressed as follows: either we try to evade frustration by evacuating it or we elaborate it. By seeking to bypass the elaboration of frustration, the mind remains dominated by the predominance of beta elements, which are derived from the primitive impressions of the senses and unsuitable as such for psychical elaboration. To reach this degree of evaluation of psychical functioning, it is necessary to count on the intervention of alpha elements, representatives of alpha function, which allow a certain degree of psychic accomplishment to be attained. The elements of the mind which guarantee its functioning are dreams, myths, hallucination, passion, etc., the veritable basic materials of the mind.

However, this function is not constructed all by itself, and is based on the mother's capacity for reverie. In other words, the infantile psyche emerges from the mother's dreaming activity, which unites the alpha functions of both partners.

Bion proposes a complex construction of the emergence of a thought via a conception. At the outset, he postulates the preconception. Is this a hypothetical hereditary matrix? The preconception precedes experience and makes it possible to guess what is expected of it before it occurs. It is when there is a conjunction between this preconception and the object that the conception is formed. But we still have to consider the realization that leads to experience. However important it may be, it certainly has fewer consequences than a negative conception; for the non-realization of the experience obliges the subject to imagine through the negative experience the virtuality of what the conception has not realized, and thus to imagine what psychical functioning thinks of this non-realization. Here we have a rich application of the fecundity of the ideas concerning the negative.

A novelty of Bion's system is to have added to the two classical factors of psychoanalysis—love and hate—a third factor: knowledge. Bion divides this factor into positive and negative knowledge (K and −K). The originality of the introduction of this factor of negative knowledge is that it allows us to imagine that when the patient says that he or she does not understand the analyst's interpretations, it is not just a question of a lack of understanding, but of an inversion of positive knowledge; in other words, the patient has an interest in not understanding what the analyst is trying to communicate to him or her. The patient understands, therefore, what must not be understood at any price. When the interpretation arouses unpleasure, it is evacuated and, thus, rendered unassimilable, and its content is expelled. If this content forces its way through the barriers in order to be introjected once again, psychical activity as a whole is annihilated. It is no longer just the unpleasant content that is negativized, but the whole of psychical activity.

It can be seen, then, that the destructive activity does not target an isolated content such as the image of the father or mother, but all the agencies representing the introjected parents. The whole of psychic activity is subject to confusion. The distinctions between waking life and sleep are blurred. Someone who is sleeping is paradoxically awake, and someone who is awake is, in fact, asleep. Findings relative to negativity have ceased to be discriminatory: *nothing* and *no-thing* are no longer distinct. The absence of thing leads to the nothing as void, oblivion. In short, absence does not lead to the creation of the no-thing, but to emptiness. Thirdness is lost. Everything that is felt to be bad is condemned to be expelled, owing to the fact that it cannot be transformed through elaboration. Under these conditions, the intervention of thirdness as a condition of signification is lacking, as Pierce had already noticed (Canestri, 2009).

When one reflects on these new theoretical constructions proposed by Winnicott and Bion, one notices that the ideas expressed by different thinkers, whose references of origin appear to be dissimilar, are in fact much closer than one would have supposed.

Transitionality is closely bound up with thirdness, bringing into closer relationship the fundamental ideas of thought with what is beyond the paradox: being and not being. The meeting point between them occurs at the level of the intersection of the subject's psychic functioning and maternal functioning, through the medium of the mother's capacity for reverie.

A complex system arising from borderline or psychotic pathology is in the process of being constructed on the basis of a new metapsychology. Even if we are still a long way off from possessing the keys to a form of psychic functioning that still has to be discovered, we are, none the less, on a promising future path, with the hope of overcoming these current impasses. We may be able to get beyond the temptation of returning to fragmentation each time we are faced with a threat of progress which is felt to be intolerable, leading us instead to prefer familiar destructivity to the danger of an unknown novelty, accompanied by unacceptable pain.

We should also mention here a new field of hypotheses and reflections in the area of infantile autism (see the work of Haag). These quite advanced references are still in the process of development; it would be astonishing if the future were not to reveal their fruitfulness for the study of borderline cases and psychoses.

The theories of Winnicott and Bion have shed light on the symptomatology of those cases that seem to resist analysis. But how are we to understand these primitive relations to the mother, since she forms an integral part of the environment (Winnicott), particularly by virtue of her capacity for reverie (Bion)? What becomes of the centrality of the Oedipus complex in all this? Can we be satisfied with linking paternal issues to neurosis, while regarding pregenital states as under the maternal influence? Should we conclude that neurotic fixations are simply later than the early fixations that are observed in cases that are considered as difficult?

This distinction does not seem satisfactory to me. Two distinct phases could be contrasted: the first, in which *maternal* (and not feminine) sexuality predominates; and the second, in which *paternal* (and not masculine) sexuality prevails. In other words, the libidinal forms could be qualified not only in relation to the child, but also in relation to the parents. Of course, it can be said that both sexualities, maternal and paternal, are observable from the beginning. But when one observes the relative importance of the two sexualities in terms of chronology and their complementarity, their influence is seen to be of varying proportions. The early nature of the maternal influence is obvious, and the fact that the paternal influence comes later is recognized by everyone. But what I wish to emphasize is the qualitative difference between them. Maternal sexuality, in its relation to the infant's libido, is more diffuse, more global, and more extensive. The mother–infant couple forms a truly symbiotic unity—the libido seems to be more free than bound. It is not without reason that we speak of a fusional relationship, for fusion is the privileged mode of this primitive relationship.

When paternal sexuality imposes its law, the quality of the libido changes. It becomes more specifically linked to the problem of the castration complex; it is related to the anxiety of the same name, which is more bound; it concerns the difference between the sexes; and it reveals the distinction masculine / castrated before the distinction masculine / feminine can be thought about. But above all, the qualitative evolution allows us to speak of a sexuality which, on the one hand, is less invasive, less marked by its tendency to diffusion which tends towards the unlimited, and yet, on the other, is more differentiated, more circumscribed, and more recognizable by identifiable signs. Admittedly, the evolution of the libido attains its specific characteristics—which now become accentuated—as puberty approaches. It may be supposed that maturation is not the only factor involved in this change and that identifications (from the primary identification to the post-Oedipal identifications) also play a role that tends in this direction. Freud has been reproached for having minimized the difference between girls and boys. Yet, the little girl lacks many secondary sexual characteristics of the woman, which is less noticeable in the boy. Examined approximately, it does seem that the essential difference pertains to the genital organs of the children of both sexes. But character differences subsist, without overlooking the role of identifications to satisfy the wish to possess the mark of the other sex. However, who can deny that little girls are often more tender, more cuddlesome, more given to effusiveness than boys who want to assert very early on their virility by despising the psychological attitudes of girls? "They are only interested in Barbie dolls," complained one four-year-old boy. In short, from the maternal sexual phase to the paternal sexual phase, a transition has occurred. For boys, the penis is an identifying marker. In this way, they struggle against the backward pull towards the maternal dimension. It is frequently maintained that no signs of the Oedipus complex can be observed in the symptomatology of many clinical situations involving non-neurotic structures. This argument, put forward by Winnicott, is debatable. It is not because the signs of the Oedipus complex are not yet noticeable that it does not exist. It continues to exist in a latent form. It is preferable to surmise its existence from discreet signs rather than to deny it.

The succession maternal sexuality–paternal sexuality does not only explain the late character of the Oedipal complex. This delayed arrival of the paternal phase is indicative of the long period of maturation necessary for the appearance of the Oedipus complex in its anthropological function. Contrary to common belief, Winnicott and Bion were not the ones who invented this. It was Freud who had first understood that the Oedipus complex is not only a developmental phase, but *first and foremost a structure*, as Lacan also maintained subsequently.

CHAPTER SIXTEEN

Recent suggestions concerning the treatment of cases resistant to the therapeutic effect of analysis

An overall view of the technical positions defended by psychoanalysts concerning the dangers to which analytic treatment is exposed reveals great disparity. The first observation, one I have already made, is that the authors point to the fact that the current population of analysands, or, more broadly, those who turn for help to psychoanalysts, does not constitute a homogenous mass but, on the contrary, forms a diverse ensemble depending on the types of structure to which they are attached. In other words, the time is over when neurosis was the exclusive model of analytic activity and when it was important to distinguish a plurality of typologies, which, taken together, formed a composite image of the analytic population. To this heterogeneity of structures there often corresponded a pluralism of techniques. This diversity was not only to be explained by the global situation of polymorphism, but also by the options chosen by psychoanalysts, not to mention the local traditions which proposed different ways of distinguishing the diverse categories of patients, of comparing them, of treating them, and so on.

Broadly speaking, in France, analysis is reserved as far as possible for the classical indications of analysis. The rule of silence is respected, interpretations are rare, short, allusive, and selective, and the transference is recognized without being systematically interpreted. Of course, I am simplifying things for the sake of argument. The transference neurosis follows a better evolution from the moment of its flowering to the moment of its resolution, which often takes a long time to manifest itself. Analyses, usually of three sessions a week, are frequently lengthy, particularly as they seek to respect the patients' resistances and only tackle them with tact.

The above remarks, which are intended to sketch an outline of French technique, are certainly schematic and insufficient. Much more would have to be said in order to give a more complete picture. But I want now to touch on a different problem, encountered in the writings of Anglo-Saxon authors, and still more frequently, those of the British Society. I will take as my starting point the technique followed by the pupils of Klein, who, today, represent the line of a new classicism. Without disregarding their differences, it would seem that the points uniting them are more important than those opposing them. One cannot fail to note how this line, which for a long time constituted an avant-garde minority, is considered today—by me at least—as embodying a classical position. It is based essentially on the belief that analysis is about interpreting the transference, conceived in terms of the directives of Klein. Regression is to be avoided, and interpretation activated.

Unlike Kleinian authors, those authors who belong to the independent group or the contemporary Freudian group have adopted a different attitude. It is not so much the exactness of the Kleinian interpretation that is contested as the usefulness in formulating it in the first place. In other words, it is considered of greater interest to leave the content of the analysand's material as it is, and to allow it to develop in its own way, without the analyst rushing to communicate the content of it by means of a transference interpretation that is supposed to modify the situation. Winnicott used to say that the interpretation was an indication of the limit of the analyst's understanding. But the one who has proved most convincing is undoubtedly Bollas (2001). He is not alone, however. Both Parsons and Stewart have defended similar positions. It would seem that these attitudes posit a return to Freud's technique, partially at least, concerning the silent elaboration which occurs in the analysand during the treatment, while allowing the process of free association to take its course; in other words, by respecting a development that is all too often prematurely influenced by the analyst's transference interpretations which risk distorting the effect of free association. It is not that we should retreat into a silent attitude, but, rather, that we should allow the patient to elaborate the material without interrupting the process prematurely.

The older he grew, the more Freud was convinced of the importance of the influence of the death drives. On the other hand, he remained equally convinced of the strength of infantile fixations and resistances. I do not think he had too many illusions about the analyst's capacity to always overcome such difficulties. It remains true that he constantly reminded us of the need to be attentive to the obstacles and resistances to recovery. Likewise, when Freud turned his attention to the three factors resisting analytic treatment, his favourable opinion with respect to benign traumas scarcely took account of their precocity, which recent clinical practice has helped us to appreciate better. If there is not much that can be said about the constitutional strength of the drives, what needs to be emphasized more than Freud did is the importance of everything that concerns binding and the fusion of the drives. But, as we have already seen, it is without doubt the early modifications affecting the ego that are the most difficult to resolve. These, at any rate, were the factors cited in 1937.

However, if we recall the defensive positions elaborated by Freud in the wake of "Analysis terminable and interminable" (1937c), importance (recognized late in the day) will have to be attributed to the notion of *construction*. We can see Freud revising his idea concerning the complete lifting of infantile amnesia and postulating the existence of traces indicating traumatic scars or surprising modes of functioning: the patient's communication reveals hallucinatory modes of functioning and perhaps also signs of somatic origin, or even a propensity for evacuative discharge, as is sometimes the case in acting out. Generally speaking, Freud's formulation regarding the patient who suffers from reminiscences has a very wide spectrum.

As I have said, new ideas have appeared with the theories of contemporary authors. I have limited myself to Winnicott and Bion, whose ideas I have set forth in a detailed manner. These contemporary hypotheses, which have proved useful, have also revealed the shortcomings of interpretations aimed at modifying forms of behaviour verging more or less on psychosis.

CHAPTER SEVENTEEN

Methodological principles of psychoanalysis and the psychotherapies

Everything I have just described highlights the fragile conditions in which the analytic setting is implemented. It is often the case that the parameters that ensure the optimal conditions for conducting an effective analytic treatment cannot be realized. This is why we attempt to transform the extremely rigorous situation of analytic communication into a less demanding form, when it becomes clear that is necessary to be satisfied with less in order to be able to move forwards. We then make the experiment of modifying the numerous requirements of the setting, such as switching to the face-to-face arrangement, a situation that the patient seems to tolerate better, and which allows the process to get going again. Many psychoanalysts have shown themselves to be in favour of this technique, after realizing that more satisfactory analytic work could be achieved face to face.

It is far from my intention here to contest the advantages of the face-to-face technique over the difficulties of applying the classical psychoanalytic method. I have witnessed many stagnant situations where the only means of getting a process going again was to abandon the classical psychoanalytic method. But noting encouraging results does not exempt us from enquiring into the differences.

It is true that the patient often feels relieved and more at ease in the face-to-face setting, yet the analyst may notice changes in the style of the therapeutic work. If something has been gained, it is not without a cost. A certain degree of *insight* becomes more accessible and the transference seems more tolerable, but it is accompanied by more protective resistances, leading to more superficial gains in insight. But, as a whole, the situation is tolerated better.

In this chapter, I do not just want to make a comparison between psychoanalysis and the psychotherapies. My aim is to clarify the methodological principles distinguishing the two techniques. To do this, it is first necessary to establish more clearly the differences between the two practices.

Wherein do these differences reside? It seems to me that what I have called the metaphorization of the setting has been modified, if not altered. Furthermore, I would say that thirdness has given way to a two-person relationship, without any effect being attributable to an identifiable third party. This thirdness, which is so indispensable to the constitution of an authentic analytic relationship, has made way for a dialogue that only accepts with difficulty the existence of a virtual, potential, third dimension. What has perhaps been modified by the new face-to-face technique has been paid for by the loss of the metaphorizing power of the analytic setting.

Going still further, it is as if the face-to-face situation had diminished metaphorization by weakening what the analytic setting implied in terms of a reference to a paternal law above the two parties present. This is where an important change occurs in so far as both parties accept that their relations are governed by a common law. It is true that it is inevitable that the setting will be subject to attacks by both partners (by the analyst, too), but the idea remains that something has been put to the test concerning this law which is necessary for the analysis to unfold. Hence, the sense of uneasiness that can arise, when switching to the face-to-face setting, concerning a potential attack on the paternal law. Can one bring a treatment to a successful outcome without referring to the setting as a paternal agency?

I am not just concerned with triangulation, which is the rule in every structure that claims to be Oedipal, but wish to go further and recall the triangular structure of the anthropological situation, or, alternatively, the necessary presence of a *de facto* triangulation

constituted by the reference to a subject born of the sexually differentiated relationship of two parents. And please spare me the objec-
tion of the artifice of adoption by two homosexual parents. Pierre
Legendre has denounced the legal options that consisted in giving
a reality to parental fantasies.

We are led to understand that in order to be productive, the
conditions of the setting require a state of psychical normality,
which is much less frequent than one might think and goes hand in
hand with an openness of mind that is not given to everyone. It is
not enough to be free of serious psychical or psychotic disorders to
offer the psychical conditions required.

If it can be said that the indications for face-to-face psychotherapy enjoy quite a large spectrum, the conditions for a good
indication for analysis are more demanding. There is no contradiction in recognizing that the more "therapeutic" effects of face-to-
face psychotherapy are beneficial. We also need to recognize that
the indications for analysis are more restricted, and its aims more
specific. In short, we must distinguish between the desire to relieve
suffering, which dominates psychotherapy, and that of analysing,
which entails work of another nature. This is the source of certain
misunderstandings that arise between supervisee and supervisor.
The first would like the supervisor to recognize that the patient
"has made progress", whereas the latter might point out, without
calling this progress into question, that the nature of it does not
plead in favour of an integration concerning recognition of the
unconscious and an evolution towards self-analysis (Busch, 2010).

The merits of both methods should not be opposed, but distinguished, while recognizing what is specific to analytic work. To do
this, we must accept that the effect we are looking for in analysis is
not limited to the analysand's "progress" and set ourselves the aim
of bringing about a sort of internal "conversion", as Klauber (1976)
once suggested at a meeting of IPA officials in the UK.

We must introduce the reference to an "internal setting" into the
comparisons between the classical and face-to-face setting. This
internal setting is the analyst who not only sees to it that the
patient's analysability is maintained, but who is also supposed to
be its guardian. The analyst sometimes succeeds in this task more
or less deeply. An analysis that is considered as successful is one
where this precious result—which it will sometimes be necessary to

support and keep alive—has been achieved. In short, the meta-phorizing agency, the paternal agency, and the symbolic function producing thirdness are interdependent. They make it possible to define more clearly what constitutes the difference between psycho-analysis and the diverse forms of psychotherapy. It is worth recall-ing that Freud based his hope on the first of these only, and it is important to note that in no case does the difference between the two techniques reside in the number of weekly sessions.

CHAPTER EIGHTEEN

Conclusions

The reader may have got the impression from reading these pages that I am excessively pessimistic about analytic work. I have, none the less, tried to stick to the essential issues by identifying the most distinctive characteristics and the most general traits, and by striving to grapple with relatively specific configurations. In any case, there can be no question of drawing up a list of all the obstacles that are encountered: such a list could not be exhaustive, and each day would remind us of omissions that every new reader could justifiably point to. Neither have I wanted to limit my descriptions to mental states of patients who ultimately become more or less well adapted to their situation and oblige the analyst to accept the imperfect nature of the outcome of his or her work. What I can say, though, is that I have tried to draw attention to the tenacity of fixations, the power of the destructive drives, the "solidified" character of masochism, the difficulty the ego has in giving up its archaic narcissistic defences, and the rigidity of resistances.

So, I want it to be quite clear that I am speaking here about the *real* "disillusions" of psychoanalytic work, that is, those that do not simply cause temporary disappointments which work out in the end. My intention is not to divert attention from the real accomplishments that only analysis can achieve, but to ensure that we are better informed about the particular forms that analytic work can take when it gets into difficulty, so that we can improve our means of overcoming impasses which stand in the way of its efficacy.

Should we become resigned when we are faced with repetition-compulsion and the interminability of an analysis, with the masochism of a patient who seeks desperately to reproduce the same sterile configurations? There would be many reasons to let oneself get discouraged. If, however, we are not tempted to throw in the towel, it is because discreet signs still allow us to retain a glimmer of hope. During recent discussions on working face to face, modes of analytic elaboration were defended which were not simply content to approximate the method inspired by the classical setting. It was suggested that it was possible to accomplish excellent psychoanalytic work face to face. This frequently defended position sought to emphasize what the diverse methods had in common. We found that there were limits to our agreement on this point, and we tried to take things further. New difficulties appeared: the impossibility of obtaining a mode of functioning that is comparable in every respect obliged those who had not let themselves get discouraged to persist in their efforts, to show imagination, and to stand firm in spite of their disappointments. Roussillon proposed another model: the *psychoanalytic conversation*. While, in the past, such an attitude would have been criticized or considered as a sign of insurmountable resistance, we came to think that it could be adopted in order to circumvent what stood in the way of effective analytic work. In other words, the appropriate course was not to get impatient, not to renounce belief in the effects of interpretation too soon, and to wait for more favourable circumstances to emerge permitting windows to be opened which would allow inside and outside to circulate freely until the moment when a little bit of analysis, even of short duration, would prove possible. Other exemplary cases could bear comparison with those mentioned above. I can recall certain presentations (Aisenstein) of psychosomatic cases which seemed closed to free association, but which, thanks to the inventiveness of the therapist, and after exchanges far removed from the usual style of analysis, often to do with themes related to books that both partners of the couple happened to have read, or films that they had both seen, or even themes concerning current events they were both familiar with, finally opened up new ideas which eludidated the analytic material (Aisenstein, 2010). These endeavours were often sterile, but sometimes the unexpected richness that emerged from them came as a great surprise to both protagonists. Without entertaining too many illusions about this technique, it may be that unsuspected avenues will open up that can be exploited in the future. However, it has to be recognized that these technical variations must be associated with psychoanalytical psychotherapy rather than psychoanalysis proper. A thousand and one objections could be made to such unorthodox ways of doing things, but nothing is worse than getting bogged down in repetition and the sense of impasse without an exit. The psychoanalytic ideal is preserved, and the fruitfulness of certain new psychotherapeutic techniques needs to be recognized.

But there is still a great distance between this position and the technical modifications used by some analysts, for we cannot conclude that anything goes. For me, and for those who share my opinion, certain measures must be proscribed. I am referring to short sessions, scansion, and other measures attesting to forms of analytic violence involving unacceptable degrees of hostility, and insensitive mistreatment, which is both deaf and blind. What has become of *benevolent neutrality*? On the contrary, analytic experience in recent years has allowed us to reflect on certain innovations proposed by Winnicott that have opened up truly imaginative ways of interpreting. Even if these approaches may seem questionable, it cannot be denied that they have the merit of being vehicles of innovation and sometimes of openness. An unexpected outcome has been that silence is recognized as having more merits than systematic interpretations, concerned with hammering home endlessly what seems not to have been sufficiently heard and understood.

In this respect, the return to a classical interpretative attitude allows us to rediscover technical practices that the Kleinian model had, to some extent, led us to forget. Bollas (2001) regards the Kleinian technique of constant and repeated transference interpretation as maintaining the resistance to analysis. The relevance of these objections has been recognized, and additional reflection has led to a reconsideration of certain excesses.

I have nothing to retract from his remarks that led me to recognize the merits, but also the limits, of the classical setting, and of its contribution to symbolization—what I have called metaphorization. We must accept the obscurities and contradictions of positions that are too clear-cut, and allow for the openings of paradoxical thought. It is better to have contradictions that are sometimes a source of obscurity than reductive simplification, which sheds light whose clarity proves illusory.

Before making a few concluding remarks on the disillusions of analysis, it is perhaps less difficult to sketch in broad outline what characterizes, for a psychoanalyst, the signs of success of the psychoanalytic method. This will no doubt be a more idealized description than the reality of what we actually encounter. By virtue of a supplementary reversal, the positive that I have described earlier allows us to get a glimpse, through its negative, of what often seems to me so difficult to describe directly.

At the risk of sinning by an excess of idealization, I will mention at random some traits that are easily recognizable: a variety, diversity, and richness of investments, with a priority for relationships with others; an absence of rigid fixations and defences; flexibility and mobility in mental functioning; the capacity to love and also to hate without allowing oneself to be carried away by a passionate attitude; the possibility of investing both parental imagos positively as well as close family relations; a compromise between loving and working that is not too conflictual; the possibility, when circumstances require it, to go through an experience of mourning without it becoming interminable; the ability to tolerate disappointments and frustrations, as well as to recognize the privilege of loving. Who can pretend to approximate such an ideal? I have only accepted citing these traits in full awareness that no human being can possess them perfectly and in their totality.

This state of perfection that I have outlined will facilitate my description of what is encountered more frequently. I have mentioned the unfortunate circumstances that can give rise to disillusions. I have already pointed up the excessively destabilizing oscillations of mood variations, and also the unfortunate consequences of the withdrawal of love, as well as the ambiguous role of flights of passion that are doomed to deception. It is understandable that against the backcloth of fragile object-relations, the transference can only be detected with difficulty. Sometimes, reactions of a psychotic, characteropathic, or paranoiac kind are allowed to break through, and feelings of disappointment or bitterness are expressed to do with the impression of not being sufficiently rewarded for one's merits. The frequency of depressive episodes gives us an idea of a narcissistic fragility that can affect each one of us. Every transference, in fact, retains its share of mystery, which is never completely elucidated.

Such is the varied nature of the forms of these disillusions. I have sometimes been reproached for describing them in too dark a light. I would like to end on a note of relative optimism, which will allow me to conclude by emphasizing the value of the analytic act. Having sufficiently pointed up its inadequacies and disappointments, it is fitting to recall the irreplaceable character of the psychoanalytic method. Although much remains to be done if we are to continue to make progress on the basis of what psychoanalysis has already enabled us to understand, it is important to stress that no other method can claim to provide an in-depth understanding into the mechanisms of psychical causality better than psychoanalysis. There is no reason in this respect to throw in the towel; on the contrary, we must be doubly courageous in face of the scale of the task that awaits us. It is better to be aware of the adversary that the analyst will have to face than to remain ignorant of it in order to entertain illusions that are bound to be disappointed.

PART II
CLINICAL STUDY

Introduction

In this part, I put the reader in contact with clinical material. On the one hand, I have presented cases that were submitted for discussion by colleagues and selected by them on account of the interest they presented regarding the difficulties of analysis they encountered in them, and, on the other, I have chosen a number of cases drawn from my own personal experience. The final result represents a wide and varied spread of clinical situations. Given the manner in which the cases presented were selected, one cannot expect to find any sort of unity in them. The material chosen was limited to its essential content. Each case, whether it was presented by my collaborators or taken from my own experience, is divided into two parts: the essential elements of the clinical material are presented first, followed by a short commentary by me aimed at drawing out the essential points or characteristics. It goes without saying that I alone am responsible for any errors of interpretation of my own making, or any other errors that I may have made.

(A) Some examples drawn from the experience of collaborators

Axelle: a countertransference equal to anything[1]

Case reported by M.-F. Castarède

This analysis had been going on for more than twenty years. After various attempts to find a suitable setting, the face-to-face situation proved to be the most favourable option. The patient led a very restricted life, unlike her brothers and sisters. She lived alone, had broken off her studies, and took care of the children of quite close friends. She had no relations with people of her own age. She seemed satisfied to look after children, with whom she said she had a "self-evident" relationship—that is, she had the feeling that she understood them instinctively, without any difficulty.

She had only one passion in her life, music, which no doubt had a lot to do with the countertransferential attachment of her therapist, who was a psychoanalyst and musicologist. But it should also be added that the therapist recognized in her patient elements that reminded her of aspects of her own history, hence the particular attachment she felt for this case. For a long period of time the therapeutic relationship was sustained by long letters from the patient to her therapist, who showed admirable patience and managed to keep the therapeutic relationship going, avoiding attempts to break it off.

This patient's childhood was marked by the sudden death of an elder brother, a bereavement her mother had never been able to come to terms with. She had embalmed him in her memory, while losing interest for the surviving sister, who herself had once almost died from drowning and was only saved *in extremis*. But once the sister had come round, she regretted that she had been saved. She would have preferred to have disappeared like that, no doubt in a relationship of rivalry and identification with the brother who had perished.

The mother, therefore, seemed deadly, always into narrative, and never into affective issues. Therapeutic work on the patient's identifications with this brother, a lost and irreplaceable object, led her to go through a process of evacuation. She emptied herself. Although strongly attached to her therapist, who had always strived to maintain a lively relationship with her, she felt disinhabited. At one point she said, "I cannot think about you when you are not there. I am going away, I am being dragged down into the void. There is something crazy about thinking that someone is there when they are not there." This reaction was no doubt related to her mother's inaccessibility, as she was absorbed in mourning the loss of the patient's brother. Moreover, Axelle saw her surviving brothers and sisters as inanimate, and her sister used to say to her, "You are like a dead rat."

The continuation of this analysis produced very few changes and an attempt to switch to psychodrama proved impossible. The therapist noticed that the face-to-face setting allowed a dialogue to be established, a "conversation" which kept the two partners in a bodily relationship, a mixture of fusional closeness and insuperable distance. She examined her countertransference, thinking that her work consisted in a construction aimed at understanding what was going on in the transference repetition and in steering away from the hazards of the relationship. The therapeutic factor resided in preserving a relation of tenderness that would allow a framing structure to be internalized. But it was not possible to count too much on an independent ego. None of Axelle's relationships involved loving commitments. Like Winnicott, the analyst wondered what would become of the patient if she (the analyst) were to fall ill. No end to the treatment was envisagable in the absence of a significant modification of her libidinal life. Music remained her main investment, and could be replaced by investments in people who were capable of sharing this with her. The last news I had was that Axelle had put an end to her therapy, although no significant change had occurred.

*   *   *

What sort of therapy was this? After analysis had proved interminable, the only acceptable setting for this relationship was face-to-face. The situation continued thanks to a number of favourable elements: a very positive countertransference capable of enduring insurmountable resistances, and, above all, the analyst's sense that there was a coincidence between the circumstances she had experienced in her own early childhood and those of her patient, which gave her the desire to help the latter overcome her traumas. On several occasions, the analyst was not afraid to intervene actively when the patient felt tempted to put an end to the therapeutic relationship. Ultimately, though, she had to resign herself to letting the patient go.

While continuing the relationship was beneficial, it had little influence on the equilibrium of the patient's life. The shared interest in music undoubtedly represented an indispensable affective communication, but the mother's mourning was probably too pervaded by insuperable guilt. There were two situations of mourning here: the mother's mourning for her child, and the patient's mourning for the mother's love, which she had not been able to enjoy after her brother's death. The question arose of knowing what would happen to the patient if something fatal happened to her analyst. It seemed to me that my listening as a third party helped the therapist to tolerate the trying aspects of this patient's treatment. I continued to follow this evolution from time to time each time the analyst felt the need for it. But today both sides have put their case.

Note

1.   The case of Axelle has already been the subject, partially, of an earlier presentation (Green, 2006, pp. 141–170).

Cendrillon

Case reported by Z

Cendrillon contacted Z at the age of twenty-seven on the advice of one of her adolescent friends who had been in treatment with her. This young woman, in great difficulty, had a "mad" mother who had often been hospitalized for delusional episodes accompanied by suicide attempts, and a father who was suspected of being perverse, without there being any convincing arguments to confirm this suspicion. The contact with the analyst was beneficial from the outset, especially as the friend who had referred the patient to her had also had a mad, unpredictable, and self-destructive mother.

Cendrillon is pretty, and displays a certain casualness, which barely conceals her great distress. She suffers physically, experiencing her body as uninhabitable. She is prey to multiple pains, in particular, headaches, for which she has been to the doctor on many occasions, and for which she has had many tests that have revealed nothing significant. One doctor diagnosed depression and advised antidepressants. She experiences these headaches as if she had a helmet pressing down on to her nose, provoking a facial paralysis accompanied by sharp pains. She feels unable to envisage the future positively like her sisters, who all have children. When she is lying in bed, she experiences strange sensations and is prey to appalling anxiety: the bed creaks all by itself and the sheets move even though she is immobile; she cannot feel any sensation in her legs and imagines that they are paralysed.

All these symptoms had set in during a period of a few months during a depressive episode when she felt she was having a breakdown. Apart from anxiety, her affects are blocked off and replaced by physical pains. Despite her distress, she is unable to cry. She is afraid of dying, but sometimes hopes she will, just to escape from her symptoms. Abandoning herself to sleep is a way of losing control of her breathing, she says.

She finds going out of her home very difficult, so, to avoid meeting people, she does not work regularly. In her work, she seems concerned to conceal the effort she makes so that her attitude does not betray her. She is afraid of disappointing her boss, who has shown esteem for her by asking her to accept a position of responsibility in an international organization. She finds it rather difficult to tolerate the pressure she is subjected to by her colleagues, who she describes as "old maids". The fear of suffering the effects of her mother's madness is difficult to bear. She questions her place in her family. She can remember having idealized it a great deal, and would like to break away from it, but is afraid of losing her security.

Cendrillon is the last of a family of six children. She has the feeling that in this family no one listens to anyone else, and that what dominates is a mixture of love and hate. Her mother has always been fragile and has made several suicide attempts by scarifying her arms. When she was a child, nobody loved her except her mother, who wanted to possess her and keep a close watch on her. Cendrillon wanted to "take her mother's pain into herself to relieve her." But she never knew what her mother suffered from, apart from the fact that she was unsatisfied with her marital relationship, which she complained about to her daughter. After her mother's last suicide attempt, her father had rented his wife an apartment so that she could put her dolls there and go and play with them like a little girl. In a state of constant agitation, she would spend her time knitting. Her physical state deteriorated and she became a mannish woman with a damaged body. Her daughter found her inanimate on two occasions, and had been obliged to call the emergency services.

Her father seemed not to notice anything and would say, "There's no point in thinking about it." During family therapy, he admitted that he did not love his daughter. Cendrillon recalls having been sent in her childhood on a linguistic exchange to a family abroad, where she had met another abusive "mad mother". She had provoked her parents into sending her to stay in this family as a means of getting away from her own family. It was during her psychotherapy that she became aware of how distressed she had been during this episode.

Cendrillon used to feel great admiration for a close brother from whom she has also become increasingly distant. She realized that she felt as if she had *two egos*, one authentic and spontaneous that could not express itself, and the other "adapted", which she wore like a mask. She would often withdraw into a state of rage that she could not get out of. In her childhood she had been operated on for a sexual malformation, which had required the opening of her little "sealed" lips. At the age of eighteen, she had had an induced abortion which she took responsibility for all alone.

The analysis was conducted in a couch–armchair setting. The patient developed a relationship of trust with her analyst, and this provided a container for her bodily anxieties, which could now be thought about. In the course of the analysis, it emerged that she had offered her *doudou* (a child's term for a security blanket) to her mother during one of her hospitalizations. Moreover, she associated the helmet that felt as if it were "pressing down on to her nose" during her headaches with the sudden bolting of a galloping horse, no doubt in connection with her mother's madness. All the mother's unpredictable and uncontrollable violence was, thus, being evoked here. The analytic work enabled her finally to free herself from the primary maternal identification. She ultimately met a man who became attached to her, with whom she managed to live for a while. Then she was obliged to realize that he did not share her desire to have a child, something she could not accept. In spite of the good understanding between them, she separated from him.

*   *   *

During the presentation of this case, I was struck by the analyst's capacity to tolerate a difficult transference relationship in an analytic setting that was applied rigorously, but not inflexibly. The patient seemed to be frightened by poorly defined somatic disorders, often hypochondriacal or delusional in character, which were analysed with patience and tact. These complaints were connected with the pathology of a mentally ill mother who had made several suicide attempts, for whom the patient had served as a punchbag. The repercussions of the patient's identification with this ill and infantile mother were evident. It was a closed family, and relations with her sisters were cold; she had a brother she liked, one of whose friends became her first love. Time spent abroad, far away from her family, had put her in contact with another "mad mother" from whom she had managed to get away. Although she was respected and valued at work and felt supported by her boss, the patient thought several times about leaving it. Thanks to her analysis, she finally met a young man with whom she had a positive relationship and took the plunge of venturing to live together. But she had to give him up, even though they were on good terms, because her friend refused to have a child. This separation was decided upon by mutual agreement.

Her relationship with her father was valued intermittently; he gave her the impression that he loved her, while keeping his distance. In spite of the unquestionable improvement in the state of this patient at the moment when the supervision with me was broken off, the future remained uncertain. The identification with maternal suffering had diminished notably with the improvement in her mother's condition.

The last I heard from her analyst was that an interesting evolution had since occurred in the patient's treatment. Owing to the transference, which had led to fresh insight, she had understood that love was concealed behind her distress and hate; she had become aware that her affective anaesthesia in fact hid very strong feelings that she had to struggle against. She realized how different things were from what she had believed. As we can see, what looked like a potentially difficult analysis ultimately had a satisfactory outcome. Only the future will tell us if these optimistic predictions can be realized.

Alceste: a negative therapeutic reaction

Case reported by X

Towards the twelfth year of this treatment, after about ten years on the couch and after a period that suggested a favourable evolution was possible, a negative therapeutic reaction set in. In an attempt to find a way out of this impasse, the analyst tried to transform the individual relationship into a triangular relationship by seeing the patient with another male analyst, and then proposed that he should undertake individual psychodrama in a group. The therapeutic process seemed to get going again, but in fact it did not last because the patient began to speak about breaking off the treatment in quite an aggressive manner.

As he was recapitulating his history, he presented strong hypochondriacal anxieties centred on sexuality. While studying abroad, he had had the impression for several weeks that his brain was decomposing. At the time he was neither hospitalized nor treated for this. On returning to France, he lived alone, without friends; he remained withdrawn, closed in on himself, and devoted himself to artistic activities in spite of having completed brilliant studies. It was at this point that he sought help. During the psychotherapy he felt depressed and every disappointment was very painful for him. He was totally intolerant of others; pathologically susceptible, he would often fly into a rage with them.

His father had committed suicide shortly after his birth and he had been brought up by his maternal grandmother. His mother, who worked, came to be with him at weekends, but as she was exhausted she would fall asleep with him quietly at her side. She had remarried when he was eight. He got on very badly with his stepfather and acted jealously towards his half-brothers. As a child, he had been sent to see several therapists of whom he had no memory except that "they said nothing to [me], or else things without any interest." In adolescence, a therapy that had left him with some positive memories was also finally broken off. Having missed the last session before the vacation, he realized on his return that his therapist was no longer waiting for him and had not kept his place.

As an adult, he was treated by his analyst, X, for approximately two years in face-to-face therapy. In spite of encouraging results, he remained in a slump of depression. Then he managed to enter professional life and had the opportunity of doing an analysis, initially four then three times a week, until the moment when the negative therapeutic reaction set in.

His sexuality was reduced to frequent genital and anal masturbation. When he was able to have contact with women he had sex with them. During his first sexual experience in adolescence he had experienced "immense but devastating pleasure" followed by a terrible feeling of betrayal when his girlfriend abandoned him. Since then, his sexuality has always been unsatisfying. As a young adult, deprived of pleasure for several years already and after experiencing strong hypochondriacal anxieties concerning his sexuality, he had the impression he was losing his creative "matter". His relations with women were marked by intolerance for frustration, strong desire, violence, and a lot of acting out involving splitting, denial, and projection.

Nevertheless, he got married and things developed positively until he became a father. It was at this point that there was a big swing towards a negative therapeutic reaction. Having lost his job, he stayed at home to look after his child, to whom he wanted to give a strict and demanding education, without being aware of his sadism. His wife ended up asking for a divorce and he suffered from not feeling supported by his analyst. An experience of psychodrama had temporary positive effects and his identification with his therapists allowed him to make new professional plans.

A few years later, on the occasion of a second birth, just when he was beginning to have dreams of the death of his children, he stopped the psychodrama. One year later, he wrote to his analyst X, saying that he had started another analysis and that he was now satisfied.

This analytic relationship had lasted seventeen years.

*   *   *

This is the complicated story of a negative therapeutic relationship that appeared after about ten years into an analysis which had given reason to hope that the process would continue in a positive way, but this was not the case at all. The analyst, at the end of his tether, tried to rescue the situation by introducing a third party, enlisting the help of another male therapist. Later, individual psychodrama in a group setting was proposed in the hope of finding a setting more adapted to the patient's needs. In this new analytic site, the handling of the transference remained delicate, since the patient found it difficult, even in role-play, to accept any other point of view than his own. His reactions were hostile, and he threatened to break off the therapy.

Although the therapeutic endeavours did not bring the expected transformations, the patient's pathology accounted for the difficulties encountered. His pleasure in sexuality was quickly abraded and castration anxiety was followed by hypochondriacal anxieties. During the period when he had lived far away from his parents' home, he proved that he was capable of completing brilliant studies. Once he had returned home, his depression worsened and his mental pain increased. He was often subject to states of rage and pathological susceptibility. His hostile and projective tendencies became more accentuated.

His personal history was marked by tragic episodes. He had never known his father, who had committed suicide when he was an infant. He was separated from his mother, of whom he saw little and who rarely had any time for him. His mother's re-marriage had obliged him to tolerate the presence of a stepfather. His childhood therapies had turned out to be very disappointing for him. As an adolescent, he had felt abandoned by his therapist who was convinced he would not return after the summer break.

When he was an adult, and still suffering from depression, the therapy with X at first gave encouraging results, to the point that analysis four times a week was proposed. Nevertheless, his sexual life remained poor. He still had the memory of a first sexual relationship that had been accompanied by immense, but destructive pleasure, but it was never repeated. When the negative therapeutic reaction occurred, he was out of work, at home, and could not suppress his violence and sadism towards those around him. In the end, his wife sought a divorce. He expected his analyst to serve as a lawyer, and his disappointment when she declined to do so led to the onset of the negative therapeutic reaction. In a letter written one year after he had broken off the treatment, he said he had started another analysis, with a man this time, with which he was satisfied. This evolution had lasted seventeen years in all.

The diagnosis is not simple. One can point to extreme narcissistic vulnerability, accompanied by castration anxiety of a very primitive form, translated by a risk of bodily disorganization and mental disintegration. His therapeutic experiences were a source of repeated disappointments, and did not succeed in filling the gaping hole of the incurable loss of his father or the lack of emotional contact with his mother. His characteropathic organization left him prey to feelings of persecution that took over from depressive states. Success was only possible far away from his parents. The first promising path he took professionally ended in failure. The patient did not succeed in establishing good relations with women, and, on the pretext of giving his own children a degree of parental attention that he had not had, he imposed a rigid and constrictive education on them. Having received nothing himself, he had not learnt to love. He seems condemned by destiny to a life of unhappiness interspersed with hopes of short duration.

Adam: a cast iron symptom

Case reported by Y

This case study is the result of twenty-seven years of analytic work, conducted by three analysts, using different techniques, without achieving any improvement in a symptom of sexual inhibition that has resulted in an absence of erection since adolescence. The last analyst consulted did not feel that his libido had been diverted from its objects, but the patient was still unable to have an erection. In addition, he suffered from a professional inhibition. He had renounced an artistic career that attracted him and did not enjoy the work he finally accepted very much, complaining that he did it badly. Two depressive episodes had obliged him to stop work.

When he consulted Y, he was about fifty. He had already done a first analysis that lasted about twenty years, during which he hardly spoke about his sexual problem. He had decided to get into analysis after his companion had left him for one of his childhood friends, which had led to a serious syndrome of depression and anxiety. He did not have a bad memory of his first analyst, praising his rigorous attitude. He had memories of walking around armed, fearing he might be attacked, and also imagined that his analyst was going to beat him, which no doubt corresponded to his unconscious wish.

A few years later, after losing his job, a new depression led him to try individual psychodrama in a group. This therapy lasted for four years but did not suit him. He felt like a child again, shameful about his limitations and his failures, and felt he was a disappointment for his therapists just as he had been for his parents. He was only able to refer to his sexual symptom once, when the other patients were absent. As the psychodrama did not succeed in modifying his feelings of infamy, the therapist decided to redirect him towards an individual therapeutic relationship. It was at this point that he met his analyst, Y. Finally, he chose to do individual therapy with Y and abandoned the psychodrama. For the past five years he has been doing analytic work face-to-face, three times a week. This therapeutic arrangement seems to suit him. He seems to appreciate the perceptual dimension that reassures him that his analyst is present, but he continues to suffer from a libidinal impoverishment in spite of some positive achievements.

During this treatment, he painted the image of his parents as two "giants" or "colossal monsters" who used to behave in an unrestrained way in front of the family, while managing to maintain a perfect image of themselves in every respect in front of their friends. The mother's behaviour was completely lacking in tenderness. The father's virility was disqualified. This did not prevent the latter from expressing disdain towards his son and handing out physical violence to him. He recalls, as a child, having had a choleric and even sadistic father, while his mother tied his sexual organs up in bandages on the pretext that he was enuretic. One can say that castration was more a reality than a fantasy, and his earlier treatments had had no effect in this domain.

During the analytic work with Y, he had a powerful fantasy of a phallic woman, "an erect woman", who alone possessed the virility to which he had never had access. He oscillated between a childlike desire to throw himself into the arms of his therapist and the desire of a lover who meets his mistress again with enthusiasm. He was dominated by the desire to hide his feelings. He managed to make a certain amount of progress at the level of his sublimations, but still felt incapable of "standing erect", as if he were deprived of a spinal column or a solid base. As the treatment continued, his homosexual and especially his incestuous tendencies were confirmed. Only once did he have the experience of a complete sexual relationship: with a foreign woman, in a far away land, after the break-up with his companion and the betrayal of his friend, as if, far away from his family and in the grip of great anger, he had been able to accomplish coitus. The treatment subsequently enabled him to recognize his identification with his mother, though still without achieving erection, and he continued to devalue himself. He said: "Perhaps I know a little bit now what it is to feel like a woman, but I know that I do not know what it is to feel like a man."

*   *   *

This patient's therapeutic journey lasted twenty-seven years. Everything began with a sexual inhibition. At the same time, a professional inhibition prevented him from following a career, symbolizing his prohibited masculinity. His development was punctuated by depressive episodes that obliged him to stop working on two occasions.

He was humiliated by the sexual success and betrayal of his childhood friend. He began by doing an analysis which lasted eighteen years, during which he made very little mention of his sexual symptoms, no doubt as a result of a sense of guilt and shame with regard to his principal symptom. This first analysis had had no effect on him, but at the beginning he experienced powerful anxieties to do with being aggressed, revealing indirectly his masochism. A second depression resulted from the narcissistic wound of losing his job. He then decided to try individual psychodrama in a group. Like a child, he felt ashamed about his inadequacies and did not dare mention his sexual symptom in front of the other patients.

He then switched to an analysis face-to-face, three times a week, which seemed to suit him better. During this treatment, he painted a picture of his parents as being wilfully abusive and cruel: they used to give free rein to their impulses in family life, while passing themselves off as models of propriety for others. Here, we can surmise indirectly his masochistic submission to his parents. The fantasy of the phallic woman who entirely monopolizes his virility is dominant. He remains like a child who cannot come of age and be a man. He has to hide what he feels. The identification with a child whose need for love is never satisfied explains his strong reparative tendencies. In his unconscious identifications, he is unable to feel like a man. He seems to have remained fixated to a series of bad sexual treatments to which he submitted masochistically. Beyond the early introjection of dead objects in relation to his infantile history, a powerful repression of the sadism induced by his parents may be suspected. The analytic work with Y has made certain achievements possible, but it remains uncertain whether the sexual inhibition he is afflicted by can be lifted totally.

From the intergenerational transmission of grief to intrapsychic questions

Case reported by Catherine Kriegel

A trauma that has not been elaborated can rebound on the next generation. The questions, therefore, concern a time prior to the elaboration of fantasy (Racamier). The danger is that of confining the issues involved within a configuration that eludes the work of interiorization. Consequently, the face-to-face setting seems to be preferable to the classical setting. I am only reporting this case owing to the singularity of the trauma.

The patient is homosexual and lives alone in an apartment that is not very welcoming and where he does not feel settled. His homosexuality is a source of disappointment. He has sometimes caught his companion deliberately cheating on him, causing him insurmountable pain. Furthermore, he presents interpretative symptoms verging on delusion. He feels observed, spied on by his ex-friend and his "accomplices".

He had learnt many years later about a tragic accident that occurred before his birth. His parents had lost four children, three boys and a girl aged between five and twelve, in an accidental death from carbon monoxide poisoning. This bereavement had plunged them into incurable depression. The patient inherited two of the first names of the dead boys, while his sister has the same first name as the daughter who died. This event was covered over in silence up until the moment when the patient was old enough to ask who the children were in a photograph that was intentionally placed in the lounge each year at Christmas time. He also learnt the meaning of the first names given to other children born after him.

As this "knowing-not knowing" was not symbolizable, the relation between this trauma and the patient's emotional problems is difficult to establish. The patient's mother suffered from severe alcoholism. Her husband avoided her and it was the patient who decided to fight against his mother's alcoholism. He used to hide her bottles. The feeling he has of not being a gratifying partner, because his rivals are preferred to him, can gradually be linked up with the impression of having been nothing more than a child of substitution, who, under no circumstances, could replace the children who had died accidentally. The patient expresses no criticisms of his hard-hit parents. They have to be protected at all costs. The hypermature child took it upon himself to cure his parents from their misfortune. They remain linked by this dependent relationship that makes the patient lose all hope of ever being loved one day by a woman.

Moreover, he secretly maintains his feminine identifications related to his bisexuality. At this stage of the therapy, he is not able to understand the meaning of his imaginary productions or to link them up with his emotional problems. Thanks to the psychoanalytic work, he has been able to recognize the paternal imago, which was previously masked or absent most of the time. In spite of his deficiencies, his father is not foreclosed. Evoking memories of his father taking him fishing, the patient recalled his sense of joy during the car journey and was gripped by strong emotions as he thought about this: "He was with me, just with me." The third dimension now exists and manifests itself in the transference. In the analytic work, the trauma that occurred before his birth has been replaced by subjective intrapsychic issues.

*   *   *

For a long time, this patient presented homosexual difficulties infiltrated by projective elements, largely facilitated by the provocations of a sadistic partner who seemed to take great pleasure in humiliating him and making him suffer. In the course of the therapy, the analyst learnt about the family tragedy in which the patient's siblings had died from accidental death. It is not certain that these deaths prior to the patient's birth can be clearly connected with the onset of his problems linked to homosexuality.

The therapeutic work is still going on, but the insurmountable character of the revelation of the death of the children born before the patient seems to have affected him profoundly, leaving no possibility of relegating this revelation to the past. He seems to be marked by these deaths to which he owes his life. Other traumatic factors have obliged him to become the therapist of his incurable alcoholic mother. Fortunately, some traces persist of pleasurable times spent with his father, which gave him the exalting feeling of at last being alone with him. How will this therapy evolve? The last I heard was that the patient's condition has improved as a result of his psychotherapy. So, here we have a case of a very severe trauma that psychotherapy has succeeded in elaborating and overcoming, at least partially. The discovery of his relationship with his father has no doubt played a very positive and reparative role.

A mysterious aphonia: Dora

Case reported by Lisa Resare

The "illness" had begun suddenly. The patient, who was about forty, and a professional musician, had to perform during a concert in which she was due to sing Mozart's *Requiem*. She was cruelly prevented from doing so by the sudden onset of aphonia. Music was linked to her deceased father, who was himself a singer. Her mother was excluded from the musical world. Since the aphonia, it had been impossible for her to sing or even to listen to music. After getting in touch with Lisa Resare, who proposed to take her into analysis, she refused to lie down on the couch. She expressed fears of being attacked from behind or, unconsciously, by the analyst.

She related her family history: as a baby she was insomniac, constantly crying and screaming, which seemed to have provoked a headlong flight into infantile sexuality; hence her bitter accusations against a seductive father who was deaf to her needs for help and protection. Her early years were marked by somatic episodes that deteriorated in adolescence.

She felt ferocious hatred towards men: "They must be punished where they have sinned," she said. After her father's death, she suffered from serious depression. In her childhood, her mother was obsessed by her daughter's intestinal evacuations and administered numerous enemas. In addition, she could not stop herself from interrupting the child's games with her father. This relationship with her mother was marked by violence. In her sessions with Lisa Resare, she would sometimes read out loud books on this subject with titles such as, *How to Avoid Harming Your Child*. She had been obsessed every day on returning from school by the fear of discovering her mother dead. As for her father, she used to have fantasies of being raped when she heard him coming up the stairs. Any material pertaining to the primal scene was accompanied by the idea of frightening sexual intercourse. When she began to tell her dreams, they were all nightmares. In her fantasies, she imagined herself violently taking possession of her cousin's penis.

The transference took the form of an identification with her therapist; she wanted to become a psychotherapist, hoping to acquire her analyst's serenity. During the treatment, she became aware of her fusional relationship with her father, transgressing the customary defences. After twelve years of therapy, she seemed to be reconciled with women and even with men, although she had no real contact with them. However, she could not make up her mind to separate from her mother. She tried to rent an apartment and to live alone, but found she was obliged to give up this idea.

Her sexuality was very poor. She had had a hysterectomy and considered that she no longer had any sexual organs. She never experienced any vaginal sensations. She imagined she was suffering from an intestinal blockage, and asked her mother to "unblock her". She had to have an emergency operation for peritonitis. "I hate my mother," she said. This hatred was accompanied by the delusional conviction that her mother was going to die. She also had suicidal ideas.

The evolution of the transference allowed her to imagine a father with a gentle face. It seems more and more probable that the aphonia that prevented her from singing was related to a lament addressed to the dead father (*Requiem*). Her hatred towards him, which she linked to his incapacity to enjoy music, found expression throughout the treatment in two quite distinct affirmations:

1. Each time she asked him for help, he looked totally bored and turned his head away;
2. His plan to rape her was crystallized in constantly repeated scenes in which her father's eyes were filled with raw desire.

Her despair culminated in a scene where she felt in bits, deconstructed, but the fact of seeing herself like that and of speaking about it was a means of resorting to the mechanisms of projective identification; the world—including the *Requiem*—was no longer in bits. The two constantly repeated reproaches took on a quite different meaning in the course of this session. The desiring father turned away from her; rape was no longer an issue, and she felt free to sing and to listen to music.

A few sexual fantasies appeared, though she made no attempts to fulfil them. None the less, she remained subject to onsets of depression and suffered from loneliness. She experienced strong emotion when listening to Purcell's *Dido and Aeneas* and admitted to having incestuous desires towards her father. At this moment, her mother's state of health deteriorated. The patient then consulted a psychiatrist and decided unilaterally to break off her analysis. Her analyst thinks—hopes—that she will return.

*   *   *

It is clear that a considerable amount of work has been done, but equally the patient still has difficulty in living independently. Her defences concerning her father have been overcome, but the perspective of her mother's death obliged her, she says, to break off her analysis, suggesting a probable struggle against the reappearance of matricidal infantile wishes.

The diagnosis of aphonia is symptomatic; it would be more accurate to say that the patient presented a pregenital "hysteria". The onset of aphonia was very significant, but it took me a certain amount of time to understand that it was unconsciously determined by a manifestation of love addressed by the patient to her father in the beyond. As a result of repression, she had developed feelings of hatred towards men. The wish to punish them in fact masked the wish to castrate them. The father was the object of fantasies tainted by violence and sexual sadism. A long period of analysis was necessary for the patient to feel reconciled with men, without however, allowing herself to let any approach her. She felt extremely ambivalent towards her mother, who kept a close watch on her daughter's bodily manifestations, in particular in the anal region. She did not hesitate to give her daughter enemas, which the latter endured passively. The mother had little tolerance for the games which father and daughter enjoyed playing together. During the treatment, the patient would read to her analyst, as if she was really addressing her mother and not a representation of her, in order to show her how she should have behaved as a good mother.

With regard to sexuality, her fantasies of being raped, standing in the way of any intimate relationship with men, disappeared towards the end of the analytic work, and were replaced by the belief that if she got interested in a man it would bring about her mother's death. In an attempt at sublimation, the identification with her analyst led her to envisage becoming a psychotherapist. She tried to separate from her mother without success. Fantasies of castration were strongly cathected. She admitted hating her mother

("I hate my mother"), but felt she had to stay with her, thus giving up her own independence, which brought her into constant conflict with her attraction for men.

When her mother's health declined, she was possessed by ideas of suicide. Her memories of her father now took on more attractive forms. As her mother's condition did not improve, she decided to put an end to her analysis. This was perhaps an ultimate sacrifice to save her mother. Will she come back?

Ariane: an unresolvable transference

Case reported by Litza Guttières-Green (and revised by her)

I am going to speak about the analysis, more than twenty years ago, of a young woman of about forty, who complained of crises of anxiety accompanied by feelings of not existing. She tried to escape from this by means of alcohol and different forms of acting out (searching for love, disappointing love affairs, and suicide attempts). She spoke of a black hole that terrified her and attracted her at the same time.

Ariane, whose mother had been ill from the moment she was born and who died when she was only six, had suffered very early on in her life from experiences of terror and feelings of hostility directed towards her father and those who took care of her. The only recollection she had, in this emotional desert, was connected with her mother's burial: she had been left at home, and, from the window, she had seen a crowd of people and her family dressed "in black". She had been afraid and had hid under the table. She had forgotten everything about her past, about her father, as well as her maternal substitutes, her grandmother, aunt, or sister. In spite of this desolate childhood, she had completed successful higher studies in a city far away from the family home and had obtained a university degree. Notwithstanding the attention and admiration she had received, and her marriage with a fellow student, followed by several babies, she spoke of this time as a "frantic headlong flight" during which she did her best to "fill holes", without managing to avoid depressive episodes.

Owing to political events, the couple had then been obliged to go into exile with two very young children. So, Ariane's life was turned upside down, and she was plunged into depression. The psychotherapeutic treatments undertaken were all abandoned. She put her marriage at risk several times by leaving her husband and then returning to him. Due to her absenteeism, she lost her job. Suicide threats, panic attacks, and alcohol had required psychiatric hospitalizations of short duration and the prescription of drugs that had no effect.

When she came to see me, having been referred by the psychiatrist at the clinic where she had been staying, she told me she had no more hope, that "death would be a deliverance". I observed that she was already putting me in a hopeless situation like the others. I told myself that it was going to be a case of handling a stormy transference, oscillating between hate and passion.

In spite of the risks of failure of which I was aware, and no doubt won over by her distress and illusions of my own omnipotence, I proposed to take her into psychotherapy.

The relationship between us was at once difficult and fragile. There was a constant sense of emergency, and the therapy was sometimes interrupted by hospitalizations. I was exposed to feelings of helplessness and had the impression of going through something similar to what she was complaining about: I had difficulty in following the flow of associations, linking them up, memorizing the material, and interpreting it. I tried hard to continue to think, in spite of the confusion I felt inside myself; I struggled to construct a history, to venture interpretations without succumbing to her masochistic provocations. Sometimes, I felt extremely sleepy during the sessions, barely managing to keep my eyes open. I told myself that I had to maintain a setting that was capable of containing and protecting her—and of protecting myself—against her destructiveness.

I read . . . Freud, Ferenczi, Winnicott, Tustin, Green, in search of answers to the problems she was facing me with.

I imagined that as her mother had been unable to establish ties with her that could survive her own death, and to give her a sufficiently secure basis, Ariane had not acquired confidence in a lasting and reliable relationship; she had withdrawn behind a mask of narcissistic indifference, whereas her unconscious grudge and hatred against her deceased mother were being relived in the transference. She forgot me during the sessions, so she said, which I interpreted as a wish to protect me against her destructiveness.

"No," she corrected herself, "when you are not there, I have to protect myself from despair."

Gradually, however, her acting out decreased, more elaborate material appeared, and real therapeutic work began. Ariane came regularly and ceased to speak of breaking off the therapy; she acknowledged her dependence and her attachment, and she also took care of her children. Although she was not freed from her anxiety, her capacity for insight led me to hope that things would develop favourably.

Her nights were haunted by dreams and she could remember them now. One of them stood out: "You were lying beside my mother. She was dying. I said to myself: 'At least *she* is going to live!'" Then she said: "I have realized that I don't know my mother, I have forgotten her; for me, she's something abstract. I speak about her instead of speaking about you."

This dream was followed by feelings of depersonalization that I linked up with her guilt about separating from her mother and the fear that I might be less reliable than a dead person.

Another dream expressed aggression towards me after I had been absent: "A large spider trapped a small spider in a cage made of its eight legs, and the small spider was looking at me with tears in its eyes as if it was appealing to me for help. It had your eyes."

I suggested to her that she wanted both to destroy me and to preserve me.

The *hole*, the *void*, which seemed to me to represent her mother's tomb in which she had taken refuge (the crypt of Abraham and Torok, 1968), were linked up by Ariane with a lack at the origin of her history: "I would like to find a sense of continuity again to fill this void," she said. She had always connected it with her mother's death because her therapists, me included, had always made this link for her, and because she did not know how to interpret it. "I think that it was before [her death], something that did not happen left a hole. I've never been able—or known how—to speak about it. I began to understand when I told you that I did not know my mother."

Ariane was trying to remember something which had not existed; she was trying to represent the unrepresentable, "the lack of self" (Roussillon, 2008). I said to myself that the loss of memory hid a breakdown that had already happened (Winnicott, 1974).

After realizing that she did not know her mother, she mentioned one of her last memories: "I was sitting beside her and she said to me: 'I am going to disappear gradually and all that will remain of me will be a little pile of shit.' I did not understand what she was saying. This memory came back to me after a dream in which I was with you in a dilapidated house. There was a smell of excrement; I got up to clean it up, but there was more and more." She associated the excrement with her mother's corpse, which she wanted to get rid of.

Me: "Your mother has become a little pile of shit, and you also felt like a piece of shit."

For her, living people, like her husband, her children, and me, were intrusive or likely to abandon you; only the dead had value. The dead, who give nothing, take nothing away. "Because you lose it anyway," she remarked.

In the next session, she told me a dream: *a workman with a terrifying face had forced her to make love with him.* She associated the workman with the distorted face with me, someone who wanted to seduce her only to abandon her afterwards ... This analysis will have to finish one day!

Attacks on linking, decathexis, disobjectalization (Green, 1986b) were at work: by destroying the traces of the past, they create holes in representation and thought which are beyond repair. In fact, what looks like an absence of memory could be connected with a sense of loss; perhaps not simply with an object loss, but also with a loss at the level of the ego or, in Tustin's terms (Tustin, 1986), a loss of its substance.

The search for historical continuity probably had a narcissistic and antidepressive purpose; by unifying a fragmented, dispersed and anarchic mind, she was struggling against the risk of psychic death.

During Ariane's analysis, buried memories and unconscious fantasies gradually became accessible, though they conserved particular characteristics. While she was able to put her fantasies into images and communicate them to me, she pointed out to me that in all her dreams the characters ["spoke"] in French, the language of the analysis, and not in her mother language. It was in the course of our analytic work that she learnt to look at them directly, in my presence; even if they remained frightening, she was able to find the words to represent them. She said: "I have learnt to speak with you."

Nevertheless, these representations had a massive, repetitive character, as if there was a link that she could not make, so that she was unable to get beyond them. Violent and sadistic images of the primal scene, barely symbolized, and explosions of devouring anality and orality appeared repeatedly.

The same dream came back several nights in a row, as if it could not discharge the excitation or give shape to the fantasy. At the heart of the representation, we find the mirror image that characterizes the dual relationship: for example, when I said to her that she feared being swallowed by me, she replied that she was the one who was going to swallow me with her greed.

Finally, something persisted that was unrepresentable, and it was unclear whether it would subsist as a scar or remain as a gaping hole.

Different interpretations of the void, the black hole, the deadly womb, did not succeed in establishing hope in a more stable way. For her, what was empty was always more important than what was full; hate was always more important than love. She said to me: "I am desperate because in spite of the changes, I continue to feel alone and empty. My life has no meaning even though I cannot say why. What we have understood and reconstituted together surrounds a hole. What is in this hole, I will never know; it did not take place, quite simply, and that is what is lacking. So I cannot know what I am lacking, nor can I have any hope of filling this void. Each time I feel close to you, I am terrorized, then disappointed; this is not what I want, so I loathe you and I loathe myself, I keep you at a distance and we have to start all over again. Won't it ever end?"

I consoled myself with what I considered to be symptomatic improvements: she seemed calmer, and less centred on herself; she spoke about those around her, and not just about her terrors.

When she told me that she would stop coming after the summer vacation, I thought it was sensible for us to prepare for the coming separation. She had decided to return to her country with her children and her husband. I told myself she was renewing her ties with a past that had come alive again. I was both relieved and worried.

But the trip went well, and we put an end to the sessions. After that, she telephoned me from time to time to ask me for an occasional session. The telephone calls became less regular, and I thought that she simply wanted to be sure that I was still alive. Then she stopped telephoning altogether . . . until this autumn, that is, when she asked to see me again.

She came back; several years had gone by, and I was horrified by her appearance: she had grown older, of course, but she seemed degraded; her husband had left her and remarried; her children had gone away to study, and had started work. They were doing well, but she did not see them much. They had their own lives. "Everyone has abandoned me, I am alone," she said with a little smile. She was not looking after herself, and had no money; she showed me her ruined teeth: "I've aged, you can see!" I asked her if she was in therapy. "No, I would like to come back to you." I refused. She understood, but she had hoped it might be possible, she said, with her little resigned smile. Staring into space, she seemed to be dreaming . . . about what? I will never know. She left again, leaving me with the feeling of having witnessed a disaster and of having been partly responsible for it.

* * *

This is a tragic example of a destiny marked from the beginning of life. The illness of an unavailable mother, whom she lost at the age of six, left indelible traces that hindered her emotional development. The pathology that had set in early saw some periods of respite, but was never satisfactorily resolved. Her memorization was fragile, without constructed memories that could resist forgetting, except for a few highly significant events. She referred vaguely to her mother's burial, but was unable to replace her afterwards by a substitute maternal figure. It was not that opportunities to meet a mother who could have taken over from the one that was missing did not present themselves, but the patient could not become attached to any of them, or accept what they had to offer by way of reparation.

In spite of all this, she was able to invest well in her studies, which enabled her to succeed quite well. She got married and had children. One gets the impression that her pathology did not prevent her from conforming to the requirements of conventional social life: studies, marriage, and children. But there seems to be no evidence of any real affective life: there are occasional bursts of emotional life that soon die out like a straw fire, while the pathological process follows its course ineluctably. Her life is marked by a succession of depressive episodes, an addiction to alcohol, and numerous suicide attempts. Any improvements that occurred were thus neutralized. She was given medication and did various psychotherapies. The treatments were suddenly broken off, without reason, and repeatedly, as if driven by irreducible masochism.

The patient is preoccupied by death, which she envisaged as a release, but none of her suicide attempts is fatal. The analyst's countertransference yields to feelings of pity and compassion and is maintained by the illusion of healing her by virtue of tenacity. The transference remains ambivalent, discontinuous, unanalysable, and is interrupted periodically by hospitalizations. In reality, can we legitimately speak of transference? It is a conventional denomination, but the evolution of the patient's affects towards her analyst seems lacking in structure, unstable and disorganized. In fact, the transference is barely identifiable, mysteriously undecipherable, and unpredictable.

When the patient takes up her treatment again, the material becomes confused, difficult to memorize, understand, and think about. The analyst has to make an effort to give meaning to what she hears. She is sometimes invaded by sleepiness. A feeling of being alternately the object of the patient's attacks and of the patient's desire to protect her against her aggression makes understanding difficult. The analyst sometimes feels disconcerted and wavers between signs that make her continue to hope and others that make her lose courage.

In the end, a real therapeutic process gets under way, the acting out diminishes, and the patient seems to recognize her dependence and her attachment. The analyst hopes cure will be possible, or at least an improvement. Very direct transference dreams are forthcoming in which the analyst replaces the deceased mother, expressing the hope that she will survive. Finally, Ariane recognizes that she does not know who her mother is, and that she can only speak about her analyst. This is a characteristic trait of transference. Although she is of foreign origin, in her dreams her mother speaks to her in French, which leads the patient to conclude that the only mother she has known is her analyst. This is the sign of a psychic event that has not so much been relived as invented during her analysis.

In the clinical picture, the psychic hole, the void, occupy the foreground, as well as an absence of a sense of continuity. The unrepresentable is the dominant feature. A memory comes back to her from a time shortly before her mother's death in which the latter tells her that after her death all that will remain of her will be a heap of shit. Ariane then says that she cannot get rid of this quantity of invasive shit. It is possible here that the shit to which the mother refers may be a representation of the expulsion, out of the patient's body, of the mother's cadaverous body. Faecalization is one of the psychic procedures representing the disorganization of a living and loving body, illustrating the manifestations of an insurmountable degree of negativity where the patient loses the substance of her body, and where the psyche cannot achieve unity and remains fragmented.

All her symptoms retain a repetitive, stereotyped, and unmodifiable character, giving her the opportunity to reproduce mirroring pregenital relations in both directions, active and passive.

She continues to be like an open wound. Her life remains devoid of meaning. The psychic work cannot fill a gaping hole, the content of which even she is unable to imagine: it is undoubtedly full of hate. Finally, because the patient expresses the wish to return to her own country, separation has to be negotiated. The hole, the void, are manifestations of a psychic decathexis which are all scars of a cathexis of the negative which can only be revived in this form. In fact, the work of the negative can never give way to a positive cathexis of desire. Eros is vanquished in advance by the destructive drives.

Her symptomaty diminishes progressively, and several years go by before she asks to see her analyst again. She finds herself without any money, without a husband, and alone, as her children have left her to live their own lives. She shows her analyst her ruined teeth and concludes by expressing the wish to return to see her, which the analyst considers pointless. It can be seen that the transference, which resisted analysis, has, in a certain way, remained intact, always ready to reappear in a compulsive mode of repetition, without any possibility of evolving. She then leaves, leaving her analyst with the feeling that she has been unable to do anything to prevent this catastrophic evolution.

One cannot claim that this unfavourable evolution has revealed all the secrets at its origin. It is most probable that the very early nature of the patient's symptoms was responsible. Only a few elements made it possible to get a glimpse and understanding of the factors that weighed negatively on this obstinate and insurmountable resistance to recovery.

(B) Personal memories of some case histories

I n this part I would like to evoke those memories that have left me with some of my disappointments. I speak of memories and not of detailed case studies, since most of the time I took no notes, even if, in my articles, I have sometimes mentioned these cases at greater or lesser length, or certain characteristics connected with them. They are memories of disappointing experiences, but not bad memories. As I was thinking about those that I am citing, I did not feel that I regretted having taken them on, even if I often found myself getting impatient in the face of their resistances, or experiencing disappointment on account of their obstinate or tenacious nature, at a time when I was still unaware of what I was subsequently to call the work of the negative. I encountered these cases very early on in my practice, often because my teachers or elders had referred them to me, overestimating, no doubt, my therapeutic capacities. I have never considered myself as a therapist capable of working miracles, but I can say that I have striven hard to remain an analyst, while taking account of what I imagined to be the needs of my patients.

What I find striking today is that these cases have never been absent from the series of analysands that I have treated, from the beginning of my practice up until today. I just hope that now I am little less clumsy or less impatient. It is not that I succeed today where I failed yesterday, but I have the impression that I understand better the causes of certain anxieties, as well as the necessity of certain defences, in people who seem unable to take the risk of making a change that would expose them dangerously. I only hope that my experience will help other analysts to avoid certain errors or even certain illusions.

I have noticed that during these long therapies a large number of patients kept up a very rich correspondence with me: they felt the irresistible need to write to me frequently and at length. Their letters corresponded to an unforced need to address themselves to me, as if the sessions were not enough, or as if they could not speak to me about what was pushing them to write to me. Naturally, I understood the role of resistance played by these missives. What could not be said was written, attenuating, of course, the effects of my presence, and in a way that bypassed free association while favouring the need for expression. Many of these letters were very rich and also often very moving. I learnt a lot from them, but I was very aware of how they bore witness to the inability of their author to respect the analytic rule. But it was that or nothing. I asked some of them to refrain from writing to me, which resulted in protests. For the others, I sometimes had pleasure in reading them. I was not unaware of the narcissistic importance of these letters that were addressed to me, but they existed to give form to a confidential personal expression, the only one possible, and also, I am fully aware, to a certain degree of harassment.

I will present these cases in the order in which I knew them. The first date from the early years my practice, when I was still rather inexperienced.

Aude: the unhappy viscountess

I owe the earliest of my disillusions to the case of a young woman whom I shall call Aude, or "the Viscountess", which was what she was in reality. She had been hospitalized in a mental health clinic (*maison de santé*) in the Paris region. Three renowned psychiatrists had been called in for consultation, of which two had been my teachers (H. Ey, P. Mâle, and H. Duchhêne). They deliberated for a long time before concluding that, although she was most probably schizophrenic, Aude could benefit from psychotherapy. They had enough confidence in the young analyst that I was to ask me to take her on.

She came to see me at my home and, as the contact we had was quite good, I agreed to take her into treatment. She was a bit lost and had the impression that no one knew what to do with her. Her father, who was divorced from her mother, had received psychiatric treatment for symptoms of a psychopathological or perverse type. Her mother, who had married again and lived in the provinces, made laudable efforts to help her daughter, but without much success. Since her divorce, she had had another child and was happy with her new husband. She was afraid of receiving her eldest daughter at home in case her pathological behaviour disturbed her young sister. The stepfather, who was tolerant and understanding, kept out of the way. The mother tried to put up with the situation, and from time to time sent her daughter to live with her grand-mother. The latter seemed to love her, but it seemed to me that she was more ambivalent than one would have thought, at least towards me.

So, she began her psychotherapy, coming very regularly to her sessions, and spoke to me mainly about her psychotic symptoms, which included intense hallucinatory activity. She was incapable of any kind of activity, apart from a certain gift for drawing. The ones she showed me seemed to me to be morbidly sad. She said little about her personal life, but seemed to love her little sister. However, she had clearly understood that she was an embarrassment for everyone. In other words, she imagined everyone was wondering, "How do we get rid of her?"

Whenever I sensed a fresh upsurge of anxieties in her, I would even see her during my holidays, when I was in Paris. I can recall her coming to see me during the Christmas holidays. I listened to her during sessions that lasted as long as it seemed necessary. I had the satisfaction of seeing her leave in a calmer, if not serene, state. But, of course, outside the sessions her symptoms became even more pronounced. At the time when she lived with her parents in the provinces, she would come to see me by train. It goes without saying that I feared an accident at each visit, but fortunately it never occurred. As it happened, her father's professional address was just a stone's throw away from mine, so it was difficult to prevent her from going to see him on leaving her sessions; what's more, he was scarcely in favour of the psychotherapy—in fact, he rejected it.

The therapy, moreover, produced very few spectacular effects, but, for more than four years, no further hospitalization was necessary and the medication prescribed by a colleague stabilized her. I could not entertain many illusions about my psychotherapy, but at least I had had the patience to wait and to contain her pathology.

However, one of her mother's friends, a pharmacology professor whom she had spoken to about her daughter, made the following irrevocable judgement: "Four years of psychotherapy, that's enough". He succeeded in convincing the family to break off the psychotherapy and had my patient hospitalized in the service of a university clinic that I knew well. I did not have to wait long to see the result: as soon as she was admitted to this service and subjected to a heavy course of drugs, an incoercible delusional activity was triggered in her, showing that her psychotic defences had been overwhelmed and that her psychiatrists had been foolhardy. After a while, the drugs ceased to have any effect. There was no further improvement. In the end, it was considered that she should leave the service and be treated as an outpatient, which was what was decided. Shortly after leaving the service, she threw herself under a metro train. After her death, her mother came to see me, and asked me why I had not warned her of this possible turn of events. I pointed out that she was the one who had made the decision, and that I had had no means of opposing it. She had trusted in the opinion of her pharmacology professor friend, who was not even a psychiatrist, but benefited from professorial prestige.

* * *

So this was the unhappy story, then, of an unquestionably psychotic female patient whom I tried to help in face-to-face psychotherapy, on a twice-weekly basis. Without claiming to have succeeded, I was, none the less, able to spare her any new hospitalization. I had the feeling that improvement would only occur after a very long psychotherapeutic treatment which might finally make it possible to tackle her problems. I had the feeling both that I was not able to achieve much and that I was an indispensable source of support for her life outside of any psychiatric institution. She found herself being shunted around between different families who sent her back and forth in turn. Her grandmother, who agreed to take care of her for a while, was no doubt appeasing her guilt feelings for having had sexual relations with her son-in-law, which had caused her daughter's divorce. At the end of the day, it was clear that Aude was not welcome. The psychotic flare-up following the forced separation with me did not result, of course, in any questions being asked either by the pharmacologist who was interfering in matters she knew nothing about, or by the chief psychiatric consultant, a confirmed organicist whom I knew, and who never felt the need to ask me for my opinion. With hindsight, I should have manifested myself and paid her a visit in the service where she was hospitalized. I had refrained from doing this, as I had not been asked to do so. I observed a principle of abstinence that I now think was mistaken, even if a visit probably would not have changed anything. There is no doubt in my mind, though, that Aude experienced this interruption as a tragic abandonment. She did not seek to see me again of her own accord. I have the weakness of thinking that this death could have been avoided.

Mélanie Blanche

One of my colleagues, who runs a reputed mental health clinic, contacted me one day to ask me if I would accept taking on a woman of about thirty years of age, who was coming out of quite a severe depression, and who, he thought, needed psychotherapy. The first meeting took place at my home. The patient came accompanied by a nurse. When I opened the door of my consulting-room, I saw an extremely sad woman, looking weighed down, with her chin on her chest, finding it difficult to express herself. After exchanging a few words, I understood that she was melancholic and of high intelligence—one could tell this in spite of her state of prostration.

Was it at this moment or only later that I learnt that she was a graduate from the *École Normale Supérieure*, and that she had also taught for a year before being obliged to stop on account of her illness? She had found a guardian angel in the person of this doctor who ran the mental health clinic. Although her condition made it unlikely that she could live alone, she was allowed to leave. There was obviously no question of her returning to work, and she seemed, moreover, to have formed an aversion to her job, even though it was prestigious. I had the opportunity, subsequently, of meeting some of her students who knew that I was following her, who told me that she was an exceptional teacher, even though she herself suffered from feelings of inferiority and thought she was a bad teacher.

No doubt impressed by the quality of her personality, and underestimating her melancholic structure, I agreed to see her three times a week, face-to-face. I did not get much out of our meetings, and simply listened to the melancholic and self-devaluating themes. I soon learnt that she had had to break off relations with her family. She felt merciless hatred for her mother. My patient accused her mother of having persecuted her her whole life long, of misjudging her personality, and of knowing nothing of her interests. Her mother, who worked as a post office employee of junior rank, apparently wanted her daughter to content herself with becoming a secretary and showed nothing but scorn for her own aspirations. As for the father, an unassuming character and a policeman by profession, he was better accepted by the patient. After several years, she was willing to see him again, alone. She felt affection for him, but wanted to be reassured as to his conduct during the Vichy regime.

She had a sister whom she liked a lot who was more in line with the parental norms; she had married, and had had two children whom my patient enjoyed seeing very much. She got on well with them and clearly cherished them. She would have liked to have more frequent contact with her sister and her nephew and niece, but they lived in the provinces and opportunities to meet were rare. She had only a few friends, who were very hard-working and only accorded a limited amount of time to social contacts.

She had no particular interest in any man. I learnt late in the day that during the year when she had been teaching, she had fallen in love with an inspector from the academy of education, who, it seems, suspected nothing. She lived completely alone, feeding herself solely on ham and yoghurts to avoid having to cook. As far as I was concerned, I felt that I had great importance for her, but the transference never led her to lead a slightly less reclusive life. I later learnt that she railed against philosophical texts—including Pascal—in order to defend her own ideals and nourish her defective narcissism. She was full of extreme requirements for purity and moral integrity.

Towards the fifth year of psychotherapy, she began to drink excessively, always the same drink, Marie Brizard, a liquor with unconscious maternal symbolism to which she had become attached. From time to time, she would go and stay for a while in the clinic, with which she had stayed in contact. Having noticed her alcoholism, the other patients made fun of her. She had no social or sexual life, but she experienced great anxiety when it was discovered that she had a vaginal prolapsus; the doctors had proposed an operation, and she was very concerned to know whether this operation would damage her genital organs, which, as we have seen were, so to speak, reduced to silence. While she was staying in a convalescent home, she was approached by a man and let him have a sexual relationship with her. This only lasted a short time and she decided to break it off on account of the difference in their cultural levels. Now and then, friends with whom she had managed to form a relationship invited her to go on a short trip with them. During one of these trips, they had a serious car accident, as a result of which Mélanie's life was in the balance. She told me that she had thought about me as soon as she had regained consciousness, and had understood how much I counted for her.

She was also invited to stay with friends who noticed that she drank. She had become very good at hiding her alcoholism, although no one was taken in by this. To stop her drinking, her friends shut her in her bedroom, where they served her meals. One day, they found her dead: she had choked to death from swallowing too large a portion of food all at once. So she died, then, from her oral greed, all alone, shut away in her room, cut off from everything. This death surprised me, and yet, at the same time, I found it significant. What remained of the brilliant student that she had been and that her students still admired? Melancholia and a persecuting mother had got the better of her. I would like to add that we never had philosophical exchanges.

*   *   *

This is the story of a chronic melancholia which was never cured and which had set in after the patient had taught for one year upon leaving the *École Normale Supérieure*. Her first love, which remained secret, was for a spiritual father, one of her inspectors from the academy of education. A second object of transference was the director of the clinic where she had been hospitalized. The third attachment was to me, her psychotherapist, and, last, she was attached to the liquor, Marie Brizard. She kept her intense attachment hidden for a long time, as well as her gratitude for my affection and my attempts to understand her. She had kept up her relations with her women friends (only to break them off subsequently), who were more concerned about their careers than about her.

She came regularly to her psychotherapy sessions, which was more or less the only occasion she left her apartment. The rest of the time, she lived reclusively, seeing no one, except when she was invited by friends. She never invited anyone herself. Her hatred towards her mother did not abate. She never tried to have another professional experience and lived on her allowances. During her psychotherapy, she went through various mental states. One of them surprised me by its violence: she started to lay into the couch as if it represented her parents' bed. She never spoke to me about her interests or what she read. I had compassion for her and also unquestionable esteem.

During her childhood, when she stayed with her grandparents, for whom she had feelings of affection, she had guessed the existence of sexual relations, though this had not given rise to any fantasy activity in her. On the other hand, another episode had delighted her: she had witnessed with joy the pilfering of a roast joint by the house cat.

I was surprised by her anxieties concerning the integrity of her body (her genital organs). The only relationship she had with a man, about which she did not say very much, did not last because he was uneducated. However, I was surprised by the intensity of my patient's alcoholism, which resisted any form of treatment, and by the degree of voracity that I had not suspected in a woman who was verging on anorexia. She died from suffocation, sequestered by her friends who had wanted to stop her from drinking. Her efforts to integrate herself socially went tragically wrong. I have often thought about her since, about her insurmountable resistances, and about the waste of her life.

Nanon: a diagnostic enigma[1]

I have already had the opportunity of speaking about Nanon. I am returning to her now because of the singular nature of her pathology. I presented her case on the occasion of a meeting that was organized in Geneva by Nicos Nicolaïdis, where Pierre Marty and myself had agreed to engage in a debate on psychosomatic praxis. In fact, this encounter never took place because Pierre Marty had passed away in the meantime. He was replaced by his close collaborators. These exchanges can be found in a monograph of the *Revue française de psychanalyse* (Green, 2010).

What spurs me to come back to Nanon's case is that with regard to this patient I felt guilty of serious countertransference errors which played a role in what I consider to be one of my most remarkable failures.

Nanon was referred to me at the age of twenty-three by a Lacanian colleague who had been her teacher at the Sorbonne. He had noticed the quality of her intelligence and she had surprised him by failing an oral examination for neurotic reasons. This failure had inflicted an intolerable narcissistic wound on her; it was the consequence of an oral examination with a teacher known for his severity and hardness, who reminded her of her tyrannical grandfather, the only person who had managed to subdue her mother.

When she came to see me, she had a grotesque pathological appearance. With a hairstyle that looked like a crown, she gave the impression of being a hysteric, aggressive and provocative, with little tolerance for passivity. Her reactions towards me indicated a phobic and evasive attitude. I did not respond to her provocations and proposed an analysis. It did not take me long to recognize patent signs in her of an intense maternal fixation. The father was eclipsed by the mother, as he was dominated by her; he seemed not to count for my patient. While she was preparing for her examinations, she had manifested very striking regressive behaviour: she would go to bed to work and have herself spoon-fed by her mother.

They were linked by a fusional relationship, and Nanon got what-ever she wanted from her mother.

She presented a great deal of anxiety, concealed by surface agita-tion and a febrile way of speaking. The analysis began at a hectic speed. Shortly after it began, she took every measure possible to manipulate her family circle and asked me to go and see her at home, a request I resisted. She shut herself in the family apartment, preventing her parents from entering it. She threw them into a state of turmoil with the result that they telephoned me and tried to put pressure on me. Via her family, she threatened to denounce me to the medical association, or the police, for non-assistance to a person in danger, although it was perfectly evident that she was trying to manipulate me. Unable to obtain what she wanted, she began to harass me with innumerable telephone calls, without giving her name. Then, by way of excusing herself, she would send flowers to my wife, or, rather, would have her mother send them. Her homo-sexuality was scarcely contained. She provoked me to transgress the rules fixed by the setting. It goes without saying that analysis was hardly possible under these conditions. There were no apolo-gies or regrets, but a permanent trial of strength in which she needed to prevail over me. She had no relations with men, except the son of one of her mother's friends, and seemed more interested in the mother than the son. The rest of the family seemed to con-sider their relations as paving the way for an engagement, although nothing had occurred between them at a physical level. Eventually, this myth was dissipated.

At the October session, she retook her exams and obtained her degree. Once the exams were over, she made plans to spend her summer holidays in a university camp, with the aim of meeting some young people. This provided her mother with the opportu-nity of preparing a bride's trousseau for her! But she did not meet anyone. Her friendships with other women were jealously guarded by her mother, who had been instrumental in breaking off her daughter's relations with a female teacher when she was at the lycée.

Without speaking to me about it, she followed up her degree in philosophy with a degree in psychology. It was a sign, I thought, that she was taking the direction of my own professional activity. She had no difficulty in negotiating the stages of this training. No doubt feeling somewhat discouraged, and considering that the analysis was making little, if any, progress, I indicated to her that I thought that the contract had been fulfilled from my side and spoke of termination, three years after the beginning of the analysis.

Her relations with men, managed by her mother, came to nothing in spite of the changes to her wardrobe that she adopted: "Womanliness as a masquerade" (Riviere, 1929). As for the transference, it remained under close surveillance. She seemed to look out for my publications, even though there was no mention of her in them at that time. She was opposed to ending her treatment and complained of vague pains in her belly until the day when she was diagnosed with a bout of haemorrhagic proctocolitis. The gastroenterologist who performed the proctoscopy said to her, "Your bowels are crying with blood." Humiliated by her illness, she announced to me, "I will never have a bout of haemorrhagic proctocolitis again." I was a bit sceptical in the face of this show of willpower. She really surprised me because, as a matter of fact, she had no further attacks. The symptom moved away from the cloaca. I myself at the time was not very aware of this pathology and so I informed myself. Feeling that my decision to terminate the analysis was probably to blame for the onset of this pathology, I backtracked and told her I had changed my mind. Was I right to do this? I felt I was responsible.

She never missed a session, but continued to struggle against the analytic process. Her persecutions via the telephone diminished, but her transference remained blocked by the recital of her projections concerning her mother. Although memories of the distant past showed that the father had once been important to her, he had given way completely to the mother. I noted that, on the couch, she adopted a stereotyped attitude, crossing her legs tightly. I finally understood that this attitude was a projection against a fantasy of being raped, or at least of penetration. She told me many dreams, which always finished in the same way: "There was no penetration."

After her studies, she was employed by an institution in Normandy. She said that she preferred "to go and make her blunders in the provinces". She never took the risk of presenting her candidature for admission to the Institute of Psychoanalysis, even though it was what she wanted. She had formed a fixation on a young female analyst whom she was sexually attracted to, without there being any physical contact between them. On the other hand, she had sexual relations with a man who did not want to share her life. In analysis, she did not speak about her sexual life, and made no reference to the emotional void of this relationship. After a while, this relationship came to an end, and, to the best of my knowledge, it was not replaced.

The patient then began to complain about breast pains and was diagnosed as having polycystic breasts. To the great surprise of the doctors, she continued to suffer, complaining to her mother and to me during the sessions. She moaned: "It hurts." Her mother finally said to her, "What do you expect me to do about it?" She replied, "I don't know; you're the mother." Needless to say, I also felt powerless. Her breasts grew bigger; a gynaecologist punctured them and drained off some brownish coloured liquid. He proposed repeating this procedure, but she refused.

In the transference, she became increasingly difficult: telephone calls, demands, reproaches for being badly treated, misunderstood. Her family considered that she was a hysteric and could no longer oppose her psychoanalysis. Her answer to them was: "No, that's not right at all, I am a psychosomatic." Then her behaviour changed seriously. She no longer respected the setting, started walking around the room, menacingly: "I want to know why my analysis is messed up. In other words, why have *you* made a mess of my analysis?" I felt myself being drawn into interminable discussions, losing my analytic neutrality. I answered the telephone, getting caught up in her acting out. I had entered into a sadomasochistic relationship with her, exasperated by the way in which she sabotaged every therapeutic attempt I made. This was where I committed my biggest countertransference errors, caught up as I was in her negative attitudes.

To tell the truth, I found it difficult to answer her questions. Her characteropathic attitude, manifesting itself in a transference full of hatred, had eventually become difficult for me to tolerate. This had been going on for more than twenty years already, and I decided to put an end to what no longer bore any resemblance to analysis. Yet, she refused obstinately to switch to working face-to-face, interpreting this suggestion as a sign of failure. I held firm and fixed a date for ending. She opposed this, but was obliged to accept what I had proposed. She then began to look for another analyst. She did the round of analysts in Paris, speaking badly of me and saying how much I had mistreated her. She eventually met colleagues of mine who were prepared to continue the work with her. Each time, she failed to take up the offer. She finally came across a colleague–friend of mine whom I had lost touch with, who agreed to take her back into analysis. She began with him and got him to put pressure on me to see her again. I refused, because I had a very bad memory of what seemed to me to have been an error on my part, and had understood that she was beyond the resources of psychoanalysis. She then left him.

I had news of her indirectly. One of my readers, who had met her, recognized her from my writings. He proposed to continue her analysis. She refused energetically, pointing out to him that she had done twenty years with me and that she had nothing more to learn. Apart from that, her physical condition was not improving. A "pre-cancerous" breast condition had been diagnosed. In the meantime, she had lost her mother. I expected her to collapse mentally, but this did not happen. A few years later, I learnt from reading the newspaper that Nanon had died at the age of fifty-four. I have no details concerning this death. It had not been possible to curb her evolution; it had followed its course until the end.

*   *   *

The hesitations concerning the diagnosis of this patient, whom I met when she was twenty-three years old, and treated for more than twenty years, were not resolved: it was most probably a case of serious hysteria, accompanied by characteropathic and psychopathic disorders in which the homosexual relationship to the mother, whom she had at her mercy, dominated. The mother herself presented psychical disorders with strong characteropathic tendencies, reducing the father to a walk-on role. Any sort of genital relationship with a man she might have loved was excluded. Her strong homosexual tendencies were never acted out, but there was a repeated passionate idealization of certain female figures, without any reciprocity on their part. The onset of the haemorrhagic proctocolitis was a total surprise for me, as was the absence of any further bout of this illness that had wounded her deeply. She insisted on practising as a psychotherapist in the provinces. She met colleagues there that I knew, who subsequently had a brilliant career in psychoanalysis. She frequented them for a while. Although it was what she wanted most, she never took the risk of presenting her candidature to a psychoanalytic institution, even though she claimed to be an analyst. She considered she was perfectly competent and had numerous conflicts with her superiors. Her skill in manipulating me got the better of my countertransference. She knew how to make me fall into the trap of her negations, provocations, transgressions, and acting out.

I still wonder how I could have allowed myself to be taken in by her. Her somatic condition deteriorated mysteriously. She had saved her rectum, but the attacks were then focused on her breasts. They swelled up and became more and more painful, but there again, she managed to manipulate her doctors, her family, and her friends. When I decided to put an end to this transference–countertransferential relationship, which left no further hope of achieving any analytic work, her attempts to convince me to see her again—"Just once, even!"—went without a response.

One further remark: when I learnt of her mother's death in the newspapers, I had the temerity to believe that she would find it very difficult to bear this loss. I was mistaken. She continued after this death to live as she had in the past. She made no attempt to have further contact with her father, nor did she make any new relationships. The new analysis that she embarked on subsequently was of short duration, and she left her new analyst without any fuss.

Her case has remained a mystery for me. No doubt the diagnosis of hysteria was erroneous. It subsequently became clear that her pathological organization consisted of a characteropathic pathological narcissism, on top of which there was undoubtedly a psychosomatic evolution for which she had refused treatment and which evolved towards a pre-cancerous state, at least as far as I know. I knew nothing of her last years.

Notes

1. This case was initially presented at André Green's seminar and first published in *Interrogations psychosomatiques* (Green, 1998 [2010], pp. 34–38).

May: a paradoxical analysis

One day, after hearing me present a case in supervision, Lacan said to me as I was leaving one of his seminars that he wanted to refer one of his friends to me, whose situation was concerning him. He added, I can still remember, "My dear Green, if you manage to see your way through this, it will not only be to your merit, but you will be very lucky." I was flattered, and accepted.

Not long after, a young woman, May, came to see me in my consulting-room. She had fine features, a very slender figure, and was endowed, it seemed to me, with sharp intelligence, even though during the first meeting she did not tell me much about herself or her difficulties. I learnt that that she had been married, but that she had since separated from her husband. Also that she had completed her university studies successfully, but she felt that they did not suit her personality very well. She was from a well-known family and took part in running her father's business, as he had died a short time before. She complained from the outset about the difficult relationship she had with her mother, who seemed to do nothing but reproach her the whole time for any number of reasons.

She was full of admiration for a brother who was only marginally younger than her. She felt as if she was his twin; he clearly meant a lot to her. He had lost his wife shortly after his marriage in a car accident, and his daughter had been brought up by their mother. She had another younger brother, but was not so close to him. It took her a long time to tell me how much she had loved her father, who had loved her silently without showing it too much. I always suspected that this discretion might be connected with a maternal jealousy that it was better not to arouse.

In her childhood, May had suffered from serious asthma, which had obliged her to wake her mother up in the middle of the night. After a while, her mother placed the bottle of ephedrine next to her daughter's bed so that she could get relief without disturbing her. Already at an extremely young age, she had seemed to her mother to be the daughter that she could not love, because she was unsatisfactory from all points of view. However, she had some uncles who were aviators and who loved her a lot; they would make signals to her while in flight to manifest their affection and to encourage her to eat, for she was a great anorexic who never fed herself properly right up until the end of her days.

The happiest relationship in her childhood was unquestionably the one she had formed with her maternal grandfather, who had taken great care of her. He taught her the names of things, of flowers and living creatures, went for walks with her, and talked to her a lot. Unfortunately, he eventually suffered a stroke and died. Her mother found nothing better to do than to hold her responsible— without there being any valid reason—for what had happened. She suffered greatly from this accusation.

I remember that she always wore long dresses that reached down to the ground to hide her shapeless figure. She was thin, and had rather unfeminine hair. She did not seem very interested in sexuality. She repeated over and over that she did not understand what I was saying to her: for instance, she could not grasp what I was thinking about when I spoke to her about "desire". She understood that for others this could mean wanting a car or a dress that would be flattering for them, but she herself wanted nothing. And yet she had fallen in love with a well-known actor; he had got tired of her quite quickly, but she remained faithful to him even though he sometimes had other love affairs. In this connection, she said that when she agreed to have sex she felt nothing, whereas the men who talked to her after having had sex with her said that she had expressed signs of pleasure; she seemed surprised by these remarks which had no resonance for her. After a while, she found a job to pay for her analysis. It was a rather surprising choice of work, for which she seemed little suited, but she managed to do it to the satisfaction of her employers. She was very attentive to her analysis and seemed interested by my interpretations, though not very affected by them. Her relationship with her mother, however, was not modified.

The death of her maternal grandfather was an irreparable loss for her, for he was not replaceable. Later, her mother suffered from back trouble and remained immobilized for a certain period of time. She also felt she was to blame for her mother's illness. Having adopted the position of a martyr who was overwhelmed by life, her mother never missed the slightest opportunity to make her feel guilty. May had a very close friendship with a childhood friend who later made a brilliant marriage, but eventually lost touch with her. She had many friends who appreciated her, the majority of whom were homosexual, and got on admirably with them. When I broached the theme of homosexuality, she replied, "It's not my thing," and that was the end of the matter. In any case, her relationship with her mother was by far the most important one. When her mother died, her emotional reaction was intense. Beside her mother's deathbed, she thought, "Why didn't you make me as beautiful as you?"—a genuine expression of love for a mother who had not seemed capable of loving her daughter.

She had lost her father suddenly from illness before the analysis. During her whole childhood she had been in admiration of her brother, who, for his part, was loved passionately by her mother. They were so close to each other that in adolescence the young people who were attracted by her were also generally attracted by him, a situation that did not arouse jealousy in her, but satisfaction. I analysed this maternal transference as best I could. I could feel I was in the father's place and the object of a silent love. As a child, she had remained alone with her father during her mother's illness and had experienced a true state of honeymoon that was interrupted when her mother came back and took hold of the reins again. Her mother constantly criticized her, kept her eye on her, pointing out her inadequacies, reproaching her for being "like her father's family" and not like hers. I am not able to say if her mother had been unfaithful to her husband; in any case, she had success with men.

I ended the analysis with May. She had a further period of analysis *a posteriori*, but I never broke off relations with her. I had too much respect for what she was, for her interests, her reading, and I wanted to help her as much as I could. She left the job that was not made for her and threw herself into activities requiring artistic skills, which she acquired diligently. She had displaced an interpretative activity connected with her analysis to her artistic work. But her personal life remained very restricted. She had a few affective relationships with men, but no sexual relationships, or very rarely. She devoted herself entirely to her work.

After the accidental death of the man that she had loved, even though their relations had been distant, she took some interest in another man who, it seemed to me, through the prism of the transference, was not very interested in her and was quite cynical, giving me the impression that he used and exploited her. He admitted to her after a while that he had got engaged to a young and rich woman who was an interesting option for him. He continued to see her from time to time. As for her, it took her a long time to get to know the real personality of this man to whom she had become attached. However, another relationship, with a nephew, the eldest son of her youngest brother, had an important place in her life; she looked after him a good deal once the transference had evolved reasonably well. He had clearly become something of an adopted son and always remained important for her. When he had grown up and become an adult, she bought herself a little dog. I witnessed her feelings for this animal, Aglaé, to whom she attributed human feelings that I had to share with her, guessing his slightest wishes and intentions. The dog had clearly become her life companion. Gradually, her ties with her family and her friends loosened.

She continued to come and see me once or twice a year, complaining about the same depressive symptoms, and was still persecuted by her mother's reproaches, even after her death. She listened to what I had to say about it with interest, appreciating the efforts that I was making to help her, even if she could not benefit from the interpretations that seemed to have enlightened her. On leaving one session, she experienced a feeling of liberation for which she was grateful to me, but this was not repeated.

I always enjoyed seeing her, even if she felt the need to apologize for disturbing me each time she asked for a consultation. One day, astonished not to have seen her for a long time, I called her apartment, expecting to learn that she had died. But there she was, on the other end of the phone. When I asked her what had become of her, I heard her reply: "I have had an attack." I asked her why she had not told me. She answered, "What would the point have been, since I couldn't come to see you?" I replied that I could come and visit her at home. "Oh! That would be nice!" I found her confined to her bed. She was paralysed on one side, but it was not serious, according to the doctors. I was struck by her solitude: "Do you see anyone?" "Yes," she answered, "but when people come to see me they just complain about their problems." "Are you bored?" "No." "So, what do you do?" "I'm waiting to kick the bucket." I promised to come back and see her. She seemed happy with that. A few days later, I learnt that she had died. I was informed that the

disorders from which she suffered, although they existed objectively, did not justify her premonition. I remain persuaded that she
had finally facilitated this outcome. I thought that my visit had been
a good-bye ceremony. Had she waited for me? She had said to me
one day, "You know, you are almost part of the family." No doubt.

I am adding here, by way of a complement, a few extracts from
the letters she addressed to me. Without overlooking the function
of resistance that they represented for her, I think they have the
merit of attesting to the complexity of the affects that May
expressed. These letters are not always dated, which perhaps
explains certain confusions. On the other hand, in choosing certain
passages and by comparing them, I think I have managed to
construct a certain coherence which has helped me to understand
my patient better, something I might not have succeeded in doing
without them.

Where to begin? In constructing her history, I learnt that the
beginnings had not been so bad. Having begun to suffer from back
problems during her daughter's childhood, her mother had put her
in her grandmother's care. May could recall a happy period during
which she felt well, in a loving environment, with her grandfather
whom she enjoyed being with very much; she also liked being
alone together with her father and brother. Three men and a grandmother. This period only lasted for a while and May soon found
herself stripped of everything, once again under her mother's
control and exposed to her rejection. She retained the memory of a
"mad" mother. It was undoubtedly at this time that she formed her
false self. She wrote to me later, "I don't know anyone who is so
well-mannered as me—it's true. Still, all that doesn't matter very
much. And, anyway, to hell with people." May had the feeling that
her mother was unsatisfied, always critical of her, treating her as
"twisted, a failure, beyond redemption", whereas she had placed a
lot of value on the brother, who was born after May, and whom
May adored in turn, no doubt in the vain hope of attracting her
mother's love. But she was only a girl, so a failure. Relations of
identificatory confusion followed:

"My muddle between my father and me . . . I have wondered if it
was me who invented that or if (and if) my mother's 'desire' wasn't
somehow involved in it. Anyway, there is no doubt that the 'little

boy' in me left when my brother died. . . . Without him, my mother could not take interest in me. Perhaps I carry that over on to you. . . . In short, I am lacking something to interest you."

An exhibitionist had shown her his penis in the metro when she was a child, and she had had no reaction: neither interest nor fear. I suggested there might be a connection with her father's penis:

"Is that what frightens me in the 'father' whom I am unable to find (is it because of that)? I have to say that my father never lost control of himself verbally, even if he was irritated, or, as he must certainly have been sometimes, angry. But I never saw him get angry. Anger was reserved for my mother . . ."

After her father's death:

"I have the impression of being denuded, without any flesh, a sort of skeleton, in short . . . In a certain way, even if I am not bored, I am actively bored by myself. That's where the waste is, and when you get irritated in turn you reflect back to me this exasperation that I have towards myself, i.e. my mother's exasperation which leaves me resourceless because I cannot interest the man in you. Well, I'm afraid of that too. In other words, I feel like a piece of shit, a 'bad egg' or at least a mess, something that's gone wrong, perhaps incomplete. . . . It's true that when I am with you, I am paralysed by you, by me, I don't know who is speaking to whom, I don't know. . . . I am very grateful to you, even if you don't realize it."

The descriptions of her mother's fits of anger are striking:

"I have realized that these 'crazy' fits of anger that invaded my mother were inevitably followed by breakdowns caused as much by the violence of the attack as by the hope that it would prevent her from getting angry. Hence her migraines, her various illnesses, her bad back, in short, her immobilization. Perhaps I have 'copied' that in my own way."

Thinking about her mother, May said, "She is innocent." But she had the feeling that she ruined everything and that her husband feared her while at the same time being won over by the seductive attitude that she adopted afterwards. Her mother seemed to deny her husband's existence as well as her children's. What's more, her father's sister, with whom my patient identified, had been put in a psychiatric clinic. This recollection seemed to be of fundamental importance.

With me, there was this duality of mad love–mad hate:

"With you I had the impression that I was not a patient 'that works'. Consequently, you were trying to get rid of me. . . . You are a safeguard for me."

She had become frozen in an attitude of lifeless immobility to avoid a catastrophe:

"I had to prevent anything from happening, either to me or to my mother, or to the rest of the family; which was the reason why I was on my guard, the reason for my inertia and mindlessness, in short, a situation of death in life that is unbearable for me and for her, but not as bad as what might have happened. . . . I had to stay there to keep guard, to watch out, to watch out for the mother in my head who replaced her and left me no room to think about anything else."

Referring to her mother:

"I must have hated her a lot, but I loved her a lot as well. I was afraid of this hate."

She wrote to me for the New Year:

"At any rate, nothing has changed in reality in my life . . . but I have the impression that for the first time in my existence, I am living or alive, as you like. It keeps me busy, it's very tiring. In any case, it's thanks to you. I have the impression I have acquired some distance towards things and people, some humour, and that I can laugh, say No and Yes and even not give a damn at all, perhaps a bit too much, about anything. . . . Let's hope it lasts!

Happy New Year."

The resurrection was short-lived. Not long after, I received a new letter:

"The last time I wrote to you it was to thank you, saying that I was for the first time consciously alive. . . . Since then, I have gradually realized that I was beginning to live in a state of panic, waking up in the morning as if the sky had fallen on to the earth, as if there was a war on. A whole string of contingent circumstances were necessary for me to realize that the fact of having shown you this meant logically and necessarily in my head, the head of an eighteen-month-old baby no doubt, that your life was in danger as a result! I think that I decided not to live because pretending, hiding, was impossible with a fragile mother, i.e. simply to keep my mother alive. Forgive me for pouring out my fear to you . . . Being alive and showing it is or was a sin because it could, or would, inevitably result in [my mother's] death. In spite of everything it was good to be alive and I thank you for that."

When, on one occasion, I gave way to impatience, she experienced my reaction as a violent rejection, reminding her of her mother's rejections:

"I made something bad out of everything good you gave me and I took pleasure in doing so, I wallowed in it, and I still came to complain. . . . I think now that I absolutely loathed you. That day, I managed to induce in you the discontent of my childhood, the exasperated hardness—which fell on me unexpectedly, though, and not when I was lettting myself go—of my mother who would suddenly burst into my bedroom in the evenings, or at night, when she was in the mood to give me sermons on just about everything, making me understand clearly that I was nothing but a piece of shit who made her feel ashamed."

She thought about me for a book; she wanted to write it for the father that I represented, to prove to me that she was something more than "just a piece of shit". She managed to complete it, receiving many compliments for it as well as genuine recognition as an author. She had "killed" me after the session in which she was convinced that I had permanently rejected her, which did not prevent her from concluding her letter by saying, "Yours affectionately."

Repetition had got the upper hand over the short period of improvement; I had lost patience, but I did not realize that I had also lost the game. After a while, there was a new development. The aunt who had been interned in a mental health clinic for

"schize . . . schizo . . . schizophrenia" became a phobogenic character who haunted her. This aunt, her father's sister, had dictated her
destiny. She ran the risk of being put in a home like her by her
mother, and for the same reasons. This fear turned into an obsession and the need to hide herself became a constant preoccupation.
A new chapter of the family mystery was revealed, throwing light
on her obsession about finishing up like this aunt. What did she
have left in her to fight against illness? One day, she wrote to me
(and that is where I will leave it as far as this correspondence, which
was a substitute for the transference, is concerned):

> "As for the truth [words taken from one of my interventions], it's
> not complicated, it's only the truth that 'works'—that is, which
> brings relief, for a while."

*   *   *

May had a face that one does not easily forget. She was slender, not
to say thin, with emaciated features, and I found her at once charm-
ing and rather ghostlike. People told me she looked lifeless. With
time, I came to think that her mother had got the better of her vitality, leaving her with nothing but the appearance of a ghost. When I
knew her, May was a member of the Paris smart set. She was a
young, solitary woman whom I suspected had remarkable intellectual gifts. A great reader, she nourished herself on Proust, whose
work she knew well, but also on other great authors of literature
such as James, Balzac, Flaubert, and so on. She read everything and
spoke about it intelligently. There was no pose, no airs. She
discussed the most sophisticated works with simplicity. I did not
know many people who had her degree of culture, and she herself
did not show this off either. She was too well-mannered to push
herself forward.

She had had a few friends prior to the car accident in which her
companion, who was driving, died. Her own life was in the
balance, and she only finally pulled through after the surgeons had
carried out intensive reparative surgery on her. Otherwise, her
health remained precarious. Her somatic state was unsteady, taking
one year with another. She lived alone and did not eat anything

because it bored her to cook, but she always had a reserve of rice in case of need. In spite of this physical condition, more dead than alive, she skied.

She came from a well-to-do background and had a taste for frequenting artists and actors from whom she could attract a certain interest, yet the psychoanalysis that she began with me was very inadequate on the relational level. Her libidinal life was lacklustre and, after a period of noctambulism, she distanced herself from this milieu. I always saw her as being fundamentally solitary. She had very superficial ties with men, who always ended up abandoning her, and yet she was very devoted to them. She seemed not to care much about anything, either people or things. None the less, she had a passion for beautiful objects and made me gifts during her analysis of some rare antiques. She only collaborated in her pater-nal grandfather's business from time to time, not wishing to get in her brothers' way. The eldest of them, whom she loved a lot, was almost her double. With me, she remained distant; I knew I had to watch my interpretations.

She was extremely refined. Although she was far from being able to benefit from the analysis, she continued to stay in contact with me, even after the end of the therapy, without ever managing to resolve the maternal transference. In spite of her resistances, she gave me the impression of understanding the interpretations that I tried to make of her psychical manifestations.

She had suffered from losing her father before the beginning of the analysis. The loss of her mother was more difficult to overcome; in fact I doubt that she ever managed this.

When she fell ill, having lost a large number of her friends, almost all of whom were homosexuals, she was terribly isolated. I broke with my neutrality to visit her at home. This only happened once. In spite of my promise to return, she did not leave me the opportunity, for she died shortly after. I had great affection for her, and a considerable amount of esteem.

* * *

I have dwelt at length on my memories of May. I confess that it is difficult for me now to add commentaries on her "case". Everything seemed so complicated to me, so heavy to bear. I could not fail to notice what I can only call her "incapacity to live".

All she had, more or less, was a female friend from childhood, from a rich family which had welcomed her as if she was one of their own children; a protective character, a clan leader, who served as a substitute father; and connections in the world of cinema and art. I could sense her extreme isolation, punctuated by health troubles that I found mysterious, about which, even though I am a doctor, I felt I understood nothing.

As for me, the more time passed, the more I had the impression that I *was* important for her *in spite of everything*. I often felt despair at being able to do so little for her. I think that I succeeded in giving her a certain understanding of psychoanalysis; she managed to convince me of this, anyway. The main benefit that she gained from it was perhaps that she succeeded in putting very distressing affects into words. Even though she may have suffered from thinking that her obstination irritated me, and that I was exasperated by her insurmountable resistances, she knew that I was the only one she could speak to. I had witnessed the passing away of both her mother and her brother, and I was astonished that she had survived all that. At the end of the day, she was able to recognize authenticity and to mistrust fabricated, fashionable, or artificial attitudes. She still had her relationship with her nephew.

It may be that the analysis distanced her from her only female friend; at any rate, she stopped seeing her, which I regretted. The few relationships she had with men, some of whom were rather cold foreigners, seemed to me to be arid. From time to time, she had esteem for the person she met, not many of whom, if any, were women. I think she spent her time feeling terrorized by an internal mother who could not recognize her, or struggling against anxieties that paralysed her. She was very, very afraid, and without any reason. I never knew anyone who got angry with her. I never heard anyone complain about her. In spite of her modesty and her self-effacing manner, I was sorry that so few people recognized the quality of her gifts.

What can I say, to conclude, about the reasons for her condition? They spoke for themselves. She had the impression that she would never, under any circumstances, be loved by her mother. She had a "crazy" mother, because she was always unpredictable, always unsatisfied, always very edgy, always irritated by this disappointing daughter. Of course, May was an X (father's family) and not a

Y (mother's family). I am not saying that her mother did not take care of her properly when she almost died in a car accident, but my patient felt that she did this more out of duty than of love. May's "true" loves belonged to the past: her deceased grandfather, then her father who loved her secretly, or the brother, almost a twin. At the end, as she admitted to me, I was almost part of the family. It was a big thing for her to make this admission. I appreciated it at its true value. Did I have any merit? Or luck? I think, above all, I was lucky to have known her.

Ange, or an implacable destiny

The case that follows was first presented in Moscow in May 2004, but I have enriched it with a conclusion.

Ange was about thirty when he came to see me for the first time ten years ago. He was a tall young man, slender and elegant, with certain mannerisms and an affectation in his voice that had a whiff of homosexuality and narcissism about them. He had got in touch with me following the recent death of his analyst. I was immediately struck by the absence of any affective reaction to this bereavement. He told me about the circumstances that had led him to do an analysis with her. After an unhappy love affair (he had been abandoned by his girlfriend, who had finally left him and emigrated to a foreign country where she had got married), he had begun a homosexual affair which subsequently ended with his friend telling him, "You've got to change something in your life." It seemed to me that this friend was reproaching him for not being homosexual enough.

Following this abandonment, and after failing a competitive examination, he made a suicide attempt that had led to a quite unforeseeable rapprochement with his father. The latter offered him a piano to console him, and told him that he loved him. Until then, their relations had been very distant. Ange had kept memories of a childhood spent with his rigid and intolerant mother who demanded precocious and constant sublimatory achievements of him (visits to museums, piano lessons, subscription to the *Comédie-Française*, closely supervised studies, and so on), without any room being made for a boy's pleasures: no sport, no fun activities with friends, no masculine complicity.

His mother's intolerance for sexuality was remarkable. One day when Ange went shopping with her to a Prisunic store, he had looked at the generous forms of certain shop assistants and had dared to say, "I like ladies like this and that", accompanying his remark with gestures outlining the contours of breasts and buttocks. The upshot of this was that he found himself at the doctor's with a prescription for Theraline syrup (a tranquillizer supposed to have effects of sexual sedation). The innuendos of his mother's reaction had not escaped him; it was as if she had considered him as crazy for having such desires. His mother, who was a seductress, often said to him, "When you are grown up, you won't love me any more; you will love other women and you will be nasty with me."

As for his father, Ange had almost no contact with him. He remembered him as being a silent man whom his mother regarded as a child on the pretext that he had not known his parents. He had a stomach ulcer and was given to great outbursts of anger. He never intervened between the boy and his mother, and had no authority over him. On the other hand, Ange could recall him having bouts of acetonaemic vomiting for which he was treated.

In adolescence, he had his first sexual adventures. The first was with a girl whom I shall call Angèle, the feminine equivalent of his first name. She was the only soft and tender woman by whom he felt loved, but he made her wait a long time before declaring himself. Even though he had had a love affair with her, sexual relations included, he never admitted that he loved her. One memory he had was of going five times in a row with her to the theatre to see *The Beast in the Jungle*, in an adaptation by Marguerite Duras of Henry James' novella. He was fascinated by this play, without knowing why. During his analysis, he discovered by chance that I had written an article on this work and he was very surprised, as if I had been watching him from a distance. The departure of Angèle, who was tired of waiting, saddened him greatly, but it did not induce him to do anything to get her back.

He then began a change of sexual orientation towards homosexuality. His choice was exclusive and involved "sodomizing men of forty". Then he alternated between homosexual and heterosexual relations. During the period when he came to see me, he had an affair with a woman whom he said was extremely beautiful and very whimsical. She led him into unrestrained pleasures that disorganized his life. He could not make up his mind about her, uncertain of his feelings as in the past.

As soon as he was on the couch, he announced that he was seropositive. He had not dared to tell me this during the preliminary meetings, fearing rejection. Initially, he pursued mixed sexual activities, now with his mistress, now with homosexual partners during passing affairs, but finally, after a few months of analysis, he decided to ask this mistress to move out of his flat, even though he continued to see her and sleep with her periodically. But he did not trust her enough to make plans with her for the future. One feature of his heterosexual relations was particularly noteworthy: he would spend a considerable amount of time scrutinizing his mistress's vagina, as if it was a disturbing foreign body. On the couch, he constantly repeated in a light tone, "I have killed my mother", alluding to the death of his first analyst, stuffing his material with mythological references from the shows he went to see (Clytemnestra, she's my mother, etc.).The early stages of the analysis were marked by quite crude sexual dreams that he clearly used for defensive purposes. He seemed to think that these dreams happened independently of his will and that consequently he did not really have to take responsibility for them. I was struck, in the transference, by the narcissistic and unemotional controlling character of his discourse. He claimed to be *"un homme de marbre"* (i.e., a cold, hard man).

He interrupted the analysis after one year and a half, for two reasons: the first was that he could not tolerate the fact that the transference was leading him to admire me more than he admired his father. In fact, what he could not stand were the envious and homosexual feelings that he felt towards me. The second reason was that he had borrowed a lot of money from his father and wanted to reimburse it in order to be free of debt. In fact, his excessive spending was encouraged by his mistress, who predicted that he was going to die soon and exhorted him to profit from life with her while there was still time. He went through a phase during which he compared himself with Dorian Gray—a comparison he subsequently had to reconsider—anticipating a physical degeneration that would render him physically and morally abominable. He was convinced that I loathed him. When the analysis was quite advanced, about three years after it began, he became aware of the meaning of his homosexual choices and, feeling guilty, he decided firmly to finish with homosexuality once and for all. He no longer acted it out, but, on the other hand, he was unable to establish any new heterosexual relationship. He had sporadic relations with women when he was on holiday, far away from me, but never in the city where we were both living. Soon, even these sporadic relations ceased.

His sexual life was henceforth limited to masturbation, about which he never told me anything, giving as an excuse the banal nature of his fantasies, which were both homosexual and heterosexual. I interpreted that he had a phobia of the vagina, which he denied, but he must have recognized this later when he spent the night in the same bed as his ex-mistress without any contact occurring between them. The years passed; he was still confined to a state of abstinence and was barely troubled by the homosexual fantasies, which he never felt inclined to give in to and refrained from speaking about.

His time was spent between reading in the morning, with the window wide open, regular attendance at shows at weekends (in his Monday session, he regularly told me that he had spent a very good weekend, denying any sense of separation and any feelings of solitude), and, finally, his major form of distraction, travel. He went round the world, very much in the style of John Marcher, the hero of *The Beast in the Jungle* after the death of May Bertram from illness and futile waiting. These voyages were always made alone. He never had anything to say about them; he had no encounters or adventures. The only exception was a trip to *Egypt*—the country I came from originally, as he knew—where he had decided to take his father shortly before his death to give him some fun. He wanted to believe that establishing good relations with him would amount to a reconciliation and erase the past. His mother, who felt pushed aside, sulked. He did not take his mother on any trips either after his father's death because she had Alzheimer's disease.

Otherwise Ange succeeded remarkably well in his work. When his mother died, he had cannibalistic dreams in which he cut her brain up into slices; the brain was strange in appearance, red like a tomato, no doubt phallic and turgescent. At a certain moment, the trips that he made outside my holiday periods amounted to provocation, which led to a parapraxis and a slip of the tongue on my part, indicating a hostile countertransference. Consequently, I decided to increase my session fee: I wanted to stop the provocation and set some limits. He understood that he had never respected paternal authority in childhood.

During the period of interruption in his analysis, he was hit by the greatest trauma of his life. Just as he had done with his girlfriend, he kept his mistress, who was still ready to live with him, waiting too long. Disappointed, she went off and married another man whom she did not love very much, but he was rich and she hoped to have children with him. She got pregnant. The announcement of this pregnancy proved to be more powerful than the mechanisms of denial that had prevented Ange from imagining the existence of a rival. This incontrovertible evidence to the contrary imposed by reality hit him like a bolt of thunder from a calm sky. He already hated the child to be born.

Let me say in passing that the analysis made it possible to construct, with a great deal of probability, the primal scene, in Rome, where he had often spent his vacation with his father and mother. His parents, who were young at the time, used to send their son off to visit monuments so that they could enjoy their siesta quietly. He had not forgotten Moses' expression in the basilica St Pietro in Vincoli (St Peter in Chains), the Via Cavour, or his visits to the Coliseum. Of course, he had a complete amnesia, due to repression, of his parents' intimate relations, accompanied, on the other hand, by a permanent and unflagging fixation on Rome. He had transformed the recollection of trauma into a predeliction for culture.

Shortly after, there was a dramatic turn of events: he took the decision to play his role to the full with regard to the child (a little girl) who had just been born—the child that had so aroused his hatred. He had been asked to be her godfather. He took care of her very actively and efficiently (much better than the father) and became an object of adoration for the child, who thought he was better suited to her mother than her own father. Today, I can say that this child was undoubtedly the most important person in his life and unquestionably the only one he loved.

I should add, moreover, that his own mother had admitted to him that she had hoped for a girl rather than a boy, who would have been called Marguerite. One day, at the end of her life, she got angry with him, reproaching him for knowing nothing about his life. Committing an extremely revealing slip of the tongue, she complained that the normal relations between "a daughter and her mother" did not exist between them. So, just as he had managed to make me commit a parapraxis revealing my negative countertransference, he had succeeded in making his mother, under the sway of anger, make a slip of the tongue revealing her refusal to accept his sexual identity. This was an indication of the way she had constantly undermined his virility. He had a dream of a woman who had a clitoris—in fact like a little penis—which prevented penetration. Not being able to penetrate her, he ejaculated on her belly. He recognized himself in the clitoris, a little penis barring entry to the man who is obliged to ejaculate outside the vagina.

Both his parents died. Ange cared for his father with devotion and affection. He cried when he died, but his grief did not last. Three years later, his mother died of Alzheimer's disease. Although he took care of her, he was remarkably cold towards her, going off travelling and leaving her care to third parties. He did not cry when she died. When it was suggested to him that he should put a photo of his father and of himself in the coffin, he added a photo of the maternal grandfather saying, "I would prefer it if there were three of us."

After the death of both his parents, at a time when he was beginning to feel attracted to a young woman with whom he clearly wanted to establish closer relations, he telephoned me at the time of his session to tell me, "I think I have made my last trip." He had been travelling with an aged cousin who had played the role of a maternal substitute since his mother's death, and he had developed symptoms that he at first associated with an allergy to quinine. But in fact they were signs of Kaposi's syndrome, for which the prognosis is very worrying. He also said to me: "Now that both my parents are dead, I have the right to be ill."

He had himself hospitalized in Paris. He returned to see me at the time of his next session, announced the news of his illness, and asked, "So, what do we do?" I replied, "We continue." This reassured him and he felt extremely grateful towards me, which he expressed by sending me a greetings card for the New Year. It took this menace of death to make him utter the first optimistic words I had heard from him expressing a sense of *joie de vivre*: "It's a nice day, so I came on foot, crossing the Luxembourg garden which was

bathed in sun. Some children were playing." Once the most danger-
ous phase of his illness had been brought under control, I thought
I noticed a slowing up and lowering of his vital capacities and his
struggle for life. Arriving at his session, he told me something that
had seemed strange to him. He had just seen his doctor who had
been happy to be able to give him a very good piece of news. His
laboratory results were excellent: "Things cannot be better," the
doctor had told him. He noticed that he had had a weird reaction.
He had said to himself, "I don't care." He tried to understand this
affirmation of indifference to these signs of rediscovered vitality. He
recounted a dream at length and came to the conclusion: "And
there I was, thinking I would soon be joining my mother. It's
depressing."

Nevertheless, he recovered his taste for living. He told me a
dream in which he was beginning to flirt with a young man, but
then stopped suddenly, saying, "We must stop, my mother's going
to arrive." He was moving towards the end of the analysis, and his
sessions were becoming increasingly hollow. For my part, I was
becoming more and more convinced that authority had been exer-
cised by his mother, with the father remaining under her domination. But, in fact, I felt that both parents were the object of unconscious hatred, no doubt on account of the primal scene, because he
had chosen to imagine that they had no sexual pleasure together.

He eventually informed me of his decision to put an end to his
treatment definitively. At this juncture, I began seeing him face-to-
face, but without much success. In his letter to announce that he was
breaking off the treatment, he assured me that he knew what he
owed me, but explained his decision by the fear of being rejected. I
think he suspected that I believed he was still attracted by homosexuality. I was indeed convinced that he was hiding his sexuality from
me, because he claimed that his masturbatory fantasies were both
heterosexual and homosexual. The desire to escape from the influence of his mother, whom he thought could never have accepted his
homosexuality, always remained with him. He concluded by saying
that he had been disappointed with psychoanalysis but also recognized that, at the end of the day, he was still alive and in good physical shape thanks to me, for which he thanked me.

*   *   *

So what were the reasons, then, why Ange's analysis could not take place? Among the reasons were, no doubt, his reticence in observing the fundamental rule, his inability to understand the principles of interpretative activity, his incapacity to express a libidinal choice of his own, as well as the omnipotence of his repression which had obliged him to silence his feelings for Angèle, who seemed to love him, without doing anything to prevent her from leaving. I sometimes thought that this silence and abstinence covered up a certain sadism towards women. Ange never manifested any sign of grief when faced with loss. He seemed to feel sorrow when he lost his father, but never when someone he said he loved went away.

He was convinced I felt hostile towards him, no doubt because of his constant transgression of the fundamental rule. His sexuality was enigmatic. His interminable observation of the vagina of his girlfriends clearly revealed that he experienced a sense of uncanniness. His homosexual practices were always centred on the sodomization of men aged forty. Although he was passive in many circumstances, he gave me the impression of not being able to bear passive homosexuality. He dominated his homosexual friends, just as his mother had dominated him. In his childhood, he had not had any masculine identification with boys of his age. He had been the perfect image of what his mother wanted—up until a certain age, at least, when he rebelled against her, remaining secretive about his life thereafter.

As an adult he invested in cultural activities, enrolled himself for courses to improve his artistic knowledge, returning to the status of student. He frequented young girls in one of these institutions, where they busied themselves with artistic initiations before finding a husband. In spite of his inclination for one of them, who had shown him affection when his father died, he did not venture to establish closer relations with her. He told me he was aware of his aggressive fantasies towards women, but never spoke about them in detail and never acted them out in any manner whatsoever. In the end, I tired of such obstinate resistance. I was convinced that he was afraid of admitting that the homosexual attraction had remained the strongest for him. He no doubt feared being rejected by me as he had been by his mother. I understood that he hid himself in order to flout the rules of the religion of his family. The only trace he kept of his maternal education was his investment in everything that concerned culture, women remaining taboo. However, I noticed that he dreamed of joining his mother in death. Since he left me, I have totally lost contact with him, although during his analysis I sometimes bumped into him by chance.

PART III

ILLUSIONS AND DISILLUSIONS OF PSYCHOANALYTIC WORK

(I) The internalization of the negative

etween the day of the first appointment I gave to Aude, the
day when I learnt of May's death, and the day of the separation with Ange, many months and years went by during
which I took care of other patients whom I tried to accompany
during their analytic journey. As I have already said, my intention
was not to give "detailed reports" of the experience that united us
through many eventful episodes. The inscriptions of our experiences constituted a rich network of memory traces—that is to say,
what my memory and my writings have retained of exchanges that
lasted for years, making them not so much patients that I treated as
familiar characters who taught me to get to know them better—
perhaps better than some of my longstanding friends.

They entrusted me with aspects of themselves that were deeply
intimate. Quite apart from the comings and goings of their transference, with some of them I felt a degree of proximity that was
rarely belied. I experienced moments of happiness with them, even
if they were too rare for my liking, and was relieved whenever I
saw their anxieties diminish, granting them respite for a while. At
other moments, their psychical state got worse, causing a fresh
upsurge of their sufferings. They were often treated by other

doctors for their physical problems, or to relieve their suffering with the help of medication. They concerned me and obliged me to be both extremely attentive and vigilant. I enjoyed our encounters, hoping for a miracle that did not happen, but was saddened to see them plunge again into a state of dejection and depression. More often than not, I tried to identify the foundations of their symptoms or to see which wounds opened up again on this or that occasion, trying to reach their personality behind the mysteries of their defences.

What can I say about it all finally? One point can hardly go unnoticed. Of the cases that I have decided to speak about, the majority are women. Of course, during my professional career I have also encountered men who have been disappointments for analysis, too. Ange is an example. But there, too, the mother was at the centre of the clinical picture.

I can recall a few other seriously ill patients whose condition I managed to improve in spite of an active delusional state of mind and who agreed to converse with me intermittently. Therapists who are accustomed to treating confirmed paranoiacs will not be astonished if I say that the delusional state of these patients could scarcely be mobilized. At the very least, I was able to congratulate myself on preventing their confinement in a mental hospital and for having enabled them to lead a more or less normal life.

So, it seemed to me that the patients I had chosen to speak about presented pathological organizations dominated by a conflict with their mother. I do not wish to simplify very complex problems, but the conflict with the maternal image has often seemed to me to be in the foreground. The father was far from being uninvolved, but he seemed somewhat indifferent or frankly pathological, even though there were no manifest conflicts with the child. What I want to suggest is that the pathology in relation to the maternal imago is much more difficult to modify. I am not claiming that the conflicts with the paternal imago can be considered as less severe, but the evolution of the analysis often shows a trivialization of the conflicts with the father, permitting a sort of reconciliation with him. A reduction of tension in the relations with the mother is more rare. It should not be imagined that the climate is perpetually tense, but when hostility is not in the foreground, anxieties about it make life impossible owing to the guilt they arouse.

When we speak about conflicts with the maternal imago, it is not enough to evoke insoluble Oedipal relations. In some cases, these feelings oscillate between insuperable feelings of hatred and the quest for love that is never satisfied. This hatred, which is difficult to interpret, is often linked to a very early wound provoked in the child by the sense of having suddenly lost his mother's love. In other cases, the therapy has allowed the patient to express the feeling of never having benefited from her tenderness or, alternatively, of having disappointed her, of having been a child who did not conform with her desires, or who did not correspond to anything she expected. Sometimes, the child had sought to monopolize the mother in a fusional and despotic relationship from which the father, who had no say in the matter, was eliminated. Sometimes, the unconscious hatred towards the mother allowed for no reconciliation and remained permanently entrenched.

As we can see, even though the variety of the scenarios involves diversely organized clinical pictures, there is a certain constancy in the central core. So, I am led to conclude that the fixation to the mother bears no comparison with the attachment that may be formed with the father. Nevertheless, it is necessary to avoid a misunderstanding here: we cannot impugn the mother's influence alone. The Oedipus complex cannot be evaluated independently of the fundamental notion of the way in which the father is loved by the mother. A woman who is preoccupied with disputing the father's role and who is incapable of showing the love she feels for her husband cannot fulfil her role as mother. This is the reason for the centrality of the Oedipus complex. But equally, the husband who effaces himself in front of his wife *vis-à-vis* his children cannot occupy his paternal role either.

As an analyst, I have quite frequently embodied in the transference a "good enough" paternal image, by virtue of which the Oedipus complex has undergone a form of reparation. But even if I have sometimes succeeded in representing an acceptable maternal image, and even, occasionally, one that is benevolent and reparative, it has never erased the patient's memory of the primitive mother, who has remained unforgettable. Efforts deployed to this end have often proved disappointing in the face of her indestructibility.

*   *   *

The cases I have called "disillusions" of psychoanalytic work can be considered, if not as failures, at least as ones that involved patients who were particularly resistant to, or rebellious against, analytic work. However, the worst is not always bound to happen and, as long as the analytic work continues, the result is not necessarily unfavourable. After analysing the various outcomes that can potentially occur, things sometimes turn out less badly than one thought they would. Above all, I have learnt to nuance my opinion. With respect to certain patients, I have told myself that they tried to fight against their suffering as best they could. For others, I have interpreted certain defensive organizations as signs of a certain analytic evolution.

Finally, it has to be admitted that these forms of resistance to recovery, feeding on destructivity, prove to be a way for the patient of hanging on and, no doubt, of surviving as best he or she can. I consider this whole clinical field to which I have directed my attention as a particularly clear expression of the work of the negative in which the action of the destructive drives predominates. This challenge thrown down for psychoanalysis must be met, and must stimulate research so that these discouraging effects can be tackled more effectively.

No satisfactory explanation is as yet available for the above observations. No description, however complete, enables us to understand the reasons for the suffering of these patients so that we can come to their help. I have just referred to the work of the negative. I proposed a description of it in my book (Green, 1993), and I cannot return to it here in detail. I argued in favour of the idea of the double role of the negative in psychoanalysis. In its most usual meaning, the negative applies to the manifestations of psychical processes affected by a sign that is inverse to that which connotes conscious processes. The example proposed by Freud is that of the aversion for a system (conscious) in relation to a *repressed* attraction for another system (unconscious). This relation characterizing the double valency of a neurotic symptom refers to the most common, most ordinary or, I would say, "normal" meaning of the relations between unconscious psychical processes and their conscious defensive form. It can be considered that this duplicity essentially concerns the psychical processes connected with the first topography. From 1920 onwards, another conception of the negative came to light after Freud's discovery of the death or destructive drives (see Green, 2007b). It should not be concluded too hastily, however, with regard to the phenomena related to the death drive, that the expression taken by the negative subsists in the earlier form of the unconscious manifestations of the first topography. If these phenomena continue to take this form in relation to the love or life drives (in their defensive form), the expressions of the negative manifest themselves differently after 1920. What underlies the negative takes the form of a refusal of the positive, not only as its reverse side or as a defence to conceal it, but that form which, in psychiatry, is called "negativism". In other words, a radical form of refusal of what is revealed by the reverse side of a positive that does not want to be recognized and is replaced by a negativized desire. In other words, by a form that depends on the destructive drives where destruction is the primordial aim, without it being possible to speak of a disguise. In this expression of the negative, the negative, deprived of its concealed positive double, is no longer involved. Destructivity comes as such, as destruction, as an affirmation of negativity, *negativity as radicality* without any relation to the positive, whose relations with pleasure, the relational dimension, the desire to give prevalence to the synthesis of Eros, give way to unbinding.

An entirely new clinical field proceeds from this, and the drive whose purpose it is to unbind, to undo, to resist linking, gains the upper hand in psychical activity. It is here that we come across certain forms of psychical activity for which the model is primordial masochism, or the form of narcissism that I have called negative.

We know that, for Freud, this basic drive couple, the life or love drives and the death or destructive drives, exists from the beginning of life. Freud undoubtedly minimized the role of childhood experiences and the scars they leave in the mind, often for a very long time after the events that caused them. These cases were marked by more or less incapacitating psychical events. When the evolution shows that these after-effects marking the organization of the mind are long term, I think that we are in the presence of what I propose to call the *internalization of the negative*. I mean that the mind has introjected these defensive primary reactions as a mode of unconscious defence, altering the psychical organization and preventing it from developing along the usual lines of the pleasure principle. In other words, the mind escapes the models of behaviour dictated by positive experiences. The outcome has made it lose its flexibility of adaptation and called for reactions dictated by acquired defensive distortions, attesting to the internalization of the negative, a form of negative primary identification.

Of course, this case is not always constituted as a model induced by pathogenic mechanisms. It is often the sign of a certain vulnerability that leaves no other option than repetition. This repetition has nothing automatic about it, but indicates a rigidity governing psychic reactions, without a capacity for adapting to circumstances better. What has happened, then, with the internalization of the negative, is that the manifestations of negativity have become identificatory introjections that are not so much chosen as obligatory; they have become what might be called second nature, artificially grafted on to a mind that has been precociously modified by pathology and its defensive reactions. The latter become so deeply rooted in the subject who has been subjected to them that they can appear for a long time to be constitutional, forming part of an innate nature. Freud often considered them as such. Today, our greater familiarity with developmental mechanisms allows us to have a better understanding of the origin of these character or behavioural traits. This does not mean, however, that they are easily modifiable, but their analysis permits a better understanding of them and can sometimes influence them. The fact that they are under the sign of the destructive drive does not mean that their manifestations are innate, even if they strongly resist giving way to manifestations that allow for easier conditions of life.

(II) Hypotheses concerning the negative beyond clinical findings

"We are living in a specially remarkable period. We find to our astonishment that progress has allied itself to barbarism. In Soviet Russia they have set about improving the living conditions of some hundred millions of people who were held firmly in subjection . . . With similar violence, the Italian people are being trained up to orderliness and a sense of duty. We feel it as a relief from an oppressive apprehension when we see in the case of the German people that a relapse into almost prehistoric barbarism can occur as well without being attached to any progressive ideas. In any case, things have so turned out that to-day the conservative democracies have become the guardians of cultural advance . . ."

(Freud, 1939a, p. 54)

The reader who has just finished these pages may reasonably consider that he or she has come to the end of the book. Everything that follows should be considered as an independent prolongation serving as an annex and constituting a sort of *post-scriptum* added to the book, but whose source of inspiration is fortunately more precise. *Illusions and Disillusions of Psychoanalytic*

Work is a book guided by analytic practice and the theory that that practice gives rise to. What is the reason for this split, then, indicating the wish to separate this conclusion from the rest of the text?

Recently, two books have fallen into my hands, which, in principle, had nothing to do with the one I was in the process of completing: *Everything Flows* by Vasili Grossman (1954), and *L'Holocauste comme culture* (The Holocaust as Culture) by Imre Kertész (1993). It was purely by chance that I made a connection between my reading of these two books. Both of them had a profound effect on me and gave me much to think about, but I thought that was the end of the matter. However, while thinking about what I had just read, the idea came to me that there might be a link between my earlier work and my recent readings, and it is this connection that I want to speak about now.

This idea seemed strange to me, and the result of these considerations only became evident to me subsequently. I finally realized that this epilogue, which might have been considered as arbitrary, was in fact motivated, and that it was akin to the connections of the same kind made by Freud from 1930 onwards. This parallel encouraged me to pursue the matter and I was now persuaded of the legitimacy of making a link between these points of view.

Everything Flows is the last novel by Vasili Grossman, a sort of testament. I had, of course, read *Life and Fate* (1959), his great novel, worthy of figuring among the masterpieces of Russian literature, and rightly celebrated by the best literary experts when it appeared in France. This was consolatory revenge after the idiotic Soviet censorship that had sought to delay its publication two or three hundred years in order to please the god Stalin. Between *Life and Fate* (begun in 1942) and *Everything Flows* (1954), a lot of water had flowed under the bridge. DeStalinization was now on the agenda. I read this novel without being able to put it down and with the feeling that I was acquainting myself with a masterpiece. Its author, who died in 1964, introduces us to a world under dictatorship. Everything in it is false for the hero, a convict released from the gulag who gets to know a "double reality", like a mental model juxtaposing his delusional world with that of "genuine" reality. Everything that Lenin had planned turned out to be a lie. Freedom was flouted and the State proved itself to be more monstrous than ever. Grossman takes the opportunity of revising the prevailing ideas concerning contemporary Russian history. Lying was standard practice; it was claimed that the Soviet Union had attained a degree of freedom unknown in the former Russia. Grossman, the Jew, reflects on the past of the Soviet Union.

This book touched me deeply. The most moving aspect of it is the disappearance of democratic values, which are henceforth falsified. While there is scarcely any freedom, it is spoken about as if it were omnipresent. The author describes with astonishing conviction the false "values" disseminated by the regime, the contrast between the hero, who has returned to his family and has no thirst for vengeance, and his former companions, who avoided exile, imprisonment, humiliating sufferings, hunger, and illness, and who deny these realities which are covered up, disguised, or painted in the official colours of the regime. The homeland of the hero, of the poor convict, has become unrecognizable. It no longer resembles what it was and is misrepresented to the taste of official truth.

I devoured this novel as if I had not been informed about the falsifications and cruelties of the Stalinist dictatorship, for hitherto I had not been touched by the reality of the Soviet State. We had become accustomed to damning Stalin in order to save Lenin's reputation as far as possible. This was, however, a vain measure of precaution, because the truth finally came out, leaving Vladimir Oulianov exposed. So be it. What was the connection, though, with *Illusions and Disillusions of Psychoanalytic Work*? I had to wait for other revelations to understand this.

As I was reading *Everything Flows*, I had not yet discovered what it was that made this novel a genuine source of psychoanalytic reflection. Although I had been interested, moved, and even fascinated by reading it, I saw only my personal reaction to a testimony of the unhappy years traversed by a victim of Stalinism. Nothing more. I had to wait for this testimony to give me the idea of a new concept with the potential to elucidate metapsychology.

Not long after, I read the latest book by Imre Kertész. I was already familiar with some of Kertész's books, since he was awarded the Nobel Prize for Literature in 2002. Before then, I did not know who he was. After that, I read *Kaddish for a Child not Born*, *Fateless*, *The Failure*, etc. I learnt that he was from a modest Jewish family and that he had translated a lot of works (Nietzsche, Hofmannsthal, Roth, Wittgenstein, and also Freud). That alone was enough to excite my curiosity. He had had the misfortune to be interned at Auschwitz at the age of fifteen, but, after being transferred to Buchenwald, he was finally liberated. In other words, he only experienced deportation for one year, a sufficiently short period to survive it but sufficiently long to be deeply affected by it.

On returning to Hungary, he suffered from the effects of Stalinist domination. Owing to an irony of fate, in order to survive he was obliged to compose opera librettos. Thirteen years after the fall of the Berlin Wall, he decided to settle in this city, which he likes "because it does not hide its past". He continued to write his novels. He never sought to flee from communist Hungary but preferred to emigrate to Berlin when he had the opportunity to do so. In his novels, he speaks of universal questions such as survival, exile, humanity, religion, and ethics. In 1992, he was invited by the University of Vienna for a symposium on Jean Améry, whom he did not know. He took the opportunity of presenting his ideas. He placed his hopes in Europe: "For if there is one hope, it's Europe." (Concerning all the bibliographical references, see the special report published by Le Nouvel Observateur on 7 May 2009. See also "Le vingtième siècle est une machine à liquider permanente", an interview between Imre Kertész and Gerhard Moser, in Catherine Coquio (Ed.), Parler des camps, penser les génocides, Paris: Albin Michel, 1999. I am grateful to Daniel Irago for having indicated this important reference to me.) It is in his last book that we can see, over and above the novelist, the appearance of a first-class thinker. L'Holocauste comme culture, like Everything Flows, moved me deeply. Vasili Grossman had written a powerful novel, but Imre Kertész has produced a philosophical work. Among the essays in the book, I will draw particularly on the eponymous essay, "L'Holocauste comme culture" (The holocaust as culture) (1993, pp. 79–92), "Ce malheureux XXe siècle" (The unhappy twentieth century) (ibid., pp. 113–136), and, last, "Patrie et pays" (Homeland and country) (ibid., pp. 137–150), in which he presents some new ideas.

Kertész analyses the thinking of our time. He detects in it a *rupture of contract*, rupture and repression (the word is Kertész's). The rupture of contract as a motor of power expresses the position of someone who opposes this rupture. Anti-semitism is a crime committed against the contract in force: "It [Nazism] broke the contract which until only recently was still believed to be eternal" (*ibid.*, p. 50). It is not my intention here to describe the similarities and differences between Nazi and Soviet camps, for Kertsész himself refrains from doing so. Later on, he contends that "... the Holocaust and European conscience are in a way interdependent" (*ibid.*, p. 57).

For Kertész, the achievement of totalitarianism was to have exiled man from himself and to have placed him outside the law (*ibid.*, p. 59). *The Holocaust created a culture.* Kertész draws on the case of Jean Amery, an opponent of Nazism who eventually committed suicide. Auschwitz not only becomes the name of a camp, it becomes that of an epoch. According to Kertész, Auschwitz is the most important event since the Cross. After Auschwitz, Stalinism extended the spirit of it. The idea of an "objective reality which exists independently of us" is fallacious and crazy, for, he says, "... I came to the conclusion that the only reality that existed was *myself ...*" (*ibid.*, p. 100). The role of the "ideological intellectual" can only be linked to political power. The duty of art is to set human language in opposition to ideology. Auschwitz was no longer just an "accident", it was "its essence" (*ibid.*, p. 117), and Kertész adds, "It is not history that is incomprehensible; it is we who no longer understand ourselves" (*ibid.*, p. 121). And here we find we are very close to Freud:

> ... I do not know if the question ... 'What is the cause of the phenomena of unprecedented violence and destruction observed in the 20th century?' should not be inversed; if we should not ask ourselves rather if the violence and destruction are not in fact initial facts which find their forms of domination. [*ibid.*, p. 121, translated for this publication]

It is *my* history, the history of our civilization, he thinks. The author's conviction is that the devaluation of life, and "the galloping *existential decline* which is destroying our era, are due to a profound depression whose roots are to be found in the experiences which shatter the course of history ..." (*ibid.*, pp. 127–128).

But the man who has freed himself of totalitarianism is unhappy because he tries to forget and searches for reasons for not returning to them: "... a civilization which does not clearly define the values that it advocates is embarking on the path of decline and annihilation" (*ibid.*, p. 135).

In 1996, Kertész delivered a speech ("Homeland, country") at the *Kammerspiele* in Munich which contained an idea that later resonated in me as a fecund thought. This text is not one of his most remarkable texts, but it contains a reference of the highest value for me. Kertész had already cited Kafka in "The unhappy twentieth century", as the greatest connoisseur of the epoch, and who had pronounced these remarkable words: "It is laid upon us to accomplish the negative; the positive is already given" (*ibid.*, p. 126). I had already read this citation in the writings of Yves Bonnefoy. In the interview with Moser, Kertész makes other references to the negative. He cites "the negative dialectic" of Adorno, which affirms that "the mind lives in the negative". (See "Le vingtième siècle est une machine à liquider permanente" [The 20th century is a permanent exterminating machine], interview between Imre Kertész and Gerhard Moser, in Coquio (1999).) He adds that if art has some kind of purpose, it is "to give form to this cultural negativity and to overcome it" (*ibid.*, p. 89). Kertész admits that he has tried to write a negative history of development showing "not how we become what we are, but how we become what we are not" (*ibid.*, p. 90, fn). In the text, Kertész reminds the audience that he has been asked to speak about his country and is led to tackle the question of the negative:

> I would define my chosen minority as a form of spiritual existence based on negative experience. It is true, I acquired my negative experience because I am Jewish; in other words, my Jewishness served me as an initiation for entering into the world of negative experience; for I consider everything that I had to suffer because I was born Jewish as a path of initiation, an initiation into the deepest knowledge of man and of the situation of man in our time. And it is because I experienced my Jewishness as a negative experience, that is, radically, that it finally led me to my liberation. [*ibid.*, p. 148]

It is worth recalling here what Kertész says about his lack of belief and his identity: "I will never be a Jewish citizen. I will never be religious." And as this Hungarian Jew continues to like the German language and chooses to live in Berlin, he concludes:

> We will have to wait a long time for my country to recognize that negative experience is important, that it has created values; and,

particularly, for it to transform this negative experience into positive acts; and to understand that it is necessary to establish a soli-
darity which is rooted in our private life and which can organize
and maintain our life independently of power, of any form of
power, while 'at the same time rejecting slavery and property'.
[*ibid.*, p. 149]

Freedom and the individual remain possessions to preserve at all
costs, over and above everything else. At the end of his book, Kertész tells us, ". . . I am happy".

And yet, many former deportees have since committed suicide:
Jean Amery, Tadeusz Borowski, Paul Celan, Primo Levi, and many
others. "The Holocaust and the existential situation in which I
wrote about the Holocaust are inextricably intertwined" (*ibid.*,
p. 219). The only solution is love. In the totalitarian logic: ". . . poli-
tics which is detached from culture and in possession of absolute
power, without scruples, causes terrible destruction; if not in terms
of human lives and material possessions, at least in terms of souls"
(*ibid.*, p. 232). What had once been values has been turned into
ideology, "making way for hatred and lies". "Why do I write?"
There is one answer and only one: "For myself" (*ibid.*, p. 255).

This brings me now to the fundamental question. Should we
think conceptually about the negative in two distinct forms which
homogeneity alone can unite but which involve two radically separate significations: one which opposes the negative as psychoanalysis allows us to envisage it, and the other which is derived
from socio-political thinking as we find it developed at length by
Kertész?

We shall be well advised not to answer too hastily. Think of
Freud. When in 2007, I wrote, *Pourquoi les pulsions de destruction ou
de mort?* (Green, 2007b), I was struck by the evolution of this
concept. Freud had begun, only timidly at first, to think about
inventing the theory of the death drive, without requiring his readers to refer to it obligatorily. As time passed, his conviction became
more firmly established. He no longer had any doubts about what
he had discovered. With better knowledge of the problem, he
extended the sphere of influence of the death drive to a domain that
he had initially left aside. When the time came, in 1930, for *Civilization and its Discontents* (1930a), three years before the appearance

of Nazism, it was in the field of socio-cultural phenomena that the action of the death drives seemed to him the least questionable. In the meantime, his elaborations concerning the superego allowed for the unification of the negative in individual clinical practice and in his cultural conception of the superego. He had, thus, succeeded in achieving a synthesis of two apparently distinct points of view— apparently distinct, but not really, in his view.

This example made me think. Was the same not true for the negative of individual clinical practice and the negative of socio-political forms of expression? *The Work of the Negative* (Green, 1993) is a theoretical innovation, the broad outlines of which I recalled in the last chapter. To a certain extent, this present book on what I have called the "illusions and disillusions of psychoanalytic work" is an extension of my earlier reflections set out in *The Work of the Negative*. The ideas presented in the book of 1993, which initially met with some resistance in being recognized and accepted, were, in the end, accepted more or less widely. Those who were at first resistant to the idea of the negative subsequently rallied around the idea of the *disobjectalizing function*. But, as I have said, it would be a mistake to present the negative in an exclusively pejorative light. I have pointed out that there was a negative—first topography—which only appeared as the reverse side of the positive that had to be discovered in the disguised forms of the repressed (the positive dissimulated under traits of the negative), and as a repressed dimension allowing what is hidden behind it to be surmised. Negative knowledge appeared as early as 1920 as the expression of the death drive, in which the negative appeared to be less a dissimulation of the repressed and more as the radical expression of a positive that is denied, rejected, and actively condemned. Here, one suspected the existence of a radical negativity that did not enter into a compromise capable of being accepted secondarily. We were faced there with an often insurmountable deadly negativity.

This was the manifestation of a form of negativity that appeared late on in Freud's work and in which he never ceased to believe, while at the same time insisting on the forms of mitigation and compromise between the erotic and destructive impulses. At the end of his life, Freud was constantly reflecting on primary masochism, the irremediable sense of guilt, self-punishment, and resistance to change.

Can we envisage other forms of relations between the individual negative observed in clinical practice and the socio-cultural negative of political forms, as Kertész proposes we should understand them, and also as Freud saw things late on in his work when he was striving to unite these two negativities into one, something we are still along way from achieving today? In what follows, I will venture to defend the idea of a unified negative, assuming diverse forms.

The speculative hypothesis that I am proposing is, no doubt, debatable, but it seems to me worthy of discussion. I have no doubt that its adoption will meet with some resistance, but this was the case, too, for all Freud's bold speculations, which were only accepted after a long period of maturation.

When we consider the negative in individual clinical practice, what do we observe? Psychic functioning seems to be subverted, and perhaps more than subverted. Compared with what we are accustomed to seeing, the determining factors of psychic functioning no longer seem to obey the usual rules laid down by the governing principles; for example, after 1924, the pleasure principle no longer governs psychic processes. Freud had accustomed us to this idea since his discovery of the compulsion to repeat in 1914. The experiences that are subject to repetition are as much those connected with pleasure as with unpleasure. There is, thus, a sort of neutralization of the direction of the phenomena compulsively repeated, even though we do not as yet have grounds for speaking of a repetition of the negative. We find ourselves in this scenario only when masochism, guilt and self-punishment, as ways of seeking unpleasure, have imposed themselves and dominate the inversion of the direction of psychic processes. In the most striking cases, masochistic, and even suicidal, behaviours have gained the upper hand. And death often eventually intervenes, if not through a patent and unquestionable suicide, at least through circumstances that suggest a suicide in all but name. In other cases, after brilliant success, the wind changes direction, and the advantages acquired are gradually dissipated. I have proposed the expression *internalization of the negative* to further our understanding of these evolutions, but it needs clarification. To say that the negative has been internalized means that it has been integrated as a direction taken by psychic processes, with the latter joining this negative direction against the natural current. In other words, without realizing it, and without knowing why or how, the new orientation seems unable to prevent itself from "making blunders", from taking bad decisions, from failing, from seeking failure and humiliation, etc. Why? What does the subject want? To be beaten, to be punished by the father, to be humiliated in front of others? So be it, but why?

Only patient and obstinate analysis, resisting the inefficacy of interpretations and the repetition of masochistic behaviours, can sometimes elucidate and even overcome repetitive forms of behaviour. One has to go back quite a long way to be able to discover the source of the patient's guilt, sanctioned aggression, and pitiless self-punishment. So much, then, for the individual negative, which leads us to suppose that these positions result from of an unconscious source, so that in the end the analyst concludes that an internal enemy, a fifth column, has taken over the reins of power. It may be necessary to take the analysis of the transference as far as that.

The other form of the negative has apparently nothing in common with the one we have just studied. Kertész, as we have seen, evokes Kafka. The negative we are concerned with here is a position that replaced the values of Western civilization, evinced by Nazi ideology. The latter, created from the beginning to the end in order to support its lies, no longer has the slightest respect for former values. Kertész is not afraid of saying that these values were derived from the traditional foundations of culture; what gave them an ideal, and no doubt idealized significance, was considered as outmoded. Ideology has but one aim: to establish by authoritarian means the falsifications on which the counter truths disseminated by certain authoritarian or tyrannical regimes are based, defending beliefs contrary to those of democracies.

Everything about it is distorted truth, statements falsifying reality, which is inaccessible for the great majority. We cannot overlook the fact that the only aim of this acted negativity is to obtain the submission of individuals who have to agree to what is imposed on them, even if there is never anything to confirm the truth of it. Everyone lies: the press, the radio, television, official propaganda speeches, statistical figures, etc. Years must go by before the reality finally emerges one day. A skilfully orchestrated culture of hate is maintained. Fanaticism, rooting out what must be condemned and executed, is systematically upheld against tolerance and is opposed to the free exchange of ideas.

What is the connection between this form of negativity and the first? Here, it is not what I have called the internalization of the negative that is involved. We are up against a different strategy. The negative has not infiltrated itself surreptitiously into an individual without his realizing it, but is the result of a violent seizure of power that has no place for sharing. It leaves no room at all for lucid discussion. It has established itself by force. It has taken the place of those who have the power to formulate the law, to speak in the name of a fragile, changing, and questionable truth.

In this case, truth is sequestered, bound, gagged, and reduced to silence. If we try to translate the acts of this negativity, we understand that they are in the service of a deliberately disseminated falsehood in alliance with violence. It is this falsehood, and this falsehood alone, which can be elected as the only authentic, the only veridical truth, the only truth that is beyond suspicion, like a religious dogma. This negativity is the product of an aggression from outside, from an "externalization" which attacks the inner truth. Nobody really believes in it; no one listens to those whose task it is to spread it around, no one backs their statements up with faith, but it is the so-called official truth, the only one that is admitted.

You can see the difference between these two negativities. The first has succeeded in passing itself off as unconscious; the second has never deluded us. It only gathers accomplices, acolytes, specialists of terror, and even those with suicidal tendencies whose families will be generously compensated, like those who sacrifice their lives in the hope of acquiring the status of martyr.

To conclude, both these forms of negativity are related in my view: in the first case, they are unable to recognize that they have carried out an inversion of the values of life by internalizing the negative; and in the second, they deliberately serve a cause which reduces the socio-political dimension to a form of highway brigandage to guarantee the domination of those who must be reduced to slavery. Language has become the exercise of a perversion.

So, there are two forms of the negative which we must link to each other by contrasting unconscious masochism and perversion. They are two forms of attack on the life of the mind: one turns against itself, and the other is subject to a cynical domination that has force of law. This, then, is my speculative hypothesis. It is not for me to form a judgement about it, but it seems to me sufficiently clear to merit discussion. It allows me to conclude that the psyche is one, and that it cannot be reduced to compartments opposing the individual and the collective. But if the psyche is indeed marked by unity, this is the result of a relation between different partners. The first case, in which the other has been internalized, involves a conflict between two positions. In the second, the other is external-ized and becomes the enemy who aspires to impose himself; noth-ing stops his thirst for domination up until the day when his system collapses. Melancholia leads psychic life, but delusional perversion seeks to take possession at all costs of all the forms of power. Most of the time, the powers of destruction ultimately fail. In any case, the psychoanalyst has the ethical duty of fighting against both of them. In the name of life. In the name of truth.

(III) An encounter at the end of the journey

W hile I was concluding these reflections on the difficulties of working alone as an analyst, I had the satisfaction of coming across a text written some years before by an author whom I have always held in high esteem and cited whenever I have had the opportunity of doing so. Invited to collaborate on a volume entitled *Les Voies nouvelles de la thérapeutique psychanalytique*, in 2006, and to write a discussion on the presentation (by France Tremblay and Gregorio Kohon) of two cases that I qualified as extreme, Anne Denis took the opportunity of presenting her ideas. I had been impressed on the occasion by the quality of her discussion, but, as time passed, I could remember only the broad outlines of her contribution. As I was finishing the present book, what Anne Denis had written came back to me, and, to my great satisfaction, I had the impression of discovering a text that coincided in many respects with my own reflections. This propitious encounter gave us the opportunity of meeting again at the end of this journey.

Denis (2006) began by presenting what she calls the "death principle", reformulating Freud's death drive. Whereas Freud's death drive is inevitable, killing or murder, except in certain circumstances of which the State has the monopoly, is prohibited. But, she adds, it is clear that murder does not only signify the physical disappearance of the other. The murderous impulse is only one part of a *death principle*. The "crime against humanity", committed seventy years ago, has obliged us to think the "unthinkable". This "unthinkable dimension" had already been anticipated by Nietzsche, and Freud was also convinced of its existence, notwithstanding the scepticism of his followers. Those authors who were victims of Nazi persecution, Robert Antelme, Primo Levi (cited by Imre Kertész), and Kertész himself, understood this well. Denis traces the effects of this death principle in human life and institutions. For her, the death principle represents a potential universal psychopathological organization (*ibid.*, p. 503). This leads her to generalize the concept of "soul murder". Those who did not experience the Shoah, but who witnessed the dictatorships of Latin America (E. Rodrigué) encountered similar fates. Denis posits a hypothesis: ". . . what triggers the murderous impulse is the psychic life of the victim" (*ibid.*). In other words, there is no soul murder without the existence of the life of the soul of the other, which is intolerable for the persecutor who, thus, wants to get rid of it. Winnicott shared this idea. Anne Denis and I both qualify this structure as a "perversion of human relations". As we have seen, we sometimes encounter this in parental perversions. For Denis, to speak of psychic life is to speak of sublimation. Only sublimation can counter the horror of this perversion.

Denis had denounced ideology as a "mechanics of mortification" before Kertész did so in his book, *L'Holocauste comme culture* (1993). The ego, with its ruses, tries to neutralize the constructive drive (Eros). Sometimes the death principle finds justifications with the ego's support, which is a way of reminding us of the presence of murder. Ideology, then, is supposed to define reality—a function that is attributed to it in totalitarian systems of thought. Here, Denis tackles the concept of meaning, congruent with that of the signifier, or even with that of word representative; rhythm is the appropriate meaning giving birth to the form and to the temporal links between heterogeneous elements. This is akin to an idea expressed by Kahn (2005): "music: is it not '*the food of love*'" (Shakespeare)? Here we are in a realm prior to significations.

I think my views are quite close to those of Anne Denis, as she has pointed out to me on several occasions. As I have done, she draws parallels between individual pathologies linked to the family and social and political experiences which deprive subjects living under totalitarian regimes of their freedom, inflicting on them all kinds of moral torture. She cites Robert Antelme and Claude Lanzmann (*Shoah*) copiously when she describes the struggle of victims in a situation of protective confinement. If we turn once again to individual experiences, we notice the co-occurrence of the affect of the psychosomatic existence of the self and of recognition of the other: "the sense of belonging to the human species always implies the other as a fellow human being" (Denis, 2006, p. 511).

Like the treatments inflicted on the victims of dictatorial regimes, soul murders are not always perpetrated by psychotics and incestuous perverts, but attest to the psychic and sexual poverty of the parental couple. It is more a question of a lack of humanity than an excess of malignant perversion. Denis cites me with regard to the mourning of a living language which disappears, where the split between *representance* and *signifiance* has taken the life out of communication. She pleads for a continuity between body and language, as is illustrated by the poetry of the maternal language. Psychic pain and the pain of concentration camps communicate with each other. They must be distinguished from mere emotional discharges that have not yet acquired the status of affect; it is as if the drive is absent from the picture. For Denis, a bodily state must not be confused with an affective state. She contends that the psychosomatic incarnation remains imperceptible for a long time, "since there exists a somatic trace of the absolute pain of the non-existence of the self". She distinguishes the *psychic* sense of existence from bodily states that can take its place. The worst pain is that of not being consoled in one's suffering. René Spitz once defended a similar idea, as if the psychic, even in pain, required its own division. This resembles malignant projective identification, which invokes reality in what it distorts owing to its perverse component: "It is; that's all". The analyst seeks to rectify this unquestionable, absolute claim. In these cases, a primary object deficiency is observable. It is no longer the representative of the contraries that is contradictory but what allows them to be united.

These observations drawn from autistic pathology are compared with the language of ideological thought studied by Victor Klemperer. For Kertész, too, ideology becomes the language of perversion. Anne Denis quotes Bailly, Saussure's successor, as I have done before, concerning "the possibility that drive duality is at play in the relation to the primal object" (*ibid.*, p. 522).

The concept of negation in psychoanalysis succeeds the forms of negation that precede it in linguistics. Abstraction and symbolization are associated. Lacan and Bion say something similar. In psychoanalysis, abstraction is underlain by drive activity. In conclusion, Denis studies the relations between meaning and signification: "Experience endowed with meaning is prior to verbal language" (*ibid.*, p. 526). Earlier I mentioned poetics: in this connection, Anne Denis writes:

> The reference to poetry ("essential for psychoanalysis") is justified even more if one thinks of it as an intermediate language between meaning and signification, as that which can unite these two heterogeneous psychic elements, because the poem is at once song and language. [*ibid.*, p. 527, translated for this publication]

It is meaning that provides the real holding, and not the object. A person enters analysis because the meaning of his or her life has been altered. For Anne Denis, the crisis of psychoanalysis is also "a crisis of meaning which drags into its defeat the connotations which are attached to it: Eros, the good, and the 'human species'" (*ibid.*, p. 530). Such is the conclusion, then, of this important contribution reflecting an inspired theoretical line of thinking with which I have more than once felt in tune.

*   *   *

All things considered, or as Louis (Althusser) would have said, "in the last instance", writing this book has made it possible to unite two poles: that of the therapist and that of the citizen. Both have taken part in the birth of the psychoanalyst. They are essential components of my identity. Many other aspects also play their part in this identity. They are more personal, and about them I will say nothing; discretion obliges. This only concerns me and those who, in one respect or another, have been important for me. One should not expect to find personal secrets here. Each person has the right to have what is secret in him or her respected.

Clinical passion, complex thinking: towards the psychoanalysis of the future

Fernando Urribarri

W hat an incandescent text! Rather than jumping straight in to discuss it immediately, let me first try to clarify a few fundamental points about the author's thinking. The dynamic core of this book makes one think of an imaginary *Diary of the Clinical Thinking* of André Green. Around this core, bundles of reflections unfold, grouped together in chapters whose titles themselves function as vanishing points towards a realm beyond the text. These perspectives allow us to penetrate more deeply into the author's work, but also stimulate us to question our own clinical and theoretical experience.

Three principle dimensions can be identified in this volume: first, a *clinical* dimension concerning the disillusions of the analytic process which leads the author to elaborate clinical considerations on the setting, its metaphorizing potentialities, and its failures; second, a *metapsychological* dimension concerning the question of destructivity which is centred around the new idea of an "internalization of the negative"; and finally, a *historical* dimension which raises the question of the crisis of psychoanalysis and proposes a new contemporary paradigm.

Illusions and Disillusions crowns the final stage of the intellectual journey of André Green inaugurated by what one could call the "turning-point of 2000". This stage was marked precisely by the crisis of psychoanalysis and the project of a new contemporary model or paradigm to overcome it. In an attempt to show the full richness of this moment and the place that this book has in it, I shall begin by tracing the broad outlines of the evolution of André Green's work and thought. I will then comment on certain aspects of the "turning-point of 2000", notably the contemporary clinical model founded on the tripod transference–countertransference–setting, and centred on the psychic work of the analyst and his internal setting. To conclude, I shall situate the concept of the "internalization of the negative" in relation to the concept of "framing structure" (conceptual articulator of the metapsychology of representation and of the theory of the setting), understood as the implicit model of Greenian theory and praxis.

André Green's itinerary: a panoramic vision

The question of contemporaneity traverses André Green's work. For me, it is its vertex: from his intervention at Bonneval, "L'inconscient freudien et la psychanalyse française contemporaine" (1962) to *Key Ideas for a Contemporary Psychoanalysis* (2002a). The result of this journey of almost half a century is the elaboration of an original theoretical and clinical model articulating a reconceptualization of the foundations of metapsychology and a renovation of the psychoanalytic method (while representing an actualization and extension of the Freudian clinical model). We will see that, after the "turning-point of the year 2000", this model would be reworked as the source or the outline of a new psychoanalytic paradigm—an enlarged and complex pluralist contemporary Freudian paradigm.

It is customary, from a classical perspective, to distinguish three main periods in the itinerary of major authors: the beginnings, the middle period of maturity, and finally, the late period. I shall follow this schema for my panoramic outline. (For an analysis of André Green's work in relation to the history of French psychoanalysis (particularly with regard to Lacan and the post-Lacanian movement), see Urribarri (2008).)

1960–1970: the beginnings

André Green began to emerge, stand out, and establish a name for himself as an author during this period, with his own themes of interest, his fundamental choices (influenced by reading the works of Freud and post-Freudians: Lacan, Winnicott, and Bion), and his own particular perspective and style. In his article, "Primary narcissism: structure or state" (1967), he introduced the theory of "negative narcissism" (complement of positive narcissism) and the notion of "framing structure for the ego" (constituted by the negative hallucination of the mother and the double reversal of the drives). He then designated as a "work of death" what he would later call the "work of the negative". These ideas, enriched by his reading of Bion's theory of thinking, eventuated in a theory of "blank psychosis" set out in the book *L'Enfant de ça* (in collaboration with J.-L. Donnet (Donnet & Green, 1973)). In the same year, in *The Fabric of Affect in the Psychoanalytic Discourse* (1973) he focused on affect with the aim of studying symbolization beyond Lacan's linguistic model. Green advocated "the heterogeneity of the psychoanalytic signifier". He was already affirming that "contemporary psychoanalysis proposes to give a theoretical basis to post-Freudian contributions". The challenges and singularities of contemporary clinical practice were the main themes of his London Report (Green, 1975). A study of the history of the parallel evolution of analytic theory and technique led him to distinguish three movements and, consequently, three models: Freudian, post-Freudian, and contemporary (within which he situates himself). Note that if this third model, defined by the investigation of mental functioning within the analytic setting, was at that time only a project in outline, the concept of the frame or setting (according to Bleger and Winnicott) already had a central role. Finally, in 1975, Green proposed a first model of borderline functioning, centred on four mechanisms: splitting, decathexis, expulsion through action, and somatization.

To sum up: the alternation between the critique of post-Freudian reductionism (Hartmann, Klein, Winnicott, Bion, and Lacan), the revision of the theoretical foundations, and the investigation of the limits of the clinical field, constituted, from the beginning, a contemporary way of thinking both in terms of its perspectives and its project. We should emphasize the correlation between the first conceptualizations of the framing structure for the ego, the process of representation ("heterogeneity of the signifier", defining representation as a basic function of the mind), and the analytic setting ("the dream is the model for the setting").

1980–1990: the decades of maturity

At the beginning of the 1980s, a series of articles, which were subsequently gathered together in *Life Narcissism, Death Narcissism* (1983b), and in *On Private Madness* (published first in English in 1986, then in French in 1990 as *La Folie privée*, though in a different version), developed and consolidated an original model of the functioning (and treatment) of borderline cases. It was at this point that psychopathological classifications yielded to considerations of the limits of analysability. "Private madness" is played out and defined in the transference and countertransference. In "Passions and their vicissitudes" (1980), he distinguishes madness and psychosis. He proposes an "aetiological myth" which aims to explain the origin of the dual conflict between the drives of the id and the drives of the other. In an attempt to elucidate borderline cases, Green proposes in his article "La double limite" (1982), a model that combines considerations of an enlarged topography (intra- and intersubjective) with the dynamic effects of the object in the setting. "The dead mother" (1983c), constructs the transferential complex of the dead mother, elaborating a paradigmatic clinical scenario of contemporary clinical thinking.

"Le langage dans la psychanalyse" (1983a) constituted a decisive contribution in the author's evolution. He not only sets out a specifically psychoanalytic theory of language but also elucidates the metapsychological foundations of the analytic method and practice. He articulates a theory of representation (double *représentance*, double *signifiance*, double reference) with a conception of the polysemy of the setting, and with a model of the double transference (on to speech and on to the object) based on the double reversal of the drive.

The 1990s were first marked by a powerful theoretical innovation, then by a work of articulation and a general conceptual organization. It was in 1990 that André Green introduced the concept of thirdness. Not long after, his most original work, *The Work of the Negative* (1993) was published. More than a concept, it is a "meta-concept", or a plural conceptual axis. The elaboration of its double structuring and destructuring dimension ranges from the most "abstract" speculation on the drives to the most "concrete" consideration of limit situations, situations of clinical impasse. Two and three years later, respectively, *La Causalité Psychique* (1995) and *Propédeutique* (1996) provided a response to the expectations of many readers who wanted an overall presentation of the general metapsychological foundations of André Green's thought. In them, we discover the new contemporary metapsychological foundations. Schematically speaking, they may be said to contain five main axes: (1) the drive-object pair, a "psychic atom" articulating the intrapsychic and the intersubjective; (2) a generalized theory of representation, enlarging Freudian theory to include the body and thinking, the other and reality; (3) an enlarged topography, correlative to the precedent enlargement, presenting the double conflict ego–id and ego–other; (4) thirdness (a metaconceptual axis ranging from the theory of "open triangulation with a substitutable third" to tertiary processes); and (5) the work of the negative (a meta-conceptual axis ranging from primary defence mechanisms to the "negative" foundations of symbolization). The consolidation and deployment of the new principles can be found in two important books of maturity: *The Chains of Eros* (1998) and *Time in Psychoanalysis* (2000b).

The late period: the turning point of 2000 and the contemporary paradigm

The "turning point of 2000" is defined by the recognition of the crisis of psychoanalysis and the project of a new paradigm. The crisis is essentially characterized by the post-Freudian fragmentation of the theoretical and practical unity of psychoanalysis, as well as by the failures exposed in the technique and identity of psychoanalysts by the modifications of practice. Orientated "towards a psychoanalysis of the future" (Green, 2003b), this turning point contains a double movement, individual and collective.

André Green has suggested that the post-Freudian crisis of psychoanalysis is a "melancholic" crisis: in other words, it is marked by the interminable mourning for Freud's death. Symptom-atically, each important post-Freudian author has wanted to replace him as the principal figure; each militant movement believed it was reviving the original situation of the pioneers and of the founding father. Ego-psychology, self-psychology, Kleinism, and Lacanism all repeated the same process, consisting in defending its own reduc-tionist model, converting it into dogma, mechanizing a particular technique, and idealizing a leader of the school. The contemporary project claims to be an antidote to the repetition of this process. Instead of a Greenian "discourse" or "system", instead of a new cant, the contemporary project aims to construct a matrix of disci-plines, an articulation of key ideas for a programme of research concerning the essential issues (theoretical and practical) of contem-porary practice.

Taking a synthetic approach, we can say that the contemporary disciplinary matrix is based on four axes. The first is a "critical, historical, and problematic" (Laplanche, in Bleichmar, 1986) con-temporary reading of Freud, which replaces the Freudian metapsy-chology and method as the foundations of psychoanalysis. The second involves a creative appropriation of the principal post-Freudian contributions, along with a cosmopolitan openness towards dialogue with foreign authors. The third corresponds to the extension of the clinical field to the treatment of non-neurotic cases. The fourth is a "tertiary" clinical model integrating Freudian and post-Freudian models (centred on the transference), based on the concept of the analytic setting. Furthermore, in this new model, Freudian vocabulary is established as a *lingua franca* and a *common ground*.[1]

The animation of the "collective" movement (trans-institutional and pluri-generational) began with the simultaneous preparation and launching of various projects: a special international edition of the *Revue française de psychanalyse*, "Courants de la psychanalyse contemporaine" (Green, 2001a) (a sort of atlas or collective cartog-raphy of psychoanalysis faced with its crisis, conceived by André Green); an open symposium of the Paris Psychoanalytic Society (SPP) at UNESCO, bringing together the scientific representatives of the two IPA institutions (SPP, APF), the Fourth Group, and the non-dogmatic Lacanian movement (SFP), on the theme of "Psycho-analytic work" (an unprecedented attempt to reunify the pluralist analytic field); and the creation of an international research group (with colleagues from the USA, the UK, Argentina, and France) on the treatment of non-neurotic structures, which (to the best of my knowledge) is the first qualitative research project at the IPA. Other interventions, publications, and symposia have been organized by our author, or "around André Green's work" (such as the Cerisy Symposium in 2005, the first devoted to a psychoanalyst during his lifetime), and last but not least, the most important collective production to date, the publication under André Green's direction of *Les Voies nouvelles de la thérapeutique psychanalytique* (2006), a volume of 908 pages containing contributions from thirty-four French and foreign analysts—a veritable survey of contemporary psychoanalysis.

If this collective work aims to construct a new scientific horizon for problems and hypotheses which define the contemporary field by sketching out its new disciplinary matrix and its general programme of research, the individual work corresponds to personal propositions, singular explorations, and original elaborations. This movement of writing produced, first of all, two almost simultaneous and complementary works of equal importance. The first, *Key Ideas for a Contemporary Psychoanalysis* (2002a), is a personal response to the challenges and key questions of the crisis of psychoanalysis. In the first part, this book deals with the problems of analytic practice; and, in the second part, it summarizes the main conceptual lines of its author's personal work. The book provides both a map of the contemporary field and a compass for getting one's bearings in it. (One could speak of "key ideas for a contemporary paradigm".)

The second, *Psychoanalysis: A Paradigm for Clinical Thinking* (2002b), is a weighty theoretical work, each text of which penetrates further into the principal themes and conceptual axes of André Green's work. Two major axes mark, in turn, the thematic direction that its subsequent principal developments would take. The first corresponds to the introduction of the very notion of "clinical thinking": it is an innovative contribution which ventures to extend the conceptualization of the specificity of analytic thinking (within the session and outside it), mobilizing in turn (and is articulated with) considerations on the foundations and variations of the setting. Green writes: "The clinical mode of thinking is defined as an original and specific mode of rationality arising from practical experience . . . It corresponds to the work of thinking involved in the relationship of the psychoanalytic encounter" (*ibid.*, pp. 9–10).

It is within this movement of thought that the important notion of the "analyst's internal setting" emerges. A second axis furthers research into the death drive and the work of the negative in non-neurotic structures. The article, "The central phobic position" (which, given its international reception, seems, like "The dead mother", to have acquired the status of a contemporary classic), brilliantly combines both axes by presenting a model of free association and a study of a singular non-neurotic mode of anti-associative work of the negative.

The last article of the volume, "The crisis in psychoanalytic understanding" (written as a conclusion to the special international edition of the *Revue Française de Psychanalyse* (2001a)), takes up all these issues again, situating them clearly within the contemporary project. As the reader will have noticed, these thematic axes and this conceptual horizon are also present in *Illusions and Disillusions of Psychoanalytic Work*. It is not a coincidence if the latter resembles a sort of "Diary of Clinical Thinking" (especially if we recognize, for example, in the words of an analysand, May, the future title of a theoretical text "Death in life").

I said earlier that this journey of almost half a century has resulted in the elaboration by André Green of an original theoretical and clinical model. The new contemporary metapsychological foundations are the object of quite a general and didactic study in the second part of *Key Ideas* . . . It seems worthwhile, therefore, to dwell a bit further on certain aspects of the clinical model.

The contemporary clinical model

After the Freudian reference to the neuroses, and the post-Freudian reference to psychotics and to children, borderline states constitute the paradigmatic cases of the contemporary model. In André Green's theorization of non-neurotic structures, the traumatic dimension of sexuality is recovered (in contrast with the post-Freudian emphasis on object relations and the destructive drives). The traumatic potentiality of the object is examined in relation to narcissism (positive and negative). The sexual drives—with pregenital fixations and a mode of functioning that is closer to that of the id than that of the unconscious—play a central role, differentiating borderline cases from the psychoses (and the contemporary model from the post-Freudian model), while, in contradistinction to the neuroses, the destructive drives and archaic defence mechanisms (splitting, denial, etc.) have a major influence.

Working with borderline states stimulates the exploration of the conditions of possibility and the limits of analysability. The concept of "setting" is introduced and explained in respect of its metapsychological foundations, its methodological (and epistemological) function, and its technical variations. Consequently, just as the importance of the analyst's internal setting is emphasized, so, too, is the plurality of its functioning during the session: the analyst's psychic work becomes a conceptual axis articulating a series of heterogeneous dimensions and operations. In this context, the countertransference is redefined: the concept of integrated or framed countertansference emerges. In contrast with silence and simultaneous translation, the dialogical matrix of the analytic method is once again valorized. The diversity of practice, with its variable settings, finds its unity (both its foundations and its conditions of possibility) in the "analyst's internal setting" as a guarantee for the method.

Transitional by nature (between social reality and psychic reality), the setting both institutes and illustrates the analytic method. Its status is at once clinical and epistemological; the setting is the condition for the constitution of what André Green calls the "analytic object"—a third object produced by the communication of each singular analytic pair. The introduction of the concept of the setting inaugurates a triadic schema (setting–transference–countertransference) for understanding the analytic process. In this new triadic schema, the signification of the setting is polysemic, including diverse logics of listening: the logics of unity (narcissism); of the couple (mother–baby); of the intermediate area (of illusion, of the transitional); and of triangulation (of the paternal law of the prohibition of incest).

In order to think about the analytic process, Green proposes the tripod "setting–dream–interpretability", with which he proposes to articulate a second tripod with a view to reflecting on the dynamics at the limits of analysability: "internal setting–act–work towards internalization". So, if for the first tripod, the dream (and its interpretation) remains the model for analytic work, for the second, the model becomes that of playing.

The setting is transformed into an instrument of diagnosis: "an analyser of analysability" (Green, 2002a, p. 27). The possibility of using or not using it as a potential analytic space in which the fundamental rule can be examined makes it possible to evaluate the possibilities and difficulties of representative functioning. Thus, with non-neurotic patients, modifications of the setting (reduction of the frequency of sessions, face-to-face position, etc.) can be justified to the extent that one is trying to establish the best conditions possible for representative functioning. From post-Freudian formalism, which classifies in terms of external parameters, we move on to a dynamic and processual definition. In contrast with the idea that psychoanalytic psychotherapies are simpler and more superficial variants of analytic work, their complexity and difficulties are henceforth given full recognition. Emphasis is placed on the need for a particular kind of psychic work from the analyst in order to render the psychic conflict situated at the limits of analysability representable, thinkable, and analysable. In both cases—psychoanalysis or psychotherapy—it can be said that the objective is the same, which is to constitute an internal setting (internalization of the setting) by virtue of which the dialogical kernel (intersubjective) of the analysis becomes a reflexive intrapsychic matrix.

Contemporary psychoanalysis develops the analyst's psychic work as a tertiary conceptual axis that attempts to include free-floating attention and the countertransference as partial and complementary dimensions. It is within this context that the idea emerges of the "analyst's internal setting" as a preconscious representative matrix. Its optimal functioning is that of the "tertiary processes" (Green) on which the analyst's understanding and creativity are based. A new concept of "integrated" (or framed) countertransference also appears. Integrated within this broader and more complex conception of the *analyst's psychic work*, the countertransference becomes a constituent part of the analyst's internal setting.

In line with the idea of the polysemy of the setting and of the diversity of the logics involved, the analyst's position is multiple and variable; it can neither be predetermined nor fixed: either as

Oedipal father or as containing mother. After the Freudian reference to the dream as an implicit clinical model and the post-Oedipal reference to the dyadic mother–infant relation, playing seems to be the contemporary reference. The analyst must *play*, both in the theatrical and musical sense and in the playful, ludic sense, depending on the scenarios deployed in the singularity of the analytic field. Moreover, the fact of recognizing that the unconscious expresses itself through different dialects favours a dialogical ideal of the "polyglot" analyst.

To summarize, we can say that contemporary psychoanalysis develops a tertiary theoretical model. This is not due to its "third" historical position, or to the importance it accords to the articulation of the two earlier models (Freudian and post-Freudian), but, rather, because of the essential role played by certain important ideas: the fundamental triangulation of all human relations, the Oedipal complex constituting the model of reference; thirdness defined as a schema of capital importance for symbolization; representation, a basic function of the mind, understood as creating a specific dimension of meaning between the body and the world; the analytic object, a third object formed out of the communication between the analysand and the analyst (by bringing their doubles into relationship with each other); the setting, a third and fundamental element of the analytic process; the triadic schema setting–transference–countertransference; the analyst's internal setting, guaranteeing the analytic third dimension, when the analytic field tends towards a dual, bidimensional dynamic; the analyst's psychic work, equally a tertiary conceptual axis, which includes free-floating attention (intrapsychic perspective, analysis of the contents) and the countertransference (bipersonal perspective, analysis of the relationship and of the container); and, finally, tertiary processes the kernel of the analyst's psychic work.

The framing structure: an implicit theoretical model of clinical practice

The idea of an internalization of the negative is explicitly linked by Green to the concept of "framing structure". Before concluding, I would like to discuss this concept, which may be considered as the implicit (articulating) model of André Green's theory and practice. So, I will just recapitulate briefly on what one can already read in the section "Prospects for future research", which concludes *The Work of the Negative*: "the framing structure is not perceptible as such, but is only perceptible through the productions to which it gives rise in the [clinical] setting" (1993, p. 211). And it is added:

> We are bound to say that it is here that the essential justification for the analytic setting lies, that is, its necessity as well as its function of revealing the internal setting which governs what happens in the perceptive and representative spheres. [*ibid.*, p. 212]

Since 1967, as I have said, André Green has elucidated and developed the Freudian conception of primary narcissism, considered as a fundamental *structure* of the psychical apparatus (and not only as a state or as a phase in libidinal development). From this perspective, primary narcissism constitutes the framing structure for the ego as a matrix of meaning (seat of the process of representation) which associates the double dimension of the drives and identificatory processes.

The framing structure is conceived of as the result of the internalization of the primary maternal setting, thanks to the mechanism of the negative hallucination of the mother. This maternal setting is carnal, bodily, constituted by the *corps-à-corps* of carrying the baby.

> The loss of the breast, occurring when the mother is perceived as a whole object, which implies that the process of separation between them has been completed, results in the creation of a mediation that is necessary to compensate for the effects of her absence and integration into the psychical apparatus . . . This mediation represents the constitution in the ego of the maternal setting as a framing structure. [1967, p.77]

"The mother", writes André Green, "is caught in the empty framework of negative hallucination and becomes a containing structure for the subject himself. The subject constructs himself where the nomination of the object has been consecrated in place of its investment" (*ibid.*, p. 85). The negative hallucination creates a potential blank space for the representation and cathexis of new objects. This structuring is also the result of the defence mechanism, prior to primary repression, of the double reversal that re-addresses to the self the circuit of the object-cathexis by transforming it into a narcissistic organization.

The Greenian perspective postulates the emergence of the psychic subject as the result of the creation of a primary narcissistic organization articulating the activity of drives and identification. Supported by maternal narcissism, this organization creates (and is created by) a framing structure that, at the same time, is a platform of cathexis and a space for representation. A source of the ego/subject, the narcissistic organization constitutes the matrix of psychic self-organization and functions as an interface, a third, intermediate space, with a relative degree of autonomy within the drive-object couple. Thereby, it establishes from the outset the tertiary structure of the mind according to the triads drive–ego–object, drive–representation–object, and subject–object–other of the object.

Globally speaking, the framing structure presents the following characteristics and functions: (1) it is the organizing matrix of primary narcissism, the basic structure of the mind, allowing for separation with the object; (2) it establishes the psychic container by means of a double limit ego–drive and ego–external object, forming an interface between the intrapsychic and the intersubjective; (3) it is the first intermediate formation and constitutes the potential space of representation; (4) it structures the unconscious dimension of the ego, and the preconscious as an internal transitional space; (5) it is the seat of the negative function and of tertiary processes; (6) it is the matrix of psychic internalization in which internalization and self-representation converge according to a principle of primary unity–identity which establishes the source of self-reference, reflexivity, and recognition.

The theoretical and clinical consequences of the introduction of the framing structure are important, for the following reasons.

First of all, it is an innovation of the theory of representation linked to the work of the negative, capable of elucidating *associative functioning in the session and its limitations*. Green proposes completing the Freudian model, centred on hallucinatory wish-fulfilment, by connecting it up with negative hallucination. The latter is the invisible reverse side, the condition and complement of unconscious representation. The framing structure seen as the kernel of narcissistic organization constitutes a matrix uniting the work of the negative and the emergence of representation.

Representation as cathexis (of the memory trace) is articulated with unbinding, in a complementary mode similar to that of the symbol and absence (of the symbolized object).

We represent that which is absent. Defined as the representation of the absence of representation, the negative hallucination of the mother constitutes the intrapsychic category of absence, a condition of possibility and support for representation. Absence is an intermediate dimension between presence and loss. It opens out on to the articulation of the dimensions of the intrapsychic and the intersubjective. Absence is conceived as the origin and sign of thirdness: the object's absence is the source of the other of the object, a germinal reference to the father, giving rise to his Law and his function. In the same way, we can note that the framing structure constitutes the condition of possibility for the establishment and deployment of primal fantasies as organizers of psychic life.

Such a theorization introduces the unrepresentable no longer only as a limit to representative or figurative binding—as is the case of the psychic representative or of thought—but as a radical alterity of representation: its complementary or antagonistic other. Now, the *unrepresentable* corresponds to the "blank" of negative hallucination as an expression of decathexis: an expression—bound or unbound— of the death drive, that is, of a work of the negative whose spectrum includes both normal decorporealization and abstraction as well as pathological splitting and disengagement. The introduction of unbinding presupposes a general model of functioning in terms of the logical sequence binding–unbinding–rebinding. On the basis of this perspective, the technique of silence is re-evaluated by considering the complementarity between silence and discourse.

Second, André Green has shown how, in Freud's work, the dream constitutes the implicit model for the creation of the analytic setting. In his turn, Green elucidates the framing structure as the foundation of the dream, both as a phenomenon and as a *model for the setting*. This perspective throws light on the diptych *model of the dream–model of the act* (Green, 2000b) in relation, respectively, to the functioning or dysfunctioning of the framing structure—either as an expression of the prevalence of *life narcissism* or *death narcissism*. As we know, the models of the dream and of the act "correspond" to both the first and the second topography as well as to representative functioning in neurotic and non-neurotic structures. This diptych attempts to account for and articulate the differences and coincidences between the classical analytical situation and the situations at the limits of analysability.

In the model of the dream, the drive is "put in chains" (the "chains of Eros") by unconscious representation, playing the role of a basic fact. The container is then sufficiently structured so that analysis can concentrate on the contents. Thus, clinical work is based on the compatibility existing between thing-presentation–word-presentation, assembled transferentially in free association. The process, as we have seen, is articulated around a tripod: setting–dream–interpretation.

Linked to the second topography—to the replacement of the Unconscious by the Id—the model of the act is centred on the instinctual impulse and the failures of its links with representation. Trauma and deadly repetition compulsion take the place of wish fulfilment. References to the failures of the primary object and, correlatively, to death narcissism, become central. The framing structure as a space for representation is overwhelmed by an evacuative, projective, desymbolizing mode of functioning. The unrepresentable erupts on to the analytic stage, defeating both free association and free-floating attention. The hypercathexis of perception functions as a counter-cathexis against representation. There is, then, reason to doubt the possibility of internalization in the actuality of the session. The process will organize itself henceforth around the tripod internal setting–act (or traumatic dream)–internalization. The construction of the psychic container and of the preconscious as an internal transitional space and seat of tertiary processes becomes a priority, and even a condition for the analysis of the content. It is in this setting that the dream, as a referent of the technique, is replaced by playing.

Third, it is now possible to speak about the framing structure as an implicit theoretical model for *listening and for the analyst's internal setting*.

The Greenian clinical model is a dynamic schema of the generativity of the discourse in the session. The framing structure functions as a model for the composition of the setting, the transference, and the analytic object. It provides the co-ordinates that allow us to situate the movements of representations, cathexes, and counter-cathexes in the session. It makes it possible, even in limit situations, to think about a minimal dynamic subject–object–other of the object, and to follow it in the associative discourse as an expression of the relations drive–representation–object. It becomes possible to evaluate, in terms of the double axis intrapsychic–intersubjective, the representative production which takes place in the session as an effect of the encounter with the absent object. The compass of listening is representation itself, according to its effects of retroactive reverberation and anticipatory annunciation in free association.

Clinical thinking can be considered as a culminating point of the theoretical model of the framing structure. It is a way of thinking about contemporary practice which seeks to go beyond the limitations of the Freudian and post-Freudian models of the transference and the countertransference. It is complementary and correlative to two other ideas which also derive their model from the framing structure: first, the active, dialogical matrix of the setting as its constant component; and second, the notion of "the analyst's internal setting" which serves as a guarantee for the analytic relation—and the functioning of the active matrix—when the classical setting cannot be utilized.

By way of conclusion, let us read André Green once again:

> In the idea of the internal setting, there is something of the order of the intrapsychic and something which permits the integration of the intersubjective. If we recall what has already been said about the framing structure, we could suppose that the internal setting is an internal/external interface. Tertiary processes, included in analytic listening, are probably the ones that play a decisive role in the internal setting. The basis of this setting can be no other than the framing structure of the analyst himself, who, by virtue of his personal analysis, becomes a source of a new reflexivity, supporting the internal setting. If we define the framing structure as that which makes it possible to constitute singularity (i.e. separation from the other, reflexivity, and self-reference), we may suppose that the internal setting constitutes—by virtue of his personal analysis—a matrix open to the singularity of the other, to his radical otherness. [Green, 2001b]

Note

1. Translator's note: in English in the original.

REFERENCES

Abraham, N., & Torok, M. (1968). Maladie du deuil et fantasme du cadavre exquis. In: *L'écorce et le noyau.* Paris: Flammarion, 1987.

Aisenstein, M. (in collaboration with S. Savvopoulos) (2010). "Les exigences de la representation". Report to the 70th Congress of French-Speaking Analysts.

Bally, C. (1965). *Le Langage et la Vie.* Paris: Droz.

Benveniste, E. (1956). Remarques sur la fonction du langage dans la découverte freudienne. In: *Problèmes de linguistique générale,* vol 1. Paris : Gallimard, 1966.

Birksted-Breen, D., Flanders, S., & Gibeault, A. (Eds.) (2010). *Reading French Psychoanalysis,* S. Leighton, D. Alcott, & A. Weller (Trans.). London: Routledge & International Library of Psychoanalysis.

Bleichmar, S. (1986). *Aux origins du sujet psychique* (Prologue by J. Laplanche). Paris: Presses Universitaires de France.

Bollas, C. (2001). Quitter le courant: de la défaite de la psychanalyse freudienne [Losing the drift: on the undoing of Freudian psychoanalysis], A.-L. Hacker (Trans.), *Revue française de psychanalyse,* special edition, *Courants de la psychanalyse contemporaine,* 65: 231–242.

Bouvet, M. (1967). *Oeuvres psychanalytiques, 1, La relation d'objet.* Paris: Payot and Presses Universitaires de France, 1969 and 2006.

Brusset, B. (2005a). Les psychothérapies et la loi: un débat d'actualité. *Revue française de psychanalyse, Le face-à-face psychanalytique, 69*(2): 1–318.

Brusset, B. (2005b). *Les psychothérapies.* Paris: Presses Universitaires de France, "Que sais-je?"

Busch, F. (2010). Distinguishing psychoanalysis from psychotherapy. *International Journal of Psychoanalysis, 91*: 23–34.

Cahn, R. (2002). *La Fin du divan?* Paris: Odile Jacob.

Canestri, J. (2009). Rêve, semiosis et interprétation. *Psychanalyse en Europe, 63*: 78–189.

Cohen, J. (1966). *Structure du langage poétique.* Paris: Flammarion.

Coquio, C. (Ed.) (1999). *Parler des camps, penser les genocides.* Paris: Albin Michel.

Culioli, A. (1999). *Pour une linguistique de l'énonciation.* Paris: Ophrys, t. 1.

Danon-Boileau, L. (2007). La force du langage. *Revue française de psychanalyse, La Cure de parole, 71*(5): 1341–1409.

Delourmel, C. (2004). Introducción a ideas directrices para un psicoanálisi contemporaneo. *Revista de Psicoanalisis de l'Asociación Psicoanalítica, 42*: 107–125.

Delourmel, C. (2005). Notes de lecture autour des idées directrices pour une psychanalyse contemporaine et de l'œuvre d'André Green. *Bulletin of the European Federation of Psychoanalysis, 59*: 174–178.

Delourmel, C. (2009). Négatif et survie psychique. *Revue Française de Psychosomatique, 2*(36): 163–180.

Denis, A. (2006). Principe de mort, destruction du sens, contresens. In: A. Green (Ed.), *Les Voies nouvelles de la thérapeutique psychanalytique. Le dedans et le dehors* (pp. 501–530). Paris: Presses Universitaires de France.

Donnet, J.-L. (2001). From the fundamental rule to the analysing situation. *International Journal of Psychoanalysis, 82*:129–140. Reprinted in: S. Flanders, D. Birksted-Breen, & A. Gibeault (Eds.), *Reading French Psychoanalysis.* London: Routledge & International Library of Psychoanalysis, 2009.

Donnet, J.-L. (2009). L'analyste et sa règle fondamentale. In: *L'Humour et la honte* (pp. 161–167). Paris: Presses Universitaires de France.

Donnet, J.-L., & Green, A. (1973). *L'Enfant de ça. Pour introduire la psychose blanche.* Paris: Editions de Minuit.

Freud, S. (1890a). Psychical (or mental) treatment. *S.E., 7*: 283–304. London: Hogarth.

Freud, S. (1900a). *The Interpretation of Dreams. S.E., 4–5.* London: Hogarth.

Freud, S. (1924e). The loss of reality in neurosis and psychosis. *S.E., 19*: 183–187. London: Hogarth.

Freud, S. (1930a). *Civilization and its Discontents. S.E., 21*: 59–145. London: Hogarth.

Freud, S. (1933a). *New Introductory Lectures on Psycho-Analysis. S.E., 22.* 1–182. London: Hogarth.

Freud, S. (1937c). Analysis terminable and interminable. *S.E., 23*: 209–253. London: Hogarth.

Freud, S. (1937d). Constructions in analysis. *S.E., 23*: 255–269. London: Hogarth.

Freud, S. (1939a). *Moses and Monotheism. S.E., 23*: 3–137. London: Hogarth.

Freud, S. (1940a [1938]). *An Outline of Psychoanalysis. S.E., 23.* London: Hogarth.

Garcia-Badaracco, J. E. (1992). Psychic change and its clinical evaluation, P. Slotkin (Trans.). *International Journal of Psychoanalysis, 73*(2): 209–220.

Green, A. (1962). L'inconscient freudien et la psychanalyse française contemporaine. *Les Temps modernes, 195*: 365–379. Reprinted in: H. Ey (Ed.), *L'Inconscient.* Paris: Desclée de Brouwer, 1966.

Green, A. (1966). Les fondements différentiateurs des images parentales. L'hallucination negative de la mere et l'identification primordiale au père. In: *Propédeutique.* Paris: Champ Vallon.

Green, A. (1967). Primary narcissism: structure or state? In: *Life Narcissism, Death Narcissism,* A. Weller (Trans.). London: Free Association Books, 2001.

Green, A. (1973). *The Fabric of Affect in the Psychoanalytic Discourse,* A. Sheridan (Trans.). London: Routledge, 1999,

Green, A. (1975). The analyst, symbolization and absence in the analytic setting. *International Journal of Psychoanalysis, 56*: 1–22, and presented at the 29th International Psychoanalytic Congress, London, July 1975. Reprinted in *On Private Madness.* London: Hogarth, 1986 [reprinted London: Karnac, 1997].

Green, A. (1976). One, other, neuter: narcissistic values of sameness. In: *Life Narcissism, Death Narcissism,* A. Weller (Trans.). London: Free Association Books, 2001.

Green, A. (1979). Psychanalyse, langage: l'ancien et le nouveau. *Critique, 381*: 134–139.

Green, A. (1980). Passions and their vicissitudes. In: *On Private Madness*. London: Hogarth [reprinted London: Karnac, 1997].

Green, A. (1982). La double limite. In: *La folie privée: psychanalyse des cas-limites*. Paris: Gallimard, 1990.

Green, A. (1983a). Le langage dans la psychanalyse (2eme Rencontres psychanalytiques d'Aix-en-Provence). In: *Langage* (pp. 20–250). Paris: Les Belles Lettres, 1984.

Green, A. (1983b). *Life Narcissism, Death Narcissism*, A. Weller (Trans.). London: Free Association Books.

Green, A. (1983c). The dead mother, K. Aubertin (Trans.). In: *On Private Madness*. London: Hogarth [reprinted London: Karnac, 1997].

Green, A. (1986a). *On Private Madness*. London: Hogarth [reprinted London: Karnac, 1997].

Green, A. (1986b). The death drive, negative narcissism, and the disobjectalizing function. In: *The Work of the Negative*, A. Weller (Trans.). London: Free Association Books.

Green, A. (1989). De la tiercéité. In: *La Psychanalyse: questions pour demain*. Monograph of the Paris Psychoanalytic Society. Paris: Presses Universitaires de France.

Green, A. (1990). *La Folie privée*. Paris: Gallimard.

Green, A. (1993). *The Work of the Negative*, A. Weller (Trans.). London: Free Association Books, 1999.

Green, A. (1995). *La Causalité psychique. Entre nature et culture*. Paris: Odile Jacob.

Green, A. (1996). *Propédeutique. La Métapsychologie revisitée*. Seyssel: Champ Vallon.

Green, A. (1997). Le langage au sein de la théorie générale de la représentation. In: M. Pinol-Douriez (Ed.), *Pulsions, représentations, langage* (pp. 23–66). Paris: Delachaux et Niestlé.

Green, A. (1998). *The Chains of Eros*. London: Rebus Press, 2000.

Green, A. (2000a). The central phobic position: a new formulation of the free association method. *International Journal of Psychoanalysis, 81,* 429. Reprinted in *Psychoanalysis: A Paradigm for Clinical Thinking*. London: Free Association Books, 2005.

Green, A. (2000b). *Time in Psychoanalysis: Some Contradictory Aspects*, A. Weller (Trans.). London: Free Association Books, 2002.

Green, A. (Ed.) (2001a). Courants de la psychanalyse contemporaine. *Revue française de psychanalyse*, numéro hors série, t. LXV. Paris: Presses Universitaires de France.

Green, A. (2001b). Unpublished transcriptions of interviews with F. Urribarri in preparation for the book *Key Ideas for a Contemporary*

Psychoanalysis, 2005; see also the reference to this in the Preface of this same book, pp. xvii–xviii.

Green, A. (2002a). *Key Ideas for a Contemporary Psychoanalysis*, A. Weller (Trans.). London: Routledge, 2005.

Green, A. (2002b). *Psychoanalysis: A Paradigm for Clinical Thinking*, A. Weller (Trans).. London: Free Association Books, 2005.

Green, A. (2002c). Le syndrome de désertification psychique. In: *Le travail du psychanalyste en psychothérapie*, pp. 17–34. Paris: Dunod.

Green, A. (2003a). Linguistique de la parole et psychisme inconscient. *Cahier de l'Herne, 76: Ferdinand de Saussure*. Paris, Éditions de l'Herne.

Green, A. (2003b). Remarques pour un temps de pause (vers une psychanalyse du future). In: *Le Travail psychanalytique*. Paris: Presses Universitaires de France.

Green, A. (2005). Preface: La voix, l'affect et l'autre. In: M.-F. Castarède & G. Konopczynski (Eds.), *Au commencement était la voix* (pp. 7–26). Ramonville-Sainte-Agne: Erès.

Green, A. (Ed.) (2006). *Les voies nouvelles de la thérapeutique psychanalytique. Le dedans et le dehors*. Paris: Presses Universitaires de France.

Green, A. (2007a). Langue, parole psychanalytique et absence. *Revue française de psychanalyse, La Cure de parole*, 71: 1761–1462.

Green, A. (2007b). *Pourquoi les pulsions de destruction ou de mort?* Paris: Panama (out of print); reprinted by Editions Ithaque, 2010.

Green, A. (2008). "Le rejet de la psychanalyse par C. Lévi-Strauss". *Texto!* Available at: www.revue-texto.net/index.php?id=1930.

Green, A. (2009). *L'Aventure négative. Lecture psychanalytique d'Henry James*. Paris: Éditions Hermann.

Green, A. (2010). Théorie. In: A. Fine & J. Schaeffer (Eds.), *Interrogations psychosomatiques*, in the collections "Débats de psychanalyse", *Revue Française de Psychanalyse*, February 1998: 17–53. [English translation: M. Aisenstein & L. Rappoport de Aisemberg (Eds.) (2010). *Psychosomatics Today. A Psychoanalytic Perspective*, pp. 1–45. London: Karnac].

Grossman, V. (1954). *Everything Flows*, R. Chandler & E. Chandler (Trans.). New York: NYRB Classics, 2009.

Grossman, V. (1959). *Life and Fate*, R. Chandler (Trans.). New York: Harper and Row, 1985.

Jakobson, R. (1973). *Post-Scriptum à Questions de poétique*. Paris: Seuil.

Kahn, L. (2005). *Faire parler le destin*. Paris: Klincksieck.

Kertész, I. (1993). *L'Holocauste comme culture: discours et essais*, C. Zaremba and N. Zaremba-Huzsvai (Trans.). Paris: Actes Sud.

Khan, M. (1964). Ego distortion, cumulative trauma and the role of reconstruction in the analytic situation. *International Journal of Psychoanalysis*, *45*: 272–279.

Klauber, J. (1976). The identity of the psychoanalyst. In: *Difficulties in the Analytic Encounter*. London: Karnac, 1986.

Lacan, J. (1966). The function and field of speech and language in psychoanalysis. In: *Écrits*, B. Fink (Trans.) (pp. 197–268). New York: Norton, 2006.

Lévi-Strauss, C., & Éribon, D. (1988). *De près et de loin*. Paris: Odile Jacob.

Linsky, L. (1974). *Le problème de la référence*, S. Stern-Guillet, P. Devaux, & P. Gochet (Trans.). Paris: Seuil.

Ludin, J. (2009). Die Entstellung, la déformation. *Libres Cahiers pour la psychanalyse, Clinique de la psychanalyse*, *20*: 55–66.

Martinet, A. (1961). *Éléments de linguistique générale* (2nd edn). Paris: Armand Colin.

Nunberg, H., & Federn, E. (Eds.) (1967). *Minutes of the Vienna Psycho-analytic Society*, Vol. II. New York: International Universities Press.

Peirce, C. S. (1931). *Collected Papers* (8 volumes). Cambridge, MA: Harvard University Press.

Potamianou, A. (1992). *Un bouclier dans l'économie des états limites: espoir*. Paris: Presses Universitaires de France.

Rastier, F. (2006). De l'origine du langage à l'émergence du milieu sémiotique. *Marges linguistiques*, *11*: 297–326. Also available online from Texto!, www.revue-texto.net/index.php?id=533.

Rastier, F. (2007). Le langage est-il une origine? *Revue française de psychanalyse, La Cure de parole*, *61*: 1481–1487.

Riviere, J. (1929). Womanliness as a masquerade. *International Journal of Psychoanalysis*, *10*: 309–313.

Rolland, J.-C. (2006). *Avant d'être celui qui parle*. Paris: Gallimard.

Roussillon, R. (2008). *Le transitionnel, le sexuel et la réflexivité*. Paris: Dunod.

Schneider, M. (2006). *Marilyn, dernières séances*. Paris: Grasset & Fasquelle.

Sebeok, T. (1974). Comment un signal devient un signe. In: E. Morin (Ed.), *L'Unité de l'homme*. Paris: Seuil.

Stone, L. (1954). The widening scope of indications for analysis. *Journal of the American Psychoanalytic Association*, *2*(4): 567–594.

Thom, R. (1968). La science malgré tout. *Encyclopaedia universalis*, Organum, vol. XVII.

Thom, R. (1980). *Paraboles et catastrophes*. Paris: Flammarion.

Tustin, F. (1986). *Autistic Barriers in Neurotic Patients*. London: Karnac.

Urribarri, F. (2008). Après Lacan: père et filiation analytique chez André Green. In: D. Cupa (Ed.), *Image du père dans la culture contemporaine* (pp. 53–63). Paris: PUF, 2008.

Viderman, S. (1970). *La construction de l'espace analytique*. Paris: Denoël.

Winnicott, D. W. (1954). Metapsychological and clinical aspects of regression within the psychoanalytical set-up. In: *Collected papers: Through Paediatrics to Psycho-Analysis*. London: Tavistock, 1958.

Winnicott, D. W. (1969). The use of the object. *International Journal of Psychoanalysis, 50*. Also in *Playing and Reality*. London: Tavistock, 1971.

Winnicott, D. W. (1971). Playing: a theoretical statement (pp. 38–52); Playing: creative activity and the search for the self (pp. 53–64). In: *Playing and Reality*. London: Tavistock.

Winnicott, D. W. (1974). Fear of breakdown. *International Review of Psychoanalysis, 1*: 103–107.

INDEX